D0680479

THE BOY WHO LOVED TORNADOES

||||||||||||||||||||||||||||||||||||||||||||||||||||||||||||||||||||||||||||||||||||||||||||||||||||||

THE

BOY WHO

LOVED

TORNADOES

A Mother's Story

Randi Davenport

ALGONQUIN BOOKS OF CHAPEL HILL 2010

FALMOUTH PUBLIC LIBRARY
FALMOUTH, MA 02540

618.9285882
DAV

Published by
ALGONQUIN BOOKS OF CHAPEL HILL
Post Office Box 2225
Chapel Hill, North Carolina 27515-2225

a division of
WORKMAN PUBLISHING
225 Varick Street
New York, New York 10014

© 2010 by Randi Davenport. All rights reserved.
Printed in the United States of America.
Published simultaneously in Canada by Thomas Allen & Son Limited.
Design by Anne Winslow.

Library of Congress Cataloging-in-Publication Data
   Davenport, Randi, [date]
      The boy who loved tornadoes : a mother's story /
   Randi Davenport.— 1st ed.
         p. cm.
      ISBN 978-1-56512-611-4
      1. Autism in children— Treatment.   2. Autistic children—
   Care.   3. Parents of autistic children.   I. Title.
   RJ506.A9D38 2010
   618.92'85882— dc22   2009031221

10 9 8 7 6 5 4 3 2 1
First Edition

FOR
CHASE
AND
HALEY

⊙ ▣ ⊙

AUTHOR'S NOTE

EACH OF US HAS A STORY TO TELL; this is mine. It comes from that most imperfect and peculiar of local records: my memory. Because of that, I have changed names and identifying characteristics of some of the people I describe. After all, they probably never imagined the things I remember them saying and doing would ever appear in a book, and they are entitled to their privacy. Changing names is not the same as changing a story. I would give anything to be able to tell a different story. But no matter the identities I disguise, the story remains the same.

DRAGON

ONCE IN A FAR AWAY valley there was a prince. The valley smelled like pine trees. There were two streams that ran through the valley. You could smell pine trees all year round in the valley. One day a terrible dragon came and was destroying the valley. A prince was risking his life to kill the dragon. The king sent out knights to help him but they were not doing any good. The valley seemed doomed and after that, the world.

—Chase, *age 9*

PROLOGUE

IN MY DREAMS, we are whole again.

I saw an image of the human brain on a science program on television. This brain had been mapped so that different parts lit up when the subject received certain stimuli. I watched as little waves of lightning flashed across this brain, bright white against the scanner's dark gray background, the palimpsest of every medical imaging device I have ever known, where something unanticipated paints out that which we expect to see.

The producers were careful to protect the identity of the subject. Despite our maps and scans, some of us still see those who suffer the symptoms of its failures as complicit in the brain's wandering actions. In the unconscious judgment of those who would assign to the illness of the brain the qualities of a doomed soul, perhaps we see how little we have progressed from the nineteenth-century phrenologists, who measured every bump and lump of the skull as evidence that only a lack of moral character, a paucity of Christian virtue, resided within.

In my dreams, Chase is whole and Zip is whole and Haley belongs to the family she remembers, as do I. But in the morning, dreams fade. When we go about our days, we still live in a world apart.

ONE

||||||||||||||

THERE WAS NO POSSIBILITY of staying with the others so Chase and Haley and I walked down the hill away from the picnic and along the creek until we came to a concrete footbridge. Haley ran ahead of us but Chase stopped at the edge of the bridge and stared intently at the trail leading into the woods. There were deep shadows under the branches and dark places where the pine needles gave way to mud and soft fluttering ferns of a bright green color. Everything moved a little in the breeze. Over our heads, pale yellow leaves shifted against dark green loblolly pine and blue sky; in front of us, the trail led up to a ridge, where the November sky opened over us like a bell.

"Chase," I said. "Come on."

"No," he said. "No."

On the other side, Haley walked backward up the hill so she could watch what we were doing while she moved away from us.

"Come on, Chase," I said. "It's okay."

He looked hard at the path behind me. His head listed a little to one side, as if his neck were a mast on a boat that had heeled over too far in deep water.

I could hear Haley scuffling through the leaves. She was nearly at the top of the hill and in another moment would follow the trail out of sight.

"All right," I said tightly. "Let's go see the waterfall."

Chase relaxed as we started back to the picnic buildings; this way, the path was out in the open and led down to the creek by a gazebo and you could see people playing softball on the next field. The park allowed you to bring in a horse to ride and a big bay with a tiny red-shirted rider delicately picked its way across the creek where the water flattened out into swampy pools. There were dogs wearing bandannas and couples with toddlers. A family dressed in identical tight shorts jostled past us just as we got to the bridge by the gazebo.

The Haw River Assembly held the picnic every year to recruit volunteers for the annual Haw River Festival, when fourth graders came from schools all over the state to go on nature walks and learn about ecology. I'd come to the picnic because I wanted us to be like other families and pictured us camped in tents at a river site for a week in the spring. I told Chase we'd paddle canoes like Indians and maybe he'd see a milk snake hanging like thick rope from a tree limb. In the evening, Haley would dance to the sound of drums by a big fire and we'd go to sleep while owls called out in the trees.

Chase refused to eat with the others, who sat outside in the bright sunshine, so we ate by ourselves in the dim living-room area of the recreation center. He kept his head down and crammed bites into his mouth until food fell from his spoon onto his lap, his legs, his little acre of floor. He didn't look up or speak to us.

Haley complained about having to eat inside and I made my usual pleading sounds: It's not that bad, Chase has trouble outside, this is just fine, we'll sit with everyone else when he's finished eating.

She ate her meal in silence and looked away from me. Afterward, Chase did not want to sit in a circle with the others. He did not want to go down to the creek to do some stream watching, did not want to toss a Frisbee with the other kids, did not want to bird-watch, touch a raccoon pelt, sing a song about the river. He stood at the back of the room instead and paced and muttered to himself while Haley tried to appear small and unnoticeable in the chair beside me.

Chase was fourteen that day, and Haley was ten. Despite my high hopes, and I had many, there was never any possibility of staying with the others. The cant of Chase's head, the soft slur of his words, the pitch and lean of his walk, his tendency to fall to staring or into convulsions, his preternatural interest in things morbid and otherwordly, his obsessions and monologues, his endless pacing and agitating, his body that served like a drain and took all of the air out of the room, all of the air and all of the energy, and all of the focus and all of the attention — these things made a wall between us and everyone else. It was as if we were on one side of a thick plate-glass window, through which we could clearly see the normal world, forever out of reach.

Having a disability in the family locks you in a space whose borders the rest of the world cannot see, and which you yourself cannot see until you run smack into its limits. Then there is nothing to do but to fall back to the center of the world. Others look in at you and wonder why you can't do anything differently and you share their sentiments. If you are me, you think that all you have to do is keep trying, keep moving, and you can overcome anything. And some days, perhaps, you feel as if you have. But on most days, you know that the only thing that has been overcome is you. For many years, I didn't realize that you can't run away from the physical fact of disability. Once it lies in the roadway behind you, even if it causes doctors to shake their heads and experts to frown, even if it cannot be named, it lies forever on the roadway in front of you.

• • •

WE FOLLOWED THE TRAIL down to the rocks where the creek spilled over into a waterfall. Haley immediately began pitching stones into the foam but Chase stood a few feet away from me. His eyes cut from the waterfall to a couple sitting on the rocks in front of us. He began to pace and swing his arms.

I'd kept up a hopeful commentary, as if I could stave off this storm, as if I could by hope and will alone cause Chase to veer in another direction. "Look what a nice day it is," I'd said. "Look how pretty the trees look. Don't you just love the color of the sky? A horse! How great! Haley, look at the horse!"

Now I offered Chase a handful of stones. He didn't look at me or shake his head. He just stalked up and down the rocks and cut his eyes from this to that. I became aware that he was talking in a low voice but I couldn't understand what he was saying or if he was talking to me or to his sister or to himself. I tossed a few stones into the creek. "If your father was here, he'd be able to make these stones skip," I said to Chase, but he looked away from me as if he hadn't heard me and stared hard at the tumbling water.

The two people on the rocks in front of us were young, maybe late teens, and sat side by side, facing the creek. The boy had his arm snugly around the girl's waist; her long red hair spread over his shoulder as she nuzzled his neck. Haley told me she wanted to go out farther on the rocks, jump down to a flat rock that was halfway across the water. I said no. She stopped and said, "Can I go up there?" There was a leg of the trail up above us where some of the family in tight shorts were noisily expressing enthusiasm about the view.

"Okay," I said.

I watched her climb. She leaned into the hill and when the incline became too steep, she put her hands down in the dry leaves and scrambled doggy-style up to the trail.

"Good job," I called, and she grinned at me and jumped up and down. But then Chase was at my elbow, patting my arm over and over. When I turned to him, his eyes were wide and dark.

"Mom, Mom," he said. "Those are profilers. That's the FBI. They're profilers."

"Who?" I said.

"Him and her," he said and gestured at the couple on the rocks. He turned away so they would not overhear him and spoke in a low voice. "They're profilers. They're after me."

"No," I said. "No. Chase. That's just a guy and a girl."

"They're profilers," he said.

"Chase," I said. "That's not true."

He said something I couldn't understand and then he turned and strode away from me, moving fast. I called to Haley and she yelled back and I said, "Now."

She slid and bumped through the leaves and roots and down the slope and ran up to me and we followed Chase. He didn't slow but kept taking long strides until he reached our car. I hadn't seen him move that fast in a couple of years. The picnic was still going on and I thought about going back to let someone know that we were in trouble. But Chase was in the car banging the flat of his hand against the dashboard, saying, "Let's go, let's go," and I had been on my own with whatever it was Chase was going to bring our way for years now. There didn't seem to be anyone to tell. Chase's voice pitched up and he said, "Come on, come on. We have to get out of here."

So I started the car and put it in gear and we were on the move again. This was my answer to everything: keep moving, stay moving, keep pushing, move, move, move. I didn't know what else to do. As we headed for the park entrance, Chase kept a lookout for the things that were after us. Haley gazed out the window. In the rearview mirror, I could see her. Her face was small and blank.

OUR FAMILY ONCE had four people: a father, a mother, a boy, a girl. The father and mother fell in love, just like most people do, and they began with a dream of a family, just like everyone begins with a dream of a life, without knowing exactly how that life will turn out, without knowing what their family will be like. They had a son, whom they named Chase, and then they had a daughter, whom they named Haley. The father's name was James but he'd taken other names in his life as if he were constantly avoiding the truth of being one person and one person alone. I knew him as Zip but after we were married, we began to get mail for someone named Art Byrd. He lived like a man in the witness protection program and watched over his shoulder as if he thought something was gaining on him. He'd been a working rock-and-roll musician and then, when that left him, a music-store manager, and then, when we left that, a house husband, and then, when he had to get a job, a man who worked on the loading dock at a big-box store. By the end of our marriage, he rarely spoke but sat on the back steps of our house and smoked Salem menthols and watched the street with a thousand-yard stare. Eventually, I came to understand that the same thing that would take Chase had taken him.

I DROVE SLOWLY out of the park, along a road that ran straight past ball fields and picnic tables and an old farm until it dumped us out on a country highway. The sun had gone behind the clouds and Chase was quieter now, although he still looked around fearfully, and occasionally glanced back over his shoulder as best as he could. His ability to turn was incomplete because his neck had been fused and no longer turned like an ordinary neck. Once he asked Haley to look and see if there was anyone behind us. Once he looked at me as if he had no idea who I was. I tried hopelessly to talk him out of his conviction that we were being followed. Haley sat quietly in the back but once she said, in a very exasperated voice, "It was just a guy and a girl on a rock, jeez." I heard myself in her voice, as if she'd picked up from me what was right to say to her brother.

Chase's ability to be stuck on something, a subject, an idea, a thing of minor relevance that was made large in his mind, wasn't new. At various times in his life he'd been obsessed with window fans, of which he was deathly afraid, and with dinosaurs, trains, railroad-crossing signs, vampires, ghosts, church steeples, tornadoes, severe weather — he watched the Weather Channel in a state of hypervigilance, so we would always be prepared — Crips, action figures, comic books, and music. His interests evolved as he grew so he wasn't stuck on all of these at the same time, and he wasn't stuck on all of them with equivalent attention, and as soon as he'd moved from one thing to the next, he left the first thing behind with utter finality.

Often, it was very hard to tell what was real for Chase and what was his idiosyncratic interpretation of what was real. He called 9-1-1 because he was convinced someone was trying to kidnap his sister. He told me that Crips followed him home from school, threatening to kill him before he could get inside. But pretty soon I realized that Chase's conviction that Crips existed in our mild suburban-style neighborhood was created by his placement in a class with behaviorally impaired children who felt utterly thwarted in their own power and talked a lot about their connections to West Coast gangs as a way to demonstrate their place in the world.

These things weren't right, they weren't true, but they were loosely associated with things that were real, and became markers not of what was real but what was real to Chase. And until he was almost fifteen, he was willing to entertain the idea that explanations other than his own might be valid. He allowed the cop to explain how important it was to see someone actually try to kidnap your sister before you report that your sister has been kidnapped. He agreed that it was pretty unlikely that LeMarcus and Gabriel were hardened Crips who also happened to have been enrolled in the seventh grade at McDougle Middle School. But he didn't let go of these ideas altogether and every so often he would tell me again about the day his sister was almost kidnapped.

When I heard these things, my guts twisted and I wanted to shake him and say, "Stop it, Chase! Stop it now!" But I didn't. I just looked at him and said, in as neutral a tone as I could muster, "You know that didn't happen, Chase." And then I set about trying to figure out what had caused this particular eruption, as if I could lay my hands on Chase's fears, his half-understood truths, and wrest them from him once and for all, as if in this act we would come together in an ancient ritual where I was asked not to sacrifice my son but instead was given a way to save him.

On Monday I'd call his therapist, his psychiatrist, his teacher at school. Maybe he needed a medication change. Maybe something had gone off-kilter in the classroom. Maybe his therapist could shed some light on what FBI profilers meant to Chase. We could put our heads together and work it out. We could change the error of his thinking. We could change the error of our ways.

TWO

||||||||||||||

WE GOT TO THE teen center around six. It was in the basement of the old post office on Franklin Street. I pulled up to the curb and set my hazards to flash and then turned around and told Chase and Haley to go inside with Melissa.

"If you each take a bag, we can get set up in no time," I said.

I got out of the car and handed Haley a bag and handed Melissa two bags. Chase came up to me and patted my arm and said, "There will be hundreds of kids there tonight, right? Right, Mom?"

"Some," I said. "I'm sure there will be some kids."

"It's going to be so cool," Chase said. He hopped up and down a little and patted my arm over and over again. "Right, Mom? Right? It's going to be really cool. And there will be hundreds of kids there, right?"

"It'll be cool, Chase," I said. "Really, really cool."

"Cool," he said.

While they made their way inside, I walked around to the rear of the car and lifted out the blue plastic cooler filled with ice and sodas and set it on the sidewalk. Jason, Melissa's green-haired boyfriend, came up to me and said, "I'll take this," and I thanked him and then got back in the car and drove to the parking lot. I turned off the engine and sat for a few minutes, maybe prayerful, maybe just in a state of hopeful wishing. Then I walked back up the street and waited at the corner for the light to change. We'd planned this party for a long time, mostly to give Chase something good to think about, to point out to him that after all he'd been through, the four surgeries on his cervical spine, there were still things to look forward to. We'd told him this would be a great way to celebrate his fifteenth birthday, now some days away, but I felt uneasy. The incident in the park was just a couple of hours behind us and when we got home, Chase had retreated to his room as if he'd forgotten all about the party while Haley and I packed paper bags with chips and pretzels and plastic cups to take into town. I'd told myself this was a good thing and that he would find some way to be more himself when the time came, but I also worried that Chase at that point was himself, that one thing didn't stand in for another, that we'd taken a turn and now we'd have to see where this road went.

The night was mild for November and boys with blue hair and huge nose rings, and girls tattooed with figures from their favorite children's books, their eyebrows and tongues pierced, had watched me lift the cooler to the curb and had watched Jason take it inside. They wore heavy black shoes with black clothes or faded T-shirts with cartoon characters printed on the front. Their clothes were decorated with things that tied or clipped or snapped, wallet chains dangling at the waist, strings and laces and safety pins and spikes and heavy steel buckles. The girls wore black lipstick and small rhinestone butterfly pins in their purple or fuchsia hair and sat in pairs or threes, fiddling with the laces on their Doc Martens or rifling through purses that contained journals with black cardboard covers clipped together with turquoise gel pens. Boys stood in small groups and joked and swore and watched the girls out of the corners of their eyes, trying to be sure the girls kept their eyes on them. Some of the boys balanced on skateboards or did vertical turns, walking in circles by alternating weight end to end.

Melissa had worked with Chase for nearly four years, ever since we came south. Together, they practiced folding laundry and emptying the dishwasher and Melissa checked the items off on Chase's goal sheet. Sometimes she'd drive Chase to a local coffee shop, where he'd order orange juice and sit at a table where he could be surrounded by kids in dark clothes with jet-black hair. Melissa herself wore red retro cat's-eye glasses. Her ears were pierced with huge, hollow rings of jade that always made me think of the pictures of African women in *National Geographic* magazine, whose earlobes hung to their shoulders. She had tattoos all over her body: the spider over her heart, the parade of toads and frogs and bears and doll-faced little girls and boys and the Jabberwocky himself crawling up her right leg in a huge spiral, Kali on her left arm, Alice in Wonderland on her right. Her hair changed to match her life story: That Time Melissa Had Blue and Purple Dreds; When Melissa First Colored Her Hair Bright Pink; The Day Jason Told Melissa Her Rainbow Hair Looks Like a Clown Wig. By the time she became Chase's daily worker, she'd settled down to a little bob that looked like the haircuts favored by Japanese anime characters.

She was patient and unflappable. Nothing fazed her. She worked with all kinds of disabled kids but usually with the hardest ones, the boys most likely to take their pants off in a mall or poop in the swimming pool, the speechless ones who screamed or rocked or bashed their heads against the wall because they could not make themselves heard or known, the ones who ran away, the ones who got into other people's cars in the parking lot at the grocery store and would not get out again, the ones who ate only blue food and drove their parents mad with having to dye the mashed potatoes. Melissa cared for them all. These events were humorous, in her view, were the things that made clear that these boys were people,

each with his particularly human way of being in the world. She
could interpret their behavior as if it were sign language or Braille
and insisted that each of these things had an internal logic, a signal or message, something that we could understand if we chose
to try.

Chase wasn't one of the worst; he and Melissa just seemed to be
a good match. He thought she was cool and she helped him with
his music. He wanted to be in a rock band but he couldn't play an
instrument. Instead, he sang and kept a microphone on a stand and
a small amp in his room, where he could practice. Melissa helped
him make posters to hang at school advertising himself as a singer.
He listed the bands he liked so the other musicians would know the
sort of music he wanted to play: Limp Bizkit and Korn and Rage
Against the Machine. He'd named his band already: Children of
Artists. He explained that this was because everyone who was in
the band would have parents who were artists, like he did. I appre-
ciated his optimistic view of us, the writer who no longer wrote, the
musician who now worked on the receiving dock at a discount store
five states away. He wanted to know all of the places his father had
played, what that had been like, in the old days, Mom, he'd say,
when you were with the band. He said these words like there was
magic associated with them, so I told him about the smoky clubs
his father played and the long hours and the low pay and the long
rides home on cold mornings just before the sun came up in a van
with a heater that didn't work and pulling into the driveway shivering and tired. I tried to make it sound awful but Chase believed in
it, just as his father had believed in it.

"And there would be hundreds of people," he'd say. "Right,
Mom? Right?"

"Sometimes," I said. "Sometimes there'd be five."

"And Dad made records, right?"

"Right," I said.

"And he was on the radio, right?"

"Sometimes," I said.

"Cool," said Chase.

There was no persuading Chase that his father hadn't been a rock star. That fall, he downloaded songs from the Internet and Melissa told him stories about her friends who were in bands. One day in early fall, Chase set up his mic and cranked Korn on the stereo. Melissa was downstairs when she heard the sound cut off and then that odd stillness that comes when some sound you expect doesn't actually make itself known — the stillness of the dead car engine after you turn the key in the ignition, or the TV when the sound drops out, or a radio with dead batteries. By the time she got upstairs, Chase had the microphone cord wrapped around his throat and was pulling as tightly as he could on each end of the cord, as if he could strangle himself. When she got him untangled, she sat him down on his bed and he leaned his head on his hands, his elbows on his knees, and sobbed that he just wanted to die.

His therapist's notes from around this time said that Chase reported no suicidal feelings. At school, however, he told the guidance counselor that he had a plan. He explained that he would drink poison or step out in front of a car. Later the counselor told me that the second way was particularly popular among teens. It would look like an accident. That afternoon, she had Chase sign a contract, promising that he would not kill himself without talking to her first.

I went through the house and removed all of the knives and the household cleaners from under the sink; I took his microphone away and took down blinds that had cords; I took shoelaces and belts, as if I were the warden of a jail, and I went to his room and removed all of the CDs by bands that spoke even distantly of

death and darkness. He protested. I told him it was my job to keep
him safe and that was what I was going to do. But he slammed the
door and screamed at me through the wood and I actually smiled,
thinking that this, at least, seemed normal.

INSIDE, THE TEEN CENTER was one large room, painted
black, strung with Christmas lights; a bar ran along one wall, and
behind that an old white refrigerator papered with signs listing
the prices for sodas and bags of chips. A basic platform stage stood
next to the front entrance. Behind the main room were two small
soundproofed rooms, painted sunshine yellow and lime green,
where kids could practice guitars or keyboards—stringless, out
of tune, missing cables and cords—and to the right of the main
room was a room with couches and arcade games. The pool table
was in front of the bar. When we got there, two kids were playing
while a third watched; another sat in the room with couches, playing a Game Boy in front of a TV whose sound had been turned
down. I put the bowls of chips and snacks on the bar and opened
the cooler. The kids at the pool table put down their cues and
ambled over and helped themselves.

Chase ignored this. Someone had left a folding chair in the
middle of the room and he sat down and stared at the space where
the band would be. His head listed to one side.

After a while, a few more kids came to the party, boys from our
neighborhood whose parents had made them come, and a couple of
disabled boys whose mothers I knew from going to mother's-group
meetings, before I gave that up to work—a boy named Christian
and two of his friends. Their parents walked their disabled children past the punk kids outside and came down the stairs and
stood uncertainly in the doorway of the teen center, wondering if
this was a place they could let their kids stay. But some of Chase's

workers came, too—the girls who'd stay with him when I had to
work late, and Mac and Danny, two young men who were seniors
in college, and Melissa. I pointed out the number of trained pro-
fessionals in the room and mentioned the band and the parents
turned away with relieved faces and told their sons they'd be back
in an hour. By the time the band started playing, there were eight
kids, including Haley. The rest of the guests were family friends,
invited to make sure that someone would show up.

The band played and the kids watched and the adults stood
around with soggy paper cups full of Diet Sprite. Every so often
Chase dragged Melissa over to a quiet corner to tell her that there
were death threats against him, that the profilers had come for him
in the park, and he wasn't safe. He told her that he was going to
live with Zack de la Rocha, the lead singer for Rage Against the
Machine. She told him he was perfectly safe and this was his party
and he should watch the band. They were friends of hers and called
themselves Amish Jihad; they knew about Chase because Melissa
had explained him to them and they had agreed to come play at
his party. There were three of them: a drummer, a guitar player,
and a bass player. When they came in, they rolled their equipment
onto the stage and came over to Chase and spoke to him in the
loud voices of confident young men and offered high fives and
handshakes. "Hey man!" they called. "It's your birthday! Happy
Birthday!" Chase grinned and slapped the hands they offered and
said things to them about the equipment that they didn't understand. They just grinned and said, "Yeah man! That's cool, dude!"
He told them about knowing Zack de la Rocha and they said,
"You do? That's cool, man!" They set up their amplifiers and did
their sound check and asked me if they should start. When they
opened the show, they said, "It's somebody's birthday here tonight
and this show is especially dedicated to him! Happy Birthday,

Chase!" And then the drummer slapped his sticks, one-two-three-four, and the guitar player hit a big power chord and twisted his body up to the mic like it was too hard to reach and began to sing, words that went with the music but words that no one could really understand.

Chase stood in front of the band and hopped up and down a few times, the way he did before he was injured, when he tried to turn his bedroom into a mosh pit, but then he sat in his folding chair and gradually leaned so far to one side that I went to see if he needed propping up. He didn't respond.

"Chase," I said. "You okay? You need something?"

He stirred then and looked at me, but I didn't see him recognize me.

"Chase, listen," I said. "It's the band. It's Amish Jihad. Remember how you and Melissa planned for this? How cool is this?"

He smiled faintly, as if it was something he was remembering to do, and raised his left hand and weakly threw the goat.

"Attaboy," I said. "Chase rules."

But he sat, motionless, unfocused, disconnected, distant, his face sliding from no expression to too much expression too quickly and too unpredictably, in ways that did not seem attached to what was happening around him. After a while, he stood up and walked away. The band stopped playing when their hour was up and began to tear down and pack up, all the familiar gestures of a rock band, the sounds so much a part of my memory that for a moment I felt homesick for my other life, when I was still with Chase and Haley's dad, when I believed that only good things would happen, that in going off with him, I'd managed to change my luck, that I myself would be transformed. I stood by the stage and felt helpless. Friends walked up to me and said things like, "Great band," before they asked if Chase was okay.

"Maybe the party's too much for him," I said, over and over again. "We'll see how he is in the morning."

I saw him from across the room. He stood at a microphone in one of the soundproofed rooms so he could sing, but his face was slack, his eyes wide, and then he drifted over to Christopher and Billings, the boys from our neighborhood whom he persisted in thinking of as his best friends although there was no evidence that much friendship existed at all. But Chase was loyal and they had been friends when they were all eleven and that was enough for him, even though he had long ago slipped away from them or they from him. From across the room, I saw the three of them together, Billings on one side, Christopher on the other, both clowning around like fifteen-year-old boys will. On other occasions, this would have been a beautiful sight, but now Chase stood in the middle, smiling widely, his eyes glassy and without any emotion at all, as if all he needed to do was move his mouth into the curve of a smile for the smile to be true.

AFTER HALEY AND CHASE went to bed, I lay down and stared at the ceiling. I was worried about Chase, but I was always worried about Chase. I hoped he could get a good night's sleep. Outside, the wind had picked up and, after a while, I stood and wrapped my robe around myself and found my slippers and stepped outside. A gleaming sliver of moon hung over the western horizon. The sky seemed bright with stars but a few clouds moved and turned the moon dark in their passing and then brightness reappeared. I walked farther into the darkness and listened to the wind move through the crepe myrtles. The night air settled me. I used to joke that after I died I wanted to be cremated and have my ashes shot out into space, where I could drift among the stars forever. Haley went to an art camp one summer; when it came time to silk-screen T-shirts, she made one for me, with a green moon and green stars against a pale background. "Because you like to look up," she said.

WHEN CHASE'S SCREAMS WOKE me, I found him shivering in the hallway. His face crumpled when he saw me, and he worked his mouth a little, and then he began to cry and pointed back at his room.

"Chase," I said. "What's the matter?"

"The executioner was outside my window," he said. "He was looking in at me."

"Your window is on the second story," I said. "No one can look in at you."

"He was," he said. "He was, he was, he was." He said something that sounded like, "It was just a head."

I walked into his room and looked out the window. "Nobody here, sport," I said cheerfully. "You're fine. It was just a dream."

"No," he said. "It wasn't a dream."

I reached under his pillow. "Where's your sleep stone?" Years before, I'd given Chase a small polished stone to help him sleep better just the way you give a carsick child a penny to hold. It worked for a while and then, like so many things in Chase's room, it vanished. I replaced it with an even more powerful sleep stone. Now I told Chase to get in bed and go back to sleep. I told him that as long as I was there, no one would hurt him. I found his old stuffed bear and I tucked it into his arms. I kissed him goodnight. I made a big deal out of checking the blinds to be sure they were properly closed and hung flat against the window glass.

"Do you want the light on?"

"Uh-huh," he said. It was a stupid question; Chase hadn't ever slept in the dark. On better nights, he could sleep with a bedside lamp turned on. On bad nights, he asked for the overhead light, which was what was on now.

"You're fine," I said again. "You're perfectly safe. Go to sleep. In the morning you'll see that everything is fine. Okay?"

He nodded glumly and then turned on his side and curled up and clutched the bear to his chest.

I shut the door carefully behind me and then made my way down the hall to Haley's room. She lay sideways across the bed on her belly with her hair spread out on the pillow, one leg hanging over the edge of the bed, her blankets on the floor. I pushed the door open so that it let a long slant of light into her dark room and picked my way through the toys on the floor over to her bed. I lifted and turned her gently and shook out her sheet and her blanket and spread them over her and then stroked her hair. She tried to push her body up on her hands as if she meant to wake up but I said, "No, shush, go back to sleep. Everything's okay. Everything's all right." She fell back into the pillow and I stood there for a few minutes, just making sure, and I thought, just as I always did, that Haley had too much to bear.

When I got in bed, I lay awake for a long time, my heart pounding. Whatever this was, it was something new. I tried to think of other times Chase had screamed in the night. For a little while, I amused myself by cursing Mitch, who'd once worked with Chase and whose brief time in our home was marked by viewings of films I'd forbidden Chase to see, like *The Matrix* or Stephen King's *It,* and then by three weeks' worth of nights where Chase had dreams from which he woke screaming every single night. Mitch had similarly been a whiz at helping Chase reach his goals and at saying seductive things to me; his time with us was very brief and his job had probably pretty much run its course the day he decided the easiest way to get a pizza into the house would be to leave Chase and Haley alone for an hour while he went to pick it up.

We'd had CAP workers since Chase was twelve. CAP stands for North Carolina's Community Alternatives Program. Designed to keep the developmentally disabled, medically fragile, or AIDs-suffering population out of institutions, CAP paid for a worker to come to our house every afternoon after school and stay until Chase's bedtime and for another who came on weekend afternoons; it paid for an occupational therapist to come twice a week and a speech therapist to come once a week. It paid for respite care so that I could go to the movies with friends or close the door to my room and lie on my bed or go to the gym or take Haley to the store.

Our first CAP worker had been an MP in the army and thought the military way was the best way and the only way. She swiftly instituted a strict system of order, followed by equally strict punishment for disobedience. Her method of communicating with Chase was to bark commands from which he shrank and retreated. She complained to me: Chase wouldn't keep up. Chase didn't even try. Chase was totally noncompliant. Chase needed strict discipline to shape him up. It didn't take long before I realized Chase was afraid of her.

Our next CAP worker was a young man named Samuel; he stayed for almost a year before getting engaged and going off to graduate school in Buffalo. After that came Ted, the Young Republican whose sole interest in working with Chase was to get some clinical experience that would help his graduate school application in clinical psychology. He complained about the way I kept house and regularly made remarks about the ways in which single mothers and black people and anyone else he could identify with unsteady domestic economies brought their troubles on themselves. After nine months, he was gone and Chase mourned his loss, for Ted had been a college student who tried to teach Chase some of the nuances of cool, along with how to pick up his room. After that, we had Mitch, who lasted three weeks, and then Andrew. And then came Robertson, about whom I tried very hard not to think.

After a time, I realized the hall light was on and someone was coming down the stairs. I sat up and reached for my robe. By the time I got into the dining room, Chase stood unsteadily at the bottom of the stairs, staring at me.

"Do you want a drink of water?"

He nodded.

I got a glass and some ice and gave him his drink, stood next to him while he drank it, and then told him to go back upstairs.

"Get some sleep," I said, and glanced past him at the kitchen clock. It read 2:13. I felt something inside me sink a little. In less than three hours, Chase would be up for the day.

Four nights later, when I came home late from work, Chase sat in the corner of the kitchen by the front windows and Melissa sat across from him, and Chase's favorite book — the one about gargoyles — lay open on her lap.

"Chase can't really be upstairs by himself right now," Melissa said. "He's pretty scared."

I put my hand on his head. He didn't shrink from my touch but looked at me, his eyes big, dark, staring.

"Did you have another bad dream?" I asked.

He didn't reply but looked around me and then flinched and looked again. I looked at the wall to see what Chase saw, but the wall was blank.

I looked at Melissa. "Is Haley asleep?"

Melissa nodded.

"Chase? What's going on?" I spoke to him in the hale and hearty let's-get-the-job-done voice of an emergency worker. I'd found myself using this voice with Chase more and more frequently. It was as if I believed my brisk voice and the firmness of my statements would, by intention alone, get him back on track. I'd begun to lose faith in this approach when Chase saw the profilers out at the state park. I'd lost more faith when Chase barely spoke to anyone but paced around the house and refused to sit still, or woke me in the night with screams. He'd gone to school on Monday but had begged me to come and pick him up in the afternoon. I told him he needed to walk home. He said the Crips were after him. I reminded him that there were no Crips in our town. He said he saw them. He said they followed him. I tried to see things as he must: the five blocks home from the school with ragged figures dressed up like hip-hop stars traipsing along behind him, maybe saying things to him, maybe calling his name, maybe waving guns or knives. I stopped. I told him that it was important for him to walk home and realize that nobody was following him and nothing could hurt him.

By this time, I'd e-mailed Dr. LJ, who'd cared for Chase ever since we came to Chapel Hill, about med changes, but Dr. LJ seemed unimpressed with my description of the changes in Chase. When I spoke with him on the phone and asked if Chase should go to the ER, he said that he didn't know what the ER could do to get Chase stable. He asked me to increase the dosage on one of Chase's meds, so that he'd be taking 12 mg a day. When I saw Chase that night, speechless and terrified in a chair in our kitchen, my faith in the effectiveness of med changes or in what I was going to be able to do slipped a little bit further away.

"Chase," I said again. "What's going on?"

He stared past me at the hallway behind me. "The nailers," he said. "They were coming in."

"The nailers? Who are the nailers?"

"They nail you to the chair and kill you," he said. His eyes brimmed with tears.

"Where did you hear about nailers?" I said. I looked at Melissa. "Is this a comic book thing?"

"I don't think so," she said. "He's been talking about them all night."

I knelt down in front of Chase and put my hands on his shoulders. "There is no such thing as a nailer," I said. "Do you hear me? They don't exist."

He nodded slowly but his eyes were dark and wet and fearful.

"Do you understand?" I said. "No such thing at all."

He nodded again. But he looked past me and watched the invisible world crawl up the wall behind me and turned and flailed his arms a little and then took a deep breath and wept.

"It's okay, Chase," I said. "It's okay. You're okay. Come on. Let's go up to bed."

He shook his head.

"There's nothing in your room," I said.

He stared at me and shook his head again.

"I'll go up with you," I said. "Come on. You'll see."

"There's the executioner," he said.

I shook my head. "No such thing," I said brightly. "Can't be."

"Mom," he said.

"No," I said. "Come on. You've got to go to bed. You've got school tomorrow."

He looked at Melissa.

"Your mom's right," she said. "It's way past time for bed."

"Okay?" I said. "You're fine. I'm home now. You're completely safe. I will not let anything hurt you. I promise. That's my job. Remember? I will always keep you safe. You're in your own bed in your own house. You are fine. I'm here. It's okay now. You don't have to be afraid anymore."

I offered him my hand and after a while he took it and leaned forward and hoisted himself out of the chair. We walked together from the kitchen to the stairs and then he walked in front of me, one hand on the wall to steady himself, his head drooping to one side, his stuffed bear in his other hand. When he got to the top of the stairs, he stopped and turned to look for me and pressed one shoulder into the wall and began to chew on his bear while I checked his room. One window blind dangled in a crazy slant across the glass; the other had been pulled down completely. I stepped around uneven piles of upended and overturned books and dragged his bookshelf back to its place under the window; he'd shoved it in front of his easy chair, which itself was pushed into position so that it could be shoved against the door. All of the sheets and blankets were off of his bed, which wasn't surprising since he'd wrapped his white blanket around his shoulders while he sat in the kitchen. Waterfalls of clothing spilled from his dresser drawers. Anything that had been on a shelf was now on the floor, along with paper with strange letters and strips of the wallpaper border he'd stripped from the walls. Only his bed and dresser were left in their original positions. Anything that could be moved had been moved, until all the furniture in the room stood at cockeyed angles to one another, all of it in front of the door.

"All clear," I called. "Chase. It's okay."

He came along the hallway and stood in the middle of the room and stared at the window. He pulled the blanket up to his head and chewed on the satin binding and didn't say a word.

I picked up the sheets and blankets, remade the bed, and he

watched me and watched the air around him, as if things would emerge from nothing.

"Come on, Chase," I said. "I'll tuck you in."

He got in bed and I pulled the blankets up to his chin.

"You're safe now," I said. "You can go to sleep now. Here," I said, and took his hand in mine. I leaned down and put a kiss in the palm of his hand, the way I did when he was a little boy, so he could hold onto it until morning.

He looked up at me from the bed. "Mom," he said. "Mom. Mom. Mom. Would you perform a mercy killing on me? Mom? Would you do a mercy killing on me please?"

"No, Chase," I said. "I won't perform a mercy killing on you."

"Please, Mom," he said. "Please, Mom, please, Mom. Mom. Mom. Please."

"Go to sleep now, Chase. You're safe. You're at home in your own bed. I'm here. I love you. Goodnight, buddy. Sleep tight."

He didn't close his eyes when I left. I went downstairs and made tea and Melissa and I sat on the sofa in the living room. My stomach felt hollow, the way it does when you stand on a high place and look down and imagine that at any moment you will slip and lose your hold and fall. I looked at Melissa. "What happened?" I said. A blind man could see what had happened but I wanted to hear it, beginning to end, from her.

Melissa stirred her tea thoughtfully. Then she said, "It started out like a pretty normal night. I sent them up to bed and Haley went quiet. But there was banging in Chase's room. And I knocked on the door and he was doing something and he was kind of freaked out. He said the nailers were going to come get him. I asked him if he wanted a story and he said yes. So I read him *Gargoyles* and told him he could leave his light on but it was time to go to sleep. I went back downstairs. More banging. I went back up to his room and he was in there, moving stuff around. The whole place was trashed. And I said, 'What are you doing?' And he looked at me and he had these big scared eyes and he said, 'The nailers are coming for me.' I told him there were no nailers but he said, 'There was a thing in my room, there was a thing in my room.' And then he shrieked, 'Can't you see that? It's right there!' And I don't know if he was hallucinating but I told him there was nothing there. He kept screaming, 'It's right there! Don't you see it? Melissa! Don't you see it? It's right there!'

"Finally I got him to lie down in bed. And I came back downstairs but then there was really horrible banging so I went back upstairs and tried to open his door. I couldn't get it open so I pushed really hard. He'd put his chair in front of the door and when I pushed it open, the chair moved and he freaked out, because he thought I was whatever it was coming into his room. He started screaming. And I came in and he was covered in toothpaste. It was all over his hands and his face and his hair. He said he was using the toothpaste to protect himself. So I got a wet washcloth and mopped him up. And then I wrapped him in a blanket and brought him downstairs and he just sat there totally scared, saying things like, 'Did you see that?'"

Melissa sipped her tea and I stared at the floor. I listened for sounds but the upstairs of my house was, for the moment, quiet.

"I don't know," I said. "Maybe he needs to go to the ER."

"He was talking about the death penalty, about how he was under the death penalty," said Melissa. "And then there was something about the executioner. He kept talking about being killed."

We sat there in silence.

"If I took him to the ER, how would that work?" I said at last. "He hates hospitals now. What if I couldn't control him? I'm not even sure I could get him there. What if he freaked out and tried to get out of the car? What if he tried to run away?"

I remembered Chase in a frenzy, trying to get out of a moving car when he was five; I remembered him constantly running away when he was seven, kicking me when he was angry, shuddering with fear before his last surgery, clutching my hand with a grip so tight my fingers went numb as we crossed the pedestrian bridge from the parking deck over to UNC Memorial Hospital in the predawn dark on the day of his last surgery. He was a big kid then, 6 feet 3 inches and 205 pounds, and a fragile kid who could be easily hurt. The surgeries had left him terrified of hospitals and I couldn't predict how he'd react to the news that we were headed to one now.

At such moments, you have to make decisions based on a mix of things, none of them quantifiable. How much of my reluctance came from my unwillingness to tempt fate by driving Chase through a dark town, when he could not be anywhere where there weren't eye-blasting amounts of light? How much came from the plain inconvenience of having to arrive at a hospital in the middle of the night? I thought of things like work the next day and Haley's school and who I might call and how any of this could be arranged, so I know that I was operating from some deep place of assessment: Is this serious enough to require that we go right now? Or can it wait six hours, until morning brings daylight and phone calls to psychiatrists? And I'd read a small story in the *New York Times* about a man who was killed on a highway in Queens. His family had tried to care for him at home but when they could not and they could not find a place to take him, they decided to bring him to the ER to see if his medication could be changed. When they got to the hospital, the man was frightened. He couldn't be controlled. He ran away, straight into traffic on a high-speed road, where he was struck and killed.

For a minute, I imagined going through with it. I pictured the three of us, Chase, Haley, and me, sitting in the pediatric ER until two in the morning. The rooms around us would be filled with other injured and sick children. At two, the pediatric unit would close and the nurses would move the kids who hadn't been treated yet over to the adult ER. Chase, who would present as a complex and difficult case, would join them. He would wait on a gurney in the hall, while Haley and I stood next to him. All around us would be things I didn't want either one of them to see.

"His doctor doesn't think he needs the ER," I said.

Melissa gave me a dubious look.

"He increased his meds. Maybe I just need to give that time to work," I said. "I think we just need to keep doing what we're doing. I think we need to get him back on track and get him moving forward again. I'll call his doctor in the morning."

"Are you sure? If you want me to stay, I'll stay."

I told her no thanks. By now, Chase was asleep and he would stay asleep until four thirty or five. When he got up, he'd play his music too loud and it would finally be just like any other day.

IF YOU SPEND ENOUGH time among parents of disabled children, someone will give you a copy of an inspirational story, which tells how a family bought their tickets for a trip to Italy and planned for their trip to Italy and looked forward to their trip to Italy but when the day to go to Italy arrived, they were told they were now on a plane that would land in Amsterdam. They were also told that they must not worry because Amsterdam, while not Italy, was also a very beautiful place, with its own wonderful flowers, its own breathtaking works of art. The point of the story comes near the end, when the narrator concludes that Amsterdam is a darn fine place, full of riches she never would have expected, and she's awfully glad she got to go there; even though it wasn't the place she wanted to go in the first place, it ended up being a very fine place, in fact, the best place in the world. The story turns on the idea that one thing can be supplanted by another, that something as simple as *X,* known as Italy, can become something else, *Y,* well-known by the name Amsterdam; in this equation, not only will Amsterdam be equally pleasing, Amsterdam will hold unanticipated delights.

I'd already landed in Italy and been in Italy for some time when I learned that Italy might not be my final destination. And when I was told that Amsterdam might be my city, not Rome, I was told that I also might be headed to Paris or Tokyo or Algiers, as well, and at some point I might be in all four places at once, we'd just have to wait and see, try to understand as things emerged, make sense of it as we went along. I was shown a Venn diagram to explain how it could be that Chase would be a citizen of all of these cities at once, as well as of others that had not yet declared themselves.

The first moment of Chase's disability was either hidden and might never be known, or simply kept happening, again and again. Often, in those days, I would lie awake and try to think it through, try to understand when everything started, try to understand where we had gone wrong. But the inescapable truth was that, instead of one first moment, there were many, from the time Chase's pediatrician said that something might be wrong right up until the time Chase's doctor told me that no one really knew what to call this thing that was wrong with Chase. Each moment brought with it a new set of words, and those words did not pin down truth. Those words destabilized all meaning: global developmental delay, severe ADHD, pervasive developmental disorder, Tourette's syndrome, obsessive-compulsive disorder, complex partial seizure, Asperger's syndrome, atypical autism, psychosis, absence seizure, epilepsy, mild mental retardation, bipolar disorder, affective disorder, grand mal seizure, seizure disorder, Capgras syndrome, schizophrenia, schizoaffective disorder, movement disorder, movement disorder not otherwise specified, affective disorder, moderate mental retardation, autism, psychosis not otherwise specified.

These diagnostic words piled up. All had some truth to them but none was essentially true. Plus, things with Chase evolved over time. When he was nearly three, his developmentalist thought Chase might be manifesting the symptoms of someone severely attention-deficit-hyperactivity-disordered but he wrote a letter to Chase's pediatrician to say that while he could appreciate why so many people had observed something different about Chase, and ADHD might one day be a diagnosis he could live with, there were other possibilities, too; he preferred to wait and see if the best diagnosis wouldn't, in fact, clarify over time.

At the time, I ignored the "other possibilities." I hung onto the idea of severe ADHD and stuck tight to it, right up until the day the developmentalist said the word "autism" instead. But even then, he hedged and said that Chase, at six, didn't quite fit. So he said it was "atypical," as if that word would mediate meaning in such a way that the entire picture would suddenly be clear. But the thing about Chase, whatever that thing was, didn't quite fit any one diagnosis, not exactly, so his diagnoses came to seem like something that was about him but not truly of him, a suit of clothes he'd borrowed from someone else.

I had a kind of label envy. I wanted to know what was wrong with Chase so I could fix it. I knew that other parents got what seemed to me then to be simple answers: Your child has Down syndrome. Your child has cerebral palsy. Your child has sustained a massive head injury in a wreck. Your child has cancer. But certainty about what was wrong with Chase never came. When he was born, no one named his disability on his birth record. He didn't take sick and emerge a different kid when the sickness was over, so different that I'd been given a sheet of paper with a syndrome labeled at the top and bulleted points describing who my child was going to be, now that he was no longer who he was.

Instead, there was suggestion, supposition, hypothesis, and a very slowly growing sense that when something went wrong for Chase, whatever it was would be complicated and it would inexorably lead to another first moment, and then another, and another. A geneticist described it to me as "stair-stepping," where original sets of skills and behaviors plateau for a while, then drop precipitously to the next level, where they again plateau for a while before dropping again. Each level seemed to bring the opportunity for more words to pile up. But the more words there were, the less meaning any of them had, and the more they depended on each other for whatever nuances of meaning they did have. If this troubled me more than it might have troubled the average person, it was because words mattered to me. Even as I knew that meanings were provisional, contextual, historically situated, unstable, I seemed to hold to the idea that the classifications of diagnosis had somehow escaped the very provisional nature of meaning that I accepted everywhere else. I simultaneously held to the idea that nineteenth-century claims about hysteria, for example, could provide us with a kind of quaint taxonomy of nineteenth-century beliefs and second, that there was stability in the diagnostic words that twentieth-century doctors offered me. I believed in the certainty and absolutism of these words because I believed that if we could name this thing, we could cure it. I could save Chase.

IN THE MORNING, Chase was pale and quiet but he dressed for school and took his meds. It had gotten cooler overnight so I told him to wear his winter coat. He put it on and pulled the hood up over his head and then went out and sat in the car.

I fixed Haley's lunch and checked her homework. We drove to school and listened to U2. School was close enough that the kids could have walked but we had gotten in the habit of a morning drive when Chase hurt his neck and we'd never gotten out of it. From there, I drove to campus. When I got to my office, I called Dr. LJ, who was working at a hospital in Raleigh that day. I left a message telling him I needed to talk with him about Chase and it was urgent. I sent him an e-mail that said the same. And then I tried to do my work.

Even though I had plenty of evidence that something was going on with Chase, the school nurse's voice on the phone surprised me.

"I just wanted to let you know that we're having a problem with Chase," she said. "He won't leave Ms. Plummer's room. He tells us he's going to be killed by an executioner."

She must have heard my silence as resistance for she plunged on in a brisk upbeat voice. I recognized the approach.

"I see many things that worry me," she said. "He's very afraid. He needs treatment. He can't come back until he's had it. We think it would be best if you came right away."

"I called his doctor this morning," I said. "But he's not going to be back in town until tonight."

The nurse paused. Then she said, "Do you think you can get him to go to the hospital?"

"I don't know," I said.

"What if I go with you?" she said. "If you can get him there, I'll meet you there, and between the two of us, we should be able to get him in."

I hesitated. "I wish I could talk to his doctor before I go to the hospital with Chase," I said.

"You understand that the school won't accept him back as student until he's been treated?" she replied. "We can't have him here when he's like this. It's not safe for him and it's not safe for us. I don't think it's safe for you and your daughter to have him at home, either. The best thing to do is to take him to the hospital. I'll meet you at the ER. If there are any questions at all, I'll be there to help."

I PARKED IN FRONT of the school in the kiss-and-go lane and left my hazards flashing. I walked down a white-tiled hallway bordered in aqua and then turned right onto a white-tiled hallway bordered in burgundy and looked through the window in the door of room 713 and found Chase sitting at a desk in Carrie Plummer's classroom. He wore his coat with the hood pulled up over his head and didn't look at us. Carrie sat on the edge of her desk, facing him, and Diane, the nurse, stood beside him.

"Here's Mom now," Diane said. Her voice was bright and firm. "Are you ready to go, Mom?"

"All set," I said. I looked at Chase. "Hey Chase. Hey buddy. We're going to go to the hospital. Do you understand?"

He didn't speak but turned ever so slightly away from me.

I walked over to him and put my hand on his back and began to rub his coat between his shoulder blades and he didn't flinch or pull away nor did he lean toward me for solace. He sat as rigid as a board with his hood pulled up over his head and his face expressionless and white.

"Don't worry," I said. "Sometimes your medication stops working and you need to have it fixed. There are doctors at the hospital who can help us do that."

He didn't reply.

"Chase," I said. I thought about the things I said even as I said them, and wondered for whom I was speaking. Chase? Myself? But I kept going. "Come with me now," I said. "It's going to be okay."

"I don't want any more surgery," said Chase. He looked at me and then looked away.

"Don't worry," I said. "You won't have any more surgery. They're just going to fix your medicine. That's going to make everything okay." I looked up at Carrie. She'd been his teacher for two years. "Do you have his backpack?"

"It's right here," she said and I realized it had been sitting on the table in front of her the whole time, Chase's black backpack that he'd picked out himself so he could seem cool. "Now listen, Chase," she said. "You get better quick and come back to school soon, all right? We'll miss you until you get back."

Diane said, "We can all drive over in my car or I can meet you there."

"It could end up being very late before we get out of there," I said. "Let me take my car and meet you."

"What about your daughter?"

"She's going home on the bus with her best friend. I called her mother at work and they'll keep her until I get back."

I carried Chase's backpack and Diane walked beside us along the long white-tiled hallway and then out through the front door of the school. It was an overcast day two weeks before Chase's fifteenth birthday. Winter was starting to make its presence known. I opened the passenger side and Chase got in and I closed the door and Diane stood casually by Chase's door with her right hand on the handle and her left hand on the glass, leaning into the car, leaning toward Chase, as if he might at any moment bolt and run, while I walked around to the driver's side and opened the rear passenger door and tossed his backpack on the backseat and then closed that door and opened the driver's-side door and got in. I checked to make sure Chase was buckled up once I got in and then reached across him to lock his door. Diane walked around to my side of the car and I rolled down my window and told Diane we'd see her over there.

"I'm right behind you," she said. I watched her walk toward the staff parking lot in my rearview mirror. Chase sat beside me, his hood pulled up, his face still and white, his eyes big and wet and full of life and ideas he couldn't express.

I stopped at the intersection of the school driveway and Old Fayetteville Road and then turned and drove east to come up into town. Just as I always did, I pointed out Chase Avenue as we turned onto Manning Drive but Chase rode without speaking and stared out the window. I found a spot in the ER parking lot and looked around for Diane's car.

"Let's wait for Nurse Kiddle," I said.

Chase didn't say anything but furtively stepped behind one of the concrete pillars in front of the ER entrance. He retreated further into his coat and stared wild-eyed at the cars passing in front of the hospital. When a white van drove by, he began to say something about FBI profilers and the death penalty.

"Let's go inside," I said. "It'll be better to wait inside."

We were sent to the pediatric waiting room, where a small girl lay in her mother's arms and a man watched television and two boys spun bright-colored spools and cogs along a wire track. We sat by the windows and Chase watched and watched the street that ran along the hospital in front of the emergency room. A nurse called Chase's name and we followed her back to a small examination room.

"Let's have your coat," she said.

Chase hunched into it more deeply and pushed his hands into the pockets and stared darkly at her.

"How do you expect me to take your height and weight with that coat on?" she said and smiled at him. "Do you want me to get in trouble for not doing my job?"

"Do you need help?" I said. "I can get the zipper for you."

He shook his head and pulled the zipper down and pulled his coat off. He held it in front of him like a blanket.

The nurse took Chase's temperature, weighed him, and measured his height. Then she led us across the hall to a dimly lit room where a striped cotton curtain separated two gurneys and a glass window faced the corridor. Diane waited for us in the doorway. She was peeling her mittens off as we came in.

"Did it go okay?" she said.

The nurse took Chase's elbow and propelled him toward the gurney closest to the door. "Just have a seat," she said. "The doctor will be in shortly."

"No trouble on the road?" Diane said.

"It was fine," I said.

"That's a relief, isn't it?" she said.

The ER pediatrician came in. She recognized Chase from his earlier trips to the ER. She listened carefully while I described the reason for our visit that day. She made notes on the chart. She asked Chase questions about how he was feeling and what was troubling him. Chase's responses seemed to satisfy her. Just before she left she looked at me and said, "Someone from upstairs will be down shortly." The ER nurse came in and asked if Chase wanted to watch TV. He didn't reply. He stared at the wall and didn't move. She left. Chase didn't say anything for a long time. Then he looked up and said, "I don't want any more surgery."

"Don't worry," I said. "You might have to stay overnight for a day or two but nobody's going to do any surgery."

"No," he said. "I'm not staying. I don't like hospitals."

"Chase," I said. "It'll be okay."

"Chase," said Diane, "when you're sick, don't you wish you were better? That's what the doctors here will do. They'll make you better and then you can come home and be back at school."

"It won't take long," I said. "You'll see."

Chase turned away from me and stared at the wall. Then the psych resident came in with her clipboard. She listened while I described the things that had been happening to Chase. She asked him many questions. He answered very few. Diane described what they had seen at school. I talked about the way in which now was different than before, but of course my statements were completely subjective, based on that most imperfect witness, bare memory, and on the shocked sense of change I'd been living with since the day we went to the picnic at Cedar Rock park.

She wrote a number of things on her clipboard and then said to me, "Wait here. I'd like to admit him but I'll have to see if there's a bed available."

While we waited, Diane told me that before she was a school nurse, she'd been a pediatric psych nurse. When she saw Chase in the classroom that day, she felt she knew exactly what she was seeing. That was why she wanted to go with us to the hospital. She said she'd seen too many cases where ERs turned acute pediatric psych patients away. This would be an unacceptable outcome for Chase. So she intended to stay with us until she knew for certain he would be admitted. She was prepared to argue his case.

But it wasn't necessary. We waited and I bought dinner for Chase at the Wendy's on the second floor and the nurse came back and gave Chase his seizure meds and we waited some more. Around eight, the nurse came back and told us they were ready for us upstairs. I don't remember how we got to the fifth floor. I do remember the nurse buzzed and someone inside unlocked the door and we were let in. I remember sitting in the unit's intake room and answering questions posed by a nurse. The room had glass walls and patients already on the unit came by, especially two teenaged girls, who wanted to get a look at the new guy. One came alone and then came back a few minutes later with another girl. Then the two walked up and down and looked in at Chase. If he saw them, he didn't let on. The nurse flipped through her papers and asked me to sign at appropriate places. I described Chase's needs. The nurse looked at me funny but kept writing things down. By nine, they'd shown Chase his bed in a room by himself and I told him not to worry. The doctors would help him in the morning and I'd be back to see him during the day. The nurse told me to come back for a meeting with the care team at eleven. I tucked Chase in and kissed him goodnight.

THREE

|||||||||||||||||||||||||||||

Before Chase, before Zip, I knew about as much about disability as anyone who has never spent much time around it knows. I saw it as something forever at a distance, a thing that happened to others, a thing apart from me, a thing with so little purchase on my life that my considerations of it were, to be generous, completely inconsequential.

When I was Chase's age, I lived in a town so close to the Hudson River that my boyfriends and I walked in a state park that was little more than a wide dirt road along the river's rocky banks and a swath of raggedy cliffs over our heads. In the fall, the trees turned yellow and stood out sharply against the low purple sky, and the cliffs looked wet even before it rained.

One cold spring, a girl who was a year ahead of me in school skipped class and took some acid or did some mushrooms or otherwise altered her consciousness and fell or flew from the lip of stone that stood between land and thin air, the steely river spread out five hundred feet below. She landed halfway down on a granite ledge and had to be airlifted out in a seven-hour rescue operation that involved a helicopter. When she finally came back to school the next year, she was in a wheelchair and couldn't speak clearly. You'd catch bits of what she said in the hallway between classes, when she was trying to get through to the aide who pushed her chair.

Her voice was loud and flat and broken. She carried her books in a
dirty white canvas sack hooked to the back of her wheelchair and
what I remember is the dirty white sack and the way she couldn't
talk, as if each of those things had become who she was, as if she'd
been erased by the fall and replaced with an object and a voice that
didn't sound like she even knew how to speak English. I looked at
her and away, in just the way I assume many others did, curious,
repelled, unwilling to be friends. I carried in me the unspoken
idea that in her disability she had somehow ceased to be human,
and now, by virtue of her damage, was a human-shaped thing in a
rolling chair at which one might steal furtive glances.

My other experiences with disability did little to ameliorate this
view of the disabled as beings among us but not of us, as if each of
their particular challenges left them a little bit less human. This
boiled down to a shameful (but I think common) idea: I could
not see myself in them and so saw nothing at all. So perfectly and
utterly are the disabled dispossessed that this notion of their sep-
arateness is, for many of us, beyond contemplation. It just never
occurs to us to think of them as people like us at all.

I MET ZIP when I was seventeen, in the very first months
of being on my own in college, and I met him as if the world had
opened up for this to happen. Some things from that time stay
with me: how much of what I did every day was a mystery to
me, how much better prepared for being in college everyone else
seemed to be. I hesitated in the dining hall and I hesitated in class.
I wrote papers and I went to the library. Everyone else went to the
Quad to play Frisbee and smoke pot while the boys in Simpson
Hall blasted "Sugar Magnolia."

I loved the college and I loved the idea of myself as part of this
college but I felt as if I hungered on the edges of things. Finally,

my exasperated older sister, who'd gone off to school the year before and seemed expert in these matters, told me that I ought to do
something, join a club, maybe work at the college radio station, for
god's sake, get out of my room, and meet people.

So I found myself early one morning toward the middle of fall
term sitting on a bus with thirty other students who wanted to get
their FCC licenses so we could go on air at the college radio station. The college was perched at the northern end of Seneca Lake,
the longest and deepest of the Finger Lakes, and a two-hour road
trip from Buffalo, where we would take the test. The first minutes
on the bus were cold while we waited for the station manager to
show up and for the engine to warm and I sat next to a boy who
would go on to become a successful investment banker. He tried to
talk with me but I didn't like the way he incessantly nodded as he
spoke, as if his head was like the head of one of those bobble-head
dogs you used to see in the back windows of people's cars. Finally,
I held my book up and said, "I have to study." He seemed relieved
and turned his attention to a book on the Spanish Armada. We
both stared at our laps for a few minutes, our books open but
unread, until someone shouted, "Here he comes." I looked up and
down the aisle and out the bus's windshield, where I could see Zip
making his way across the gray parking lot.

He wore a long green army coat, a black beret, black boots,
jeans, and round glasses that made him look like a revolutionary,
Che Guevera, maybe, or someone from dark Russia. He had black
hair that fell down over his shoulders in a sleek pelt. As he walked,
he smoked and, even from a distance, I could see how hard he
pulled on his cigarette. The wind flipped the hem of his coat up
and open and blew his hair across his face; he lifted his hand and
pushed his hair out of his eyes and dashed the cigarette he smoked
to the ground. A minute later he jumped up on the bus where the

rest of us waited. Someone said, "About fucking time." Everyone else clapped. He grinned and shrugged and swung into the seat behind the driver and we were off. Later, he'd tell me that he saw me the minute he got on the bus but I don't remember this.

He was an upper classman. He ran the student radio station and his band played local bars. He was an American Studies major and had written his baccalaureate essay on the Green Lantern. He told me later that there was no critical apparatus to support work on the Green Lantern so he carefully made the whole thing up, from the names of essays and books consulted to phony authors to fake publishing houses. This may have been the first of many times I believed him when a more skeptical response might have been called for.

The college employed a self-promoting Famous Professor of English; allegedly, it was an honor to take a course with this man and you had to go to his office and get him to sign a permission slip before you could register. Rumor had it that before he signed that form, he made you recite passages from books like *Moby Dick* or obscure stories by Nathaniel Hawthorne. Once you were in, he had strict rules about attendance and locked the door to the classroom smartly at the beginning of each class. Nothing could induce him to open the door once it was locked and tardy students would be shamed for their tardiness even as they stood outside of the door, begging to be let in. He was clearly a man who believed in public spectacle as a form of discipline.

One day, the Famous Professor arrived late to class and discovered that Zip had locked the door. Zip later described this act as the logical result of a rule that applied to the class in its entirety. He had no patience for those who claimed superiority over others and lampooned pomposity whenever he encountered it. He was contemptuous of most of the faculty. Later, after he dropped out of school and worked for the college treasurer, he told me he enjoyed notifying faculty who had fallen out of political favor that they would be moved from their swank departmental offices to new offices made out of closet space in the basement of the administration building. He said this had happened more often than I might imagine.

No matter what he told me, I believed him.

I knew him as a brilliant, creative man with an impish sense of humor, a man who could speak insightfully on just about any subject that might come up, a man who had the ability to cut quickly to the heart of the matter. He also was one of the gentlest people I have ever met. In college, we were friends, not lovers. I had other boyfriends, a rotating roster of hopefuls, the rugby player, the art historian, the chemistry major, until I finally settled on a boy who dreamed of being a writer, the son of a famous literary agent. Zip and I only saw each other at the radio station and at parties. He later told me he would fake reasons for me to be at the station when he was there, like the time he set up phony election-night coverage of the local races, supposedly reported from the county Democratic headquarters but really broadcast from the student radio station in the basement of Murphy Hall. He'd called me up and asked me to come and be the girl reporter. They had too many guys on the air.

WHEN I WAS EIGHTEEN and finished with my first year of college, I took a summer internship at Fountain House in New York City. In those days, in the mid-seventies, hundreds of people who suffered from serious mental illnesses were being dumped into the community as, one by one, the big state hospitals closed. Just like now, there were supposed to be community placements for all of the people who'd previously lived in institutions but for many

people, maybe even for most people, there were no such placements and so they wandered the streets without food or medical
care or shelter. New Yorkers recoiled at the sight of these homeless, who raised in them the nearly instinctual fear of the mentally
ill that is commonly recorded across Western history. That fear,
which feels almost biological in our experience of it, stems from
our widely held and unconsciously doctrinaire conviction that
mental illness is a thing chosen by the afflicted, a moral failing
and a deep personal flaw, rather than an illness that emerges in a
single organ with symptoms as specific as the symptoms of failure in other organs. For no other illness do we throw its sufferers
out in the street and shudder when they come near us, not heart
patients or liver transplants or folks with pulmonary disease. But
those who suffer from epilepsy have been demonized across the
ages as the possessed, locked up in asylums in the nineteenth century for fear that their disease might be contagious. The psychotic
appear among us in popular culture as wise fools or mad men on
the heath, with some contravening force from God at work in their
brains; since the advent of film, they've appeared most popularly
as the wielders of chain saws and knives and hatchets, as cannibals
or demons, strewing the land they pass through with death, dis-
memberment, the bodies of the innocent. Even now, as they gather
by the sides of roads, begging, or sit in piles of smelly clothes on
our city streets, we offer nothing but contempt for the choices this
person has made. We turn our heads and say to ourselves, I had to
get a job; that man needs to get a job, too.

Fountain House offered job coaching and life-skills training
and group housing in little apartments scattered around the city
to those who suffered from schizophrenia. If you were a client, you
could just show up and spend the day at the clubhouse, talking to
social workers if you felt like it, keeping to yourself if you didn't.

You had a place to go during the day and once you got there, you could learn or practice job skills, have something like a social life, learn to live in an apartment with others, find ways to care for yourself, or you could simply have a meal and a place to sit when it was pouring rain outside.

As an intern, it was my job to learn the skills that we wanted our clients to learn and then pass my wisdom along. I rode the bus every morning from New Jersey into midtown and passed through the clamorous riot of the Port Authority Bus Station, where I was often accosted by men sporting large plumed fedoras who assumed I needed another line of work, and by desperate people who were running cons and scams — the three-card monte games, the pleas for money just to buy a bus ticket home because unbelievably someone had stolen all of their cash not ten minutes before. From there, I walked a few blocks to Hell's Kitchen where Fountain House occupied a five-story brownstone.

On the fringes of the acceptable world, its location was representative of the borderland still commonly occupied by the disabled no matter where they live. In the 1970s, Hell's Kitchen was only marginally a neighborhood where you'd want to spend time. Forty-ninth Street was narrow and lined with overflowing steel trash cans; over on Ninth Avenue, there were a few bodegas with crusty windows and newspapers piled out front; in between, you found brownstones with inscrutable graffiti sprayed on their old stone steps and rusty chains with padlocks strung through their wrought-iron gates. You had to walk many blocks to a D'Agostino's grocery. On Eighth Avenue, there were a few shabby Laundromats, as well as storefronts for businesses with uncertain purpose, but no barbershops, newsstands, dry cleaners, florists, dime stores, cobblers, or other businesses that suggested that this was a place where life of some sort was lived.

They took my measure fairly quickly at Fountain House. I was
trained to chop lettuce and to run a Xerox copy machine; I spent
several weeks teaching a client how to feed paper into the machine,
pretending that the machine's many Xeroxing options didn't have
me a little baffled and overwhelmed, too. Mostly I spent my time
hanging around with the clients in one of the social activity rooms.
They weren't much older than me: Ricky, who at nineteen knew all
the good bars for hearing live music and who acted like this whole
thing was a big mistake; he was merely humoring everyone while
it was sorted out. He didn't talk about it much but, given half a
chance, he'd tell you that he didn't belong at Fountain House the
way the others did but had landed there as the result of the work of
unseen enemies who were scheming to make his life hard; as soon
as everyone got that simple fact straight, he was going to go back
to Long Island, where he would maybe start a vending-machine
service. Susan, who often talked with me about hair and clothes,
had a somewhat disconcerting habit of watching smokers tap their
cigarettes as they smoked and tapping her own cigarette in return;
the taps were a form of communication oblique to everyone else
but as translatable to her as Morse code. Billy, who was planning
on going back to school and had even begun by taking a single
evening class at the New School; he played piano so beautifully
you'd tear up when you heard him but he did not survive his leap
from a rooftop one morning.

The older folks were more distant; in some cases, they'd been in
hospitals their whole adult lives. They looked to others to structure
their days, and if no one did, they sat by themselves and talked to
no one and looked at nothing. One sat in the same chair under the
same window wearing the same shirt and the same expression on
his face every day. I read the file of another: long ago, she'd been
a troublesome teenager with a tendency to disobey her mother's

rules; her shrink had her lobotomized, which led to permanent psychosis and forty-one years in a state hospital.

I WAS NOT COMPLETELY inept at my job but I wasn't very good with Fountain House clients, either. I was frightened much of the time, not of the clients but of doing or saying the wrong thing, of someone finding out that I was no good at the very things at which I was assumed to excel. My fear caused me to appear as a tourist among people in possession of a great deal more local knowledge than I, or to lack empathy, or worse. I could see that others around me cared and I told myself that I cared, too, and that the experiences at Fountain House were especially good for someone like me, who longed to write but didn't have the first idea what in her life mattered enough to write about.

In those days, I didn't possess anything like clear sight. I was much in debt to Sylvia Plath and Anne Sexton for the poems I wrote, but what my writing revealed was not my own deepening humanity but my shallow fascination with the mad, among whose members I often secretly thought I myself should be counted. I romanticized madness as a moral condition, just as our Western tradition taught me to, and I relentlessly failed to see the biological components in madness, the symptoms and subtexts that belong to organ malfunction.

If we romanticize madness, it is because we have, from the Enlightenment forward, elevated the brain of the individual to something other than mere biology. We believe that our very rationality gives us special status, perhaps just as pre-Enlightenment scientists knew that when the body's fluids circulated in unbalanced ways, our black bile would lead us to madness, to despair. When I worked at Fountain House, I had no awareness of any of this. I'd read Virginia Woolf and the Romantics and the Beats, the whole canon of those who called the public's attention to their distress. But it would be years before I realized that I'd believed in a heroic view of madness, as something that existed simultaneously in excess of reason and also as personal choice.

One day, in the late summertime, when Billy still played piano for us, Sulah—my supervisor—announced that we needed to check on Robert, a boy who used to come to Fountain House every day and liked to work in the kitchen. She also thought I should see the inside of a state psychiatric hospital, and so I rode with the treatment team out of the city to the small part of Pilgrim State that was still open. I'd imagined our destination would be one of the huge Gothic monsters that everyone thinks of when they hear the words *insane asylum*. I was, in fact, looking forward to seeing one of those places on the inside. But we stopped at a long, low mid-century building with a flat roof and few windows. Inside, the hallway was long and dim with doors to patient rooms opening off of it, each room like a brightly lit cell, each door open.

We found Robert sitting on a mattress with no sheet, wearing a hospital gown, his knees tucked up to his chin. He was tall and dark-haired and so emaciated you could see his blue veins through his milky skin. He didn't look at us. His face was expressionless, flat and blank as a plate. Sulah talked to him as if he could hear her, telling him about things we were up to at the clubhouse in the city, the wonderful things he was missing out on, that he had to get well and come back to us soon. His expression never flickered nor did he turn his head or smile or cry or even lick his lips. He sat on the bed nearly naked while the unit nurse found a vase for the bouquet of daisies we'd brought and talked to Sulah and said how much better he was doing. "Look at him," she said. "He's sitting up today." I watched him for signs of life, for his chest to rise and fall or for a glimpse of emotion in his eyes. But I saw none of these things. Instead, he stared unblinking at the wall and I stared at him until Sulah said it was time for us to go.

THE NEXT SUMMER, Zip and I both got jobs working for the summer conference program at the college. Late on a July night, after we finished checking the visiting Mormons into the dorms, we went to my apartment and I made scrambled eggs and we sat next to each other on the sofa with only one small lamp burning, sat in the near dark with the drapes moving in a night wind until fewer and fewer cars passed on the street below us, until finally the street was empty and the light at the intersection blinked from yellow to red to green for nothing, as if nothing existed but the widening space in the living room, as if our room had joined the night sky and was everything in the world the universe was. It seemed amazing to me that a room lit by just one low-wattage bulb could suddenly feel so spacious, could feel like it was expanding. And Zip made jokes but every so often I caught a solemn look on his face and then a kind of tenderness for which I was not prepared. We sat like that until the sky grew light and the living room came back up around us in the gray predawn light and I reached over and snapped the light off and we sat awhile longer and smelled the lake on the breeze and pretty soon after that, a car or two began to pass the building and then we knew the sun was up because the light in the room turned from gray to pink and then to that golden early light that feels new every day. We sat close enough that I could smell him and he could smell me; all night, we'd lolled and drunk and didn't touch one another. He never even brushed my hand, my hair, my face. When the sun was up, he stood and stretched and headed for the door. Our neighbors had begun their early morning drumming; they'd been to India and brought back tablas, which they played as daylight

came every day. After Zip left, I lay on the sofa and listened to the
drums and to his footsteps on the stairs and then I lifted myself on
my elbows and watched him cross the street and turn the corner
and disappear.

He had girlfriends: Emily, who loved horses; Marilyn, who
must have reminded him of his mother; and Jen, the tall blonde
who left him because, she said, Zip and I were in love with each
other and anyone could see it. I was always in his orbit, somehow.
Later, he told me that he used to watch my apartment from his
bedroom window and, when the lights came on at the end of the
day, try to imagine what I was doing.

Sometime during his senior year, he stopped going to classes.
He quit the radio station and he rarely appeared on campus. He
moved to Keuka Street and lived with his college roommate in
a third-floor apartment across the street from Cosmo's Bar. Late
one afternoon toward the beginning of winter, I walked down the
hill from the college, down through old brown leaves, down past
the graying lawns of the big houses that looked out over the lake,
down to the place where the sidewalks heaved and broke. I waited
at the corner for the light to change and then climbed the cracked
brown linoleum stairs to his apartment. I hoped to talk some sense
into him. I hoped to get him to change his mind.

Every apartment door had been shellacked the same dark brown
as the stairs and the air reeked of fryer oil from the crummy pizza
joint below. I could hear music from someone's apartment and
dishes clattering. When Zip answered the door, I followed him
into his living room where an umber sofa covered with yellow
flowers and brown leaves and a gray plaid upholstered chair that
must have come with the place stood next to a drum kit and a
pile of cords. Thin light filtered in through dingy sheers at the
window.

He told me that his classes were stupid, that he knew more than the professors, that college was a monumental waste of time and an even bigger waste of money. I asked him how many credits he needed to finish his degree. He couldn't say. Six, perhaps. Maybe nine. Six probably.

"That's less than one semester," I argued. "Worst case, it's just one semester."

He shrugged and reached for his cigarettes and tapped the pack against his leg to settle the tobacco and then pulled out a cigarette and let it hang from his lip while, in a practiced move, he slid his Zippo across his thigh, in one quick snap, to open it, and then in another quick snap back, to light it. He raised the flame to his face and didn't look at me.

Outside, early darkness had begun to fall, a winter dark peculiar to upstate New York, a big darkness that left one with the sense of being in a vault of a place, the sky high and the stars far away.

"What are your plans?" I said. I picked at the button on my shirt and didn't look at Zip. For reasons that I could not explain, I took his quitting school hard, as if it had something to do with me.

"I've got a job, if that's what you mean," he said.

"That's not what I mean."

"I'm not going back," he said. His face went still and quiet. I could see that the subject was closed. "Let's talk about something else," he said. "I'm sure we can talk about something else."

I MOVED TO NEW YORK after I graduated. I found a temporary position at a film animation studio and I stayed with my college boyfriend and his roommate in the down-at-the-heels place they'd rented on the Upper West Side; I went to work in the mornings and my boyfriend stayed in our room and worked on his first novel. At night I would lie across the mattress on the floor and listen to people throw glass bottles down into the courtyard. Later, after I went to work for an ad agency, I took an apartment on East Twenty-fifth Street, between Second and Third. It had one large room, one brick wall, a tiny kitchen, a bath, and a view of the Empire State Building if you stood in exactly the right spot and craned your neck exactly the right way. I showed it off whenever anyone came by. I could walk to work from there and walk home in the evenings, picking up groceries at D'Agostino's or talking with the Korean grocer or stopping in at the bodega to buy something and say hello to Abdul. After work, I wrote and eventually finished a novel that was so bad it took my breath away.

On nights when I did not write, I went to clubs—Mudd and the original Ritz on Eleventh Street and CBGB's and the Peppermint Lounge and places whose names I no longer remember. I began to wear black clothes exclusively and subscribed to Diana Vreeland's mantra, *Elegance is refusal*. My name started appearing on the lists for promotional parties at the clubs. Every year, at Christmastime, I went to parties thrown by filmmakers and commercial directors at places like Roseland Ballroom. This was the early eighties, so everywhere I went, someone had coke. I began to visit a diet doctor who kept an office on Beekman Place; like my colleagues, I followed his diet, which was essentially a schedule of amphetamines and Quaaludes. On several occasions I fell in clubs and felt strangers lift me up from the floor.

My college boyfriend asked me to marry him. But when he asked, he hedged his bets and asked if he were to ask me to marry him, would I say yes? I stared at him.

"Is that a proposal?" I said.

"That depends," he said. "If it is, what would you say?"

"For chrissakes," I said. "I can't answer that unless I know what you're asking."

He smirked at me. "Isn't that your answer?" he said.

"I don't know," I said. "What was the question?"

He looked away. "If I asked you to marry me, would you say yes?"

I kept my gaze level. "No," I said. "Not if you asked me that way."

We passed the winter and the question did not come up again. In the spring, I discovered that he had been having a three-year affair with my best friend and I decided I'd be better off without both of them.

At night, I lay awake in my apartment and listened to the sounds of my building; one night, these included the sound of police with dogs on the roof because a man with a gun had been seen going that way. They brought him down and passed by my door on the way to the elevator, his wrists knotted into handcuffs behind his back like a bunch of strange grapes.

I had no idea what I was doing. I had come to New York to marry my college boyfriend and become a famous writer but, after five years, I was alone, trapped in a job I disliked, in a place that scared me. I couldn't see anything in front of me but more of the same.

Zip called me in December and said he was in Connecticut to visit his parents for the holidays and did I want to get together? I gave him directions to my apartment and he was late and then he got lost. When he was almost an hour overdue, I gave up on him and took the elevator in my building down to the lobby and pushed through the front door and crossed from one dark side of Twenty-fifth Street to the other dark side, digging my hands deeper into my pockets, and walking sharply on high-heeled boots with my shoulders back and my head high, so I wouldn't look like a potential crime victim. I saw him standing on the corner, a dark form in a pool of cool yellow light, his dark hair tucked into his dark coat, the tip of his cigarette burning red as he blew streams of smoke out over Third Avenue. He told me that he was late because he'd been stopped and detained by the Port Authority police, who felt that he looked like a member of the FALN, a Puerto Rican terrorist group prone to making bomb threats all over the city. He must have guessed my disbelief because he made two fists and crossed his wrists and twisted his fingers together behind his back to show how he'd been handcuffed and taken away.

"Just for getting off the bus?" I said incredulously.

"This is the kind of thing that happens to me all the time," he said. "You know that."

"Why didn't you call me?"

"I didn't have your phone number. And then I had the directions written down but you told me a building with a doorman—"

"I told you a building next to a building with a doorman," I interrupted. "I told you 209 East Twenty-fifth. Next to the building with the doorman."

"I knew I'd get here eventually," he said.

IN JANUARY THERE WERE long phone calls back and forth and in February I took a bus back through the frozen fields of upstate to visit him; in March he pinned a silver eagle to my sweater. He said it had been his father's when his father served in World War II.

One April morning, while I lay half asleep in his bed, Zip sat down next to me and picked up my hand. The window was open and a breeze moved in the sheers and the curtain strings rattled a little against the window frame. He held my hand. He leaned over me. He asked me to marry him. I didn't say yes that day but when I left town and went back to New York, he called every day and asked the same thing, again and again, until I gave in. He had a ring made for me and he asked if men got rings on their engagement, too. When I told him no, he seemed so disappointed that I gave him the Hopi ring I bought when I was a girl.

But his question stopped me cold, as other things should have but until that day had not. It was the question of a person who lived outside of the regular customs and beliefs of our society, who drew a blank when confronted with actions based on ordinary social behaviors and expectations; he was genuinely puzzled and wanted to do the right thing but he had no idea what the right thing might be. I decided to overlook it. I was very lonely and a new life with Zip offered me a way out of the mess I'd made of my life in Manhattan. He told me when I came to live with him there would be no drugs and I would learn to rest and I would have to eat and I was only to think about what I needed to do in order to write. He was in a band and I was going to be a writer and it was all going to work out fine, provided I just trusted him and trusted us. He promised to buy me a big house where we could have kids and dogs and I could write and he'd have a music room. He convinced me that the world was wide open to us, and we could be artists together forever.

I took up my place in the story that he told himself about us and I set my hand to a contract that said love meant that we would both believe this forever. His world, the one he proposed, the one he offered, was far better than the world I saw myself, where I was every day miserable and afraid. And his view matched my dreams and I thought that all we needed to do was work hard and we could make all these things come true.

FOUR

||||||||||||||||||

Neurosciences was but one part of UNC Memorial Hospital and
had six floors and a Medivac heliport on the roof. The ER was in
the basement. While I waited for the elevator, a man carrying a
small suitcase walked up behind me, and then a man with a tool
belt strapped around his waist, and then a woman with thin gray
curls, and another woman who had two small girls with her, one
in each hand. We rode up together.

I turned left out of the elevator and walked through a lobby to
a hallway hung with a single small sign: CHILDREN'S UNIT FIVE
NORTH/ADOLESCENT UNIT FIVE SOUTH. Arrows pointed in the
appropriate directions. I turned right and then left and walked
down a long hallway to a set of double doors. On the wall to the
immediate right of the doors, a buzzer flanked a small glass window covered by a blind. I pressed and heard something buzz inside
the door. After a minute, a tiny woman lifted the blind and looked
at me and said, "Can I help you?"

"I'm Chase's mom," I said, and she flipped through the pages
on her clipboard and made a check next to something she found
written there and looked back at me.

"Just a minute," she said. "I'll come around and let you in."

I waited. There was a sign on the door announcing that escape
precautions were in place and advising me of visiting hours, the
appropriate times to bring food, and the likelihood of patients

being involved in therapy groups if I arrived at certain times of the day. The door opened and she waved me inside. She closed the door behind me and turned the key in the lock and then turned to look at me. She gestured at the duffle bag. "We'll have to go through that," she said.

I looked at the bag and then at her. "It's just clothing," I said. "His teddy bear."

She nodded. "It's policy," she said. "We have to remove anything that might be used to cause a patient harm: strings from sweatshirts and sweatpants, belts, shoelaces, jewelry, pens, pencils, razors of any description, metal utensils for eating."

I held the bag. "All of Chase's pants have drawstrings in the waist," I said. "He can't do zippers."

She frowned. "We'll have to take a look at that. Maybe you can bring him some jeans from home?"

"He can't do zippers," I said. "He has to wear pants with elastic waists, the kind that tie in front."

She took the bag from me. "We'll have to see," she said. "Maybe if we can pull the strings out, it will be okay." She pulled Chase's bear out of the bag. "I think you can have this," she said. Then she pointed at a room across from the nurse's station and told me he was just through there. A sign had been taped to the doorframe that told us in big letters that the person inside that room was on *Seizure Precautions* and *Fall Precautions*.

The unit could house ten adolescents at a time. The nurses' station was in the center and faced the dayroom, where patients ate their meals, watched TV at prescribed times, and occasionally tackled one of the jigsaw puzzles piled on a window ledge. To the left of the nurses' station, the unit hallway led to a set of double doors, closed and locked, which connected Five South to Five North; just inside those double doors was the Snoozlin' Room with lava lamps and murals of life under the sea and black lights and beanbag chairs that patients could earn the right to retreat to if they managed their unit responsibilities well. Between the Snoozlin' Room and the unit's main entrance, the room where Chase and I sat for the intake interview also housed a small library of books on adolescent depression and related disorders, which the staff encouraged parents to borrow and read. They'd also loan you CDs with titles like *You and Your Adolescent*. I was attracted to these in the way of a teenager who constantly revisits the scene of a car wreck he's caused, but I never borrowed them. I was pretty sure they were going to be more about "You" than about "Your Adolescent": a whole litany of charges about what a terrible parent I must have been for my child to wind up here.

An enclosed terrace with chairs, a Ping-Pong table, and a foosball table ran the length of the dayroom; on days when the weather was fine, you could stand outside and look out through the mesh screens to the street and parking lot below. Facing this was a short hallway with a classroom where group therapy sessions were held and where families could meet in privacy. Across the way, a music and movement room held a treadmill and an electronic keyboard. There were two isolation rooms where patients could be held if they became hard to handle.

Several teenagers in the dayroom watched me as I walked toward Chase's room. Chase had his back to me but turned when I said his name. I held his bear out in front of me and he took it and hugged it and put the snout in his mouth and stared at me.

"How was your night?" I said. "Did you sleep?"

He nodded.

"It's not so bad here, is it?"

He didn't reply.

I crossed the room and sat on the desk. Patients who'd been

in this room before had scratched encouraging remarks into the surface, mostly things like, *Die you mother fuckers die* or just brief bleats, like *Fuck you!!!*

"You'll be home before you know it," I said. "A few days. Maybe a week. It won't take long."

He nodded and took the bear out of his mouth. "I don't like hospitals," he said.

"I know," I said. "But this won't be like those other times. This will be pretty quick."

"I want to go home," he said. "I don't like it here."

"I know," I said. "But the doctors need to fix your medicine."

"And I'm not going to have surgery?"

"No," I said. "No surgery."

He crossed the room to look out the window. "The nailers were outside last night," he said. "I could see them. They were right here."

"That's what everyone's worried about," I said. "The nailers."

He didn't reply.

"Can you tell me who they are?" I asked. "What they are like?"

"They come up to you and they kidnap you and they hold you down and nail you to a chair," he said. He began to weep.

"They're not real," I began, but he shook his head.

"They were outside, Mom. Right outside last night."

I found some toilet paper in the bathroom. "Can I help you wipe your face?" I said. He stood still and held his face still and I gently wiped his tears and then held the toilet paper in front of his nose and told him to blow.

"It'll be okay," I said. "It's going to be okay."

He didn't answer but looked at me with haunted eyes. Then he took two steps back. I turned and looked. A doctor in a long

white coat stood in the doorway; his medical students crowded the
doorway behind him. He said he was from Neurology. He wanted
to know if they could come in. I nodded.

"They tell me that Chase is having problems with delusional
material," he said to me. "How do you see that?"

"He sees things that aren't there, he's afraid the FBI is out to
get him, he thinks the executioner is going to kill him, he stays
up at night because he's afraid of the nailers. He wants me to kill
him," I said.

The doctor didn't look at me. He watched his hand as he wrote
notes in the chart. "We're just going to do a brief exam," he said,
glancing up. "Sometimes the kinds of things you're describing can
be related to seizure activity and we want to see if that's what's happening here. He's had generalized absence seizures, tonic-clonic
seizures, complex partial seizures?"

I nodded.

"All right," he said and wrote something in his notes. "Do you
happen to recall if there was ever any part of the brain that seemed
to have more seizure activity than the rest? Or were they all generalized?" He paused. "What I mean is that sometimes the tests
will show seizure activity in one part of the brain but not in the
whole brain."

"There's an EEG that shows activity in his left temporal lobe,"
I said. "I can't remember when that was."

He made a note and then looked up at Chase. "Hey big buddy!"
he said. "Wow, you're a tall guy! How tall are you? Hey! Give me
five! Can you do something for me? Can you follow my finger?
Don't turn your head, just follow my finger with your eyes. Good.
Now the other side. Good. Can you look straight at me and touch
your finger to your nose? No, look straight at me and then touch
your finger to your nose. There you go. Good. Now hold your

hands out, like this. No, like this. There. Okay, you can relax. I'm going to hold my hand up and I want you to push as hard as you can against my hand with your hand. Just like that. Good. Now the other side."

Chase's hands shook as he tried to do what the neurologist asked him to do. The tremors made it impossible for him to hold his palms flat. He tried to touch his nose with his finger and missed, nearly poking himself in the eye.

After a while, the neurologist asked Chase to sit in a chair and hold a paper bag over his mouth and nose. "Breathe really fast into the bag until I tell you to stop," he said. Chase held the bag flat against his face and weakly blew in and out.

"No, no," said the doctor. "You need to open the bag up, here, like this." He took the bag from Chase and opened it and held it up. "Now," he said, "put the open bag over your mouth and nose" — he guided Chase's hands up to his face — "and keep it there while you blow. Go ahead, now. Blow."

We stood in an earnest half moon around Chase — the neurologist, the neurology students, and me — and watched Chase blow into the bag. He looked out at us as we watched him.

"You're going to have to go a lot faster than that," said the neurologist. "Go faster. Big breaths. You can do it."

Chase blew a little faster.

"Keep it up. Don't stop until I tell you to stop. Wait, what are you doing? Are you stopping? Do it again! Keep going! Way to go!" He smiled at Chase in an encouraging way. "Attaboy!"

Chase blew halfheartedly into the bag. The neurologist kept an eye on his wristwatch. When five minutes had passed, he told Chase to stop.

"Great job," he said. "That wasn't too bad, was it?"

Chase looked pale and sat with his hands limp in his lap.

"I guess we'd better get an EEG," the doctor said and made another note. "We'll do that in the next day or so," he said and glanced at me. "Someone will let you know the results."

THE READER OF THE EEG noted that he checked seventy-two separate instances but saw nothing that looked like unusual electrical activity in the brain. After that, the attending ordered basic metabolic studies, to see if something might be out of whack chemically, but these came back without findings, too.

I GOT READY TO drive Haley to school in the morning and early daylight spread around us. Our driveway sat in front of our house, next to a garden I'd planted with the kids almost as soon as we moved in. We had dogwood and crepe myrtle and cherry, and roses and daylilies and iris, and camellia and Chinese beautyberry and a tall maple that turned red each fall. I wanted this house to be the house of Chase and Haley's childhoods, the place they remembered first. I did not want to erase the house we'd left in the Midwest, not exactly, and I knew I couldn't do that in any case. That we are what we bring forward from the past is a fact that is inescapable and true, but I wanted Chase and Haley to make a distinction between then and now and to remember that when we lived here, I made for them a home, a place at peace, and in so doing, corrected, as best I could, the things that hadn't gone so well before.

Haley walked up around the garden to the car and brushed past the glossy dark green leaves of the camellia and started to get in the backseat, her usual spot, but I leaned across the front seat and popped the passenger-side door open and told her she could sit in front, in Chase's spot, until he came home. She hoisted her backpack and carried it around the back of the car and got in front next to me and stood the backpack on the floor behind her knees and then tucked her hair behind her ears.

We drove, just the two of us in our silent car, past packs of cheerful children walking in colorful crowds with their mothers. Some of the women had dogs on leashes and the dogs padded happily alongside the children. I watched the children and I watched the dogs and I watched the road roll out under us and just out of the corner of my eye, I watched Haley.

"There's Megan," Haley said. "And Trev." She turned in her seat and waved as we drove past and then she faced front again. "They didn't see me," she said.

"Are those kids from your class?"

She shook her head no. "I just walk home with them sometimes."

The crossing guard waved to us, just as he did every morning, and then we turned left onto the road that ran in front of the school, with its old cow pasture and its borderland of McMansions on one side, the long scrubby lawn of the school on the other. I eased into the kiss-and-go line behind a long line of cars and Haley stared out the window.

"Haley?"

She glanced at me.

"You okay?"

"I'm fine," she said.

"Do you have your homework?"

"Mom."

"You have to be sure to turn it in," I said.

"I will."

"I'll be home early this afternoon," I said.

"I know."

"You know?"

"You told me already."

"Well," I said. "Okay then."

I kissed her and she got out of the car and slung her backpack over one shoulder and headed for the door. "I love you," I said. All around her, kids ran from the cars, but Haley sauntered as if the world needed to come to her, as if she set the pace. I watched her as I pulled away and thought again how much like her father she was, from her strong, lean shape to the way that Chase's sudden absence revealed that she was many things but most of all, she was a mystery to me.

WHEN WE MOVED SOUTH, I'd taken a job at a local university as executive director of a center for undergraduate excellence. All day long, I thought about bright kids and the things faculty could do to help them excel. This job had many challenges but perhaps the biggest one was this: students came to my office and talked to me about their hopes and dreams and asked me questions as if I had answers.

My office was just across campus from the hospital, so at lunchtime I could go over and see Chase. On his first day, Pam, the nurse we'd met the night before, had somehow convinced him to sit at the lunch table with the other patients. He had a seat at the end, with an empty seat across, and he sat with his arms wrapped around his waist leaning forward, his attention on something not on the table or past the table, his neck strangely straight and still. He shifted a little and then sat with his elbows propped on his knees and his chin cupped in his hands and stared at the edge of the table. The girls who'd walked up and down the hallway when he was admitted sat to his right. The bony girl ate only two tiny spoonfuls of the vanilla ice cream on her lunch tray and the other, a pudgy blond girl with dull skin and very shiny eyes who wore low-slung jeans and a striped shirt, leaned into her and said something and the thin girl smiled and looked at Chase and then looked away. The pudgy girl ate her lunch slowly, with elaborate ease, and watched Chase and then looked at the other girl and laughed. Lunch was some sort of Sloppy Joe–style of sandwich, hamburger and tomato sauce spilled across a bun, a bowl of peas, ice cream, and a flabby piece of cake with sad white icing and one droopy chocolate squiggle. Chase ignored all of it. I sat down across from him and began to talk in my cheerful emergency-worker voice: "Chase, look, it's lunch! Let's see what we've got here! That looks pretty good, buddy, don't you think?"

Pam picked up his tray. "If you want to visit, let's go to one of the other tables," she said. "It'll be more private."

"That'll be fine," I said. "Come on, Chase. Let's go sit over here."

He stood up and fell in beside me as we walked to a small table pushed up against the wall. He sat down across from me and stared at me.

"How're you doing, sport?" I asked. I reached over and touched his arm. "This is okay, right? This is going to be okay?"

He wrapped his arms around his waist and leaned forward.

"I'm going to California," he said. His mouth twisted.

"What?"

"I'm going to California," he repeated.

"Chase," I said. "Buddy. You know that's not true."

He tensed up. "I'm going to live with Zack," he said. "Zack de la Rocha." He nodded vigorously and then came the terrible smile, without mirth or joy, a grimace of a grin.

He stood up and began to pace up and down the dayroom between the nurses' station and the windows, swinging his arms in wide arcs, speaking to no one. A boy who was done with his lunch stood across the unit with the telephone against his ear and he watched Chase as Chase walked up and down, up and down, and

I watched the boy watching Chase for a minute and then looked back at my son. Every so often he'd look darkly at me and then flick his fingers in my direction. I picked up the cellophane pouch containing Chase's plastic flatware.

"Do you want me to open this for you?" I held the packet out to him as he passed close to the table but he walked on as if I did not exist, until the nurses spoke to him. They cajoled him to sit down. He briefly stared at me and then turned and walked into his room, where he stood at the window and stared down into the roadway below. Behind me, the kids at the lunch table picked up their trays and slid them back onto the cafeteria cart and then drifted toward the classroom.

Pam picked up Chase's tray. "We'll save this for him, in case he gets hungry later," she said. She waited for me to say something but when I didn't, she said, "Maybe you'd like to try to visit another time? Maybe tomorrow? After he's had a chance to settle in?"

After that, I was outside and heard the lock turn on the world inside and made my way down the long silent white hallway on my way back to the car.

AT NIGHT, THAT FIRST WEEK, Haley and I ate our dinner and after the table was cleared, I did the dishes and she did her homework. If we finished when there was still enough time, we set up the Sorry! board and played until bedtime. At first I took it easy on her and didn't knock her men off the board but after she gave me a fierce look and ruthlessly knocked my men back to start, I decided to step it up a bit. Still, she beat me every time.

Card games were even worse. I told her that even though she was only ten, she had a future as a card sharp in Vegas and she cackled with glee and dealt herself winning hands again and again and again. She also played chess well, and I never could beat her at checkers and that was not for lack of trying. There was something exact, almost mathematical, in Haley's ability to look down at a board and strategize moves, tally the odds, make what otherwise looked like an intuitive move. I asked her how she did it and she said it was easy. She couldn't understand what baffled me and marched her men forward and piled up kings and came back at me from the rear and took all of my pieces. She kept a poker face until I said something and then she would grin, her eyes flashing, and take another one of my men.

After Haley was in bed, I turned on the TV and watched without changing the channel and without checking the listings. I took comfort in the murmurings of strange voices. Sometimes, I even stopped thinking of Chase, or of what seemed to be happening with Chase. It was the moment that I thought of Chase again that I realized that I had stopped thinking of him. At such times, I tried to understand how renewed presence could emphasize absence so acutely. I didn't know if it was better to try to hold Chase constantly in my thoughts, which was clearly impossible, or if it might be better to allow myself to forget, when the act of forgetting felt like an act of betrayal, if not something even worse.

THE NEXT SATURDAY, I brought Haley to the hospital with me so she could see for herself that the doctors were taking good care of Chase. I brought some more clothes for him and the nurse took these from me and dropped them behind the nurses' station where they could be inventoried. A dark-haired boy who would have looked like a high school jock if it weren't for his brooding and bruised expression and his wrists wrapped in fresh white gauze sat in one of the blue vinyl chairs in the dayroom and stared out the window for a while and then asked when he could turn on the television. We sat at a table under the windows that looked into the terrace area. I asked if we could go out there, but Pam told me that Chase hadn't earned the points to use the outdoor area yet.

"He's in his room," she said. "I'll go get him."

"Wait," I said. "Did he have a good night?"

"I wasn't on," said Pam. "I don't know." She paused. "I think so," she said. She looked at me and smiled. "He'll be fine. Don't worry. What does he like to eat for breakfast?"

"Cereal," I said. "Pop-Tarts. You know. Nothing special."

In the morning before school, Chase often liked to stroll out of the house on the walk leading from the driveway to our front door wearing his T-shirt and pajama bottoms, socks on but no shoes, swinging his arms and pacing up and down. If he was in a good mood, he'd crow like a rooster; other times, he made the sound of the gargoyles in his favorite book, which also sounded like a rooster crowing, except the sound he made was somewhat louder and more sharply screechy. I'd lean out the door and yell at him to put shoes on his feet so he wouldn't wear holes in his socks, but all of his socks had holes in them anyway. The morning had a feeling, a softness of air when I opened the door to call to him, the dark pines across the street, the way the air smelled like North Carolina. The morning had Chase, grinning at me and crowing.

"I'm just asking because he didn't eat anything this morning," said Pam. "We thought maybe it was because there wasn't anything he liked on his tray."

"Try Pop-Tarts," I said. "He likes Pop-Tarts. Or maybe frozen waffles," I said. "Something like that."

"How much help does he need with things like the shower?"

"Someone will have to teach him," I said, "and then someone will have to supervise him while he showers, to make sure he washes."

"So he's not independent?"

"No," I said. "He's not independent."

She paused as if she had to consider what it was she had to say. Then she stepped away from me. "I'll go get Chase," she said.

He didn't say anything when he saw us. Haley sat across from me and picked up a puzzle and hunched forward, her thin shoulders curved like the wings of a bird; she worked for a while on a long stretch of dark water below a boat on an otherwise bright blue sea.

"Do you want to play Uno?" I said. "Chase?"

He didn't reply.

"I'll play," Haley said. She picked up her puzzle and began to break it into pieces over the box, the dark water disappearing into fragments, the bow of the boat breaking apart.

"Chase, we can be on the same team," I said. I dragged another chair back to the table where Haley was waiting. "You can sit here," I said. "I'll be your partner."

Pam looked up from her work behind the nurses' station. "Chase," she said. "Sit down with your mother." She paused and waited for him to respond. "Sit down with your mother," she said again.

He sat and looked at the pile of cards in front of us.

"Draw to see who goes first," Haley said. She looked at Chase. He sat with his hands in his lap. Then he reached forward to the pile and pulled a card. Haley drew her card. They compared. Haley won the draw.

She dealt the cards and I fanned Chase's cards into a hand with everything organized by color first, and then numbers within colors, and held the hand for him, where he could see it if he looked.

Haley studied her cards before she played one, and then, quickly, two more, in a quick run. She looked up and grinned at

Chase but he looked at the floor at his feet, his chin held in his
hands, his elbows on his knees.

"Chase," I said. "Your turn."

He didn't move.

"Look at your cards," I said. "Here. Just point to the one you
want to play."

He turned and looked at the cards and pointed to a yellow six.

"You've got to play a red or a four," I said. "That's what's on
the pile."

He pointed at a red card. His hands shook with tremors.

"That's right," I said. "That's good." He watched me discard his
red nine on the pile. Haley dropped a blue nine and a yellow nine
on the pile and looked at Chase. He pointed to the yellow six.

"Right," I said. "Good idea."

When the unit's front door buzzer sounded, Chase stood up fast
and warily and his chair fell over. The nurses looked up. Haley put
her cards down and looked at me. I stood up and put my hand on
Chase's arm and said his name. He ignored me and looked at the
front door and when the nurse opened it, he backed away from me
and then away from the man who leaned over the counter to sign
the log and then turned to face the dayroom. The man was maybe
fifty years old and wore worn-out tennis shoes and dark blue trousers and a shirt crossed with pale plaid. He carried a white paper
sack and a gray cardboard drink carrier with two tall paper cups
balanced in the cup holders. He looked around the dayroom and
headed for the lunch table. Chase began to step away from me.

"Chase," I said.

He shook his head and his breath caught in his throat and his
face twisted and he began to cry as he walked quickly to his room.
Haley didn't say anything. "Wait here," I said. "I'll be right back."
I followed Chase to his room.

Chase had wedged himself in the corner on the far side of the room and had pulled the desk in front of him. His face was white even though the room was eye-blinding bright with afternoon sun and I crossed to turn the knob that would flatten the blinds.

"What's the matter?" I said. "What's wrong?"

"He's a profiler," he said. "He's a profiler."

"He's just a guy who's here to visit his kid," I said. "Chase."

He shook his head. "No, no, no," he said. "He's a profiler. He manages the death squad. He's going to kill me."

"Look," I said. "Here's Brown Bear." I picked up his bear and held it out to him and he grabbed it and clutched it and began to chew on the bear's snout.

"It's just some guy, Chase," I said.

Pam came into the room. "What's the matter, Chase?"

He chewed on his bear and didn't speak.

"Is your daughter still outside?" Pam said. I nodded.

"You can't leave her alone here," Pam said.

"I know," I said.

"We'll look after Chase," she said. "Don't worry. We'll take good care of him."

As soon as she saw me, Haley stood up. I picked up the cards and straightened them and put them in their box and stroked her head. The unit was quiet. I signed out and the nurse opened the front door for us. She smiled at me and said, "Try not to worry. Try to have a good day."

I looked at Haley. "I'm sorry this didn't turn out so well," I said. "Your brother's just having a hard time. Maybe we can come back tomorrow."

"No, thank you," said Haley. She walked beside me and her face was serious and still. Without looking, she reached over and took my hand and we walked to the elevators and she held my hand until she could push the button for down. She waited quietly.

"Maybe on Thursday?" I said gently, but she shook her head.

"No, thank you," she said again. "I'd rather not."

"That's okay," I said softly. "Maybe another day."

We waited for the elevator. Haley let go of my hand and walked over to the window and looked down at the street below.

"Mom," she said.

"Yes."

"Can I go over to Bonnie's house this week?"

"We'll see."

"That's what you always say."

"I'll look into it. We'll try to work it out."

"I don't think you want me to."

"I want you to," I said. "I just need to figure out how."

She kept her back to me and stared out the window. I could hear the elevators moving in the elevator shafts but otherwise it was very quiet.

"Never mind," Haley said at last. Her voice was small, bitter.

"Haley," I said. "I'll try. Things with your brother are a little uncertain right now. It makes it hard to plan."

"Just forget it," she said stiffly. "Pretend I didn't even ask."

FIVE

||||||||||||||||||

Chase hadn't been in the hospital very long before I began to think about Zip, as if I could raise from his memory some clue that would help Chase. In retrospect, things that appeared to have one meaning in the moment took on new meanings in the remembering. We fell in love in New York City and we stayed in love during the years the Strangers played roadhouses strung out on the web of country highways around Syracuse, Rochester, and Ithaca. This was in the early eighties, when Zip's band looked like it was going to break out and be successful. When the van pulled up at Sam's or the Tom Jones or the Penny Arcade, the roadies wheeled blocky amplifiers into the club, carried lights latched to long poles and tripods of steel on their shoulders, walked with coils of black cable slung over their chests like bandoliers. The band carried their instruments and when the amps and monitors were in place, they lifted their guitars out and slid the cases behind the stage, which was usually nothing more than a raised plywood platform and sometimes wasn't even that, and plugged in.

When we got to the club, I'd pick up my notebook and jump down from the van and walk through the fading late afternoon light across a gravel parking lot and into the bar, where the barman set me up while the band did the sound check. I wrote stories in clubs all over upstate New York in those days, wrote in dim light leaning over the bar, the sound of the band banging things together for their show beside me, behind me, around me. In between sentences, I watched the bartender wash glasses, dipping them into a basin of sudsy water and then wiping them down with a towel. When the glasses were done, he'd take the towel and wipe the bar, moving in a slow, languorous way, watching the band set up, asking me to lift my notebook and my glass so he could make a pass over the bar in front of me.

I stopped writing just before the show started and would always walk back to the van and slide my notebook under the front seat. When I came back in, Zip had already changed into his stage clothes: black jeans and a black shirt. He had a rock-and-roll body, tight and wiry, and the strong hands of a bass player. Mickey, the lead guitar player, favored bottle-green velvet trousers on stage, with a white jacket, his sleeves rolled up to his elbows. The whole band wore skinny ties but Mickey wore his pulled askew, over an open collar, as if he would otherwise suffocate.

Zip was not someone who dreamed of being in a rock-and-roll band and thought the gods had selected him. He worked and worked and worked, writing songs and practicing. The Strangers rehearsed whenever they weren't playing a show. Pretty soon, the shows were the rehearsals, because they'd been booked into so many places, they spent all of their time on the road. They had an old orange van and they stashed their gear in the back and hired a couple of teenage boys from town to serve as roadies. When the shows started, Bert's girlfriend Lainey and I got up and danced, which was our job as band girls. The idea was we'd get people out of their seats and on their feet and it always worked. Men came up to us and asked for dances but I would always retreat and say, "I'm with the bass player."

Zip's songs were popular, especially a song protesting war and a love song he wrote for me. People bought the 45s the band cut of his songs, and his songs got picked up by the Rochester radio stations. At shows, fans stood down in front and waved their arms and screamed for the song about war until Ed started the telling opening drum part, a series of soft staccato beats on the high hat and then Zip struck the first power chord and Mickey, who played lead, looked across at him with a wry smile and stepped back so Zip could stand in the lights alone during the first verse. By the time Mickey played the whining riff that sounded like bombs whistling toward the distant ground, it was time for the chorus and the lights came up on the whole band and flashed and strobed and smoke poured from the smoke machine and the crowd screamed the words that Zip sang.

I always wondered if anyone actually listened to the lyrics. Zip wrote the song in an effort to understand his father's Second World War life on a B-52 in the Pacific Theater. Zip grew up with the consequences of that war all around him, his father haunted by the burning of rice-paper cities, a cipher of a man, drunk, unemployed, who spent most of his waking hours in the basement, where he tried to put out a magazine for the lighting industry, where he stayed for hours on end, where he kept the phone that he used to call me one night when years had passed since Zip left home to tell me to tell Zip that he loved him, to tell me that he wanted me to know that he loved his son, and maybe things hadn't gone the way anyone expected, but he loved him, he loved him, he loved him. I gave the message to Zip when he came in and his face darkened and he turned away. And then he wrote the song and the song was like a prayer for understanding. They didn't speak that night and I don't think they ever spoke again.

NOT LONG BEFORE ZIP and I got married, he got a call from a big and well-respected record label. Their A & R guy had heard the Strangers' demo and said he liked the songs—especially the war song and the love song—and they'd be interested if the Strangers would be willing to find a new lead singer. They did not mean Zip. They meant Bert, whose reedy voice had a tendency to slide off pitch. When Zip gave Bert and Ed and Mickey the news, no one said anything for a few minutes. Sunlight sparkled on Ed's Pearl drum set and Mickey crossed his leg, right over left, and then shifted and crossed his leg left over right.

Then Bert said, "We're not going to do that." He looked from face to face. "We're not fucking going to do that. Are we?"

And everyone was quick to reassure him. Of course they wouldn't do that. Of course they'd go on as before. Mickey stood up and stretched and said, "Fuck 'em if they can't take a joke. Let's just try another label."

I stopped holding my breath.

When we got home, I asked Zip if the decision was final and he said, "We're not going to get rid of Bert. It wouldn't be ethical to kick him out now." He spoke fiercely, so I knew how much it hurt him to do what he thought was the right thing.

That summer, while the band was playing an outdoor gig, Zip stopped in the middle of a song and lifted his bass from his shoulders and over his head and walked over to an oak and held the bass by the neck and swung the bass against the tree again and again and again, the way you swing a bat at a ball. He hadn't unplugged the bass before he began to flail the tree, so the first chords were of a strange, strangled, roaring chord and the audience thought this was a cool new part of the show. But then they realized their mistake and a dismal silence fell as Zip slammed his guitar against the tree until the strings popped and the terrible roaring chord ceased and then there was just the whacking sound of the instrument on the tree and then the neck came off and he sent it sailing away, end over end, spinning like the single spoke of a wheel. Then Zip walked off the stage. Mickey and Bert and Ed stood with their arms hanging limply at their sides. Kevin, the sound guy, was the only one to go after him.

BUT IT WASN'T QUITE OVER. To pay off the bank loan for the sound system, the band had to keep working. This became complicated for several reasons: not long after Zip put down his guitar, Mickey decided that the time was right to try to drown Zip by holding him face down in a sink full of water. After Bert and Ed pulled him off, Mickey went home to his apartment and tried to open his wrists with a pair of kitchen scissors. Then he called Bert to tell him what he'd done. The wounds were superficial but he spent a night in the hospital and showed up the next day with his forearms wrapped in white bandages to tell everyone that he needed alcohol treatment. He was leaving the band.

After that, Bert and Ed began to attend Bible study meetings held at the home of the minister of a cultish Christian group called the Way International and Bert's regular expression was replaced with a strange glittery look around his eyes and a mirthless smile. He began to walk the way crazy people walk, as if he weren't fully anchored to himself or the ground. He received Christ, married Lainey, his long-time girlfriend, and proselytized about our immortal souls and our heathenish behavior, which included indulging in Christmas lights during the holidays. Ed, too, found his way to the Lord, and Zip and I began to joke uncomfortably that the town had been subjected to the *Invasion of the Body Snatchers*.

Bert and Ed and Zip put together a working three-piece called the Trapdoors, strictly cover tunes, and played parties and weddings and little bars during happy hour. Then they resurrected the Strangers and replaced Mickey with a keyboardist and made a new demo tape, with Bert's screechy voice still warbling over half of the songs, but this incarnation of the band rarely played anywhere. Zip went to work in a music store and Strangers' fans came in to see him as if they couldn't believe their eyes. Mostly they wanted to shake his hand but sometimes they said things like, "When are you guys going to play out again, man?" Or, "What was the deal at that show?" Eventually, however, they stopped thinking of Zip as Zip of the Strangers and he became Zip who ran the instrument department at a local music store and rang up sales at the cash register.

In the early evening, before Zip had to go to a Trapdoors gig, he'd refuse to eat and then would lie doubled up on the bathroom floor, the side of his face pressed against the cool tile, his knees against his chest. He told me that he felt dizzy and faint before he had to play and he said this was a sign of how much he hated doing what he had to do. I suggested a doctor. He said no. He drank. I thought he was starting down his father's road and I took all of the beer in the house and poured it down the drain. Still, even when the alcohol was gone, he'd fall. Around this same time, he began to faint. I'd hear him in the bathroom, a soft full sound as he hit the floor. I'd find him lying next to the bathtub with his eyes still rolling and I'd help him up when he was ready. He was always disoriented afterward. Most of the time, he'd whisper, "Just let me lie here for a minute. I'm okay."

I grew irritated with his falls because I believed they were part of his drinking, something he chose, something of his own volition, something he was doing on purpose, something he was doing to me, something he was doing to us. It never occurred to me to call an ambulance; I was too angry for that. Years later, I described these episodes to one of Chase's doctors and he nodded and said, "All kinds of things can cause syncope but from what you describe, it sounds like a seizure."

There was money from the band and money from Zip's job at the music store, but there wasn't really enough and I never planned to be a woman who owed a man anything for her support so I worked off and on at odd jobs: I sold ad space in a TV guide put out by the local cable company, I proctored civil service examinations, I taught a creative writing class at a local art school. I kept writing. I had the idea that I would sell something I wrote, something that would make me famous, so I wrote another extraordinarily bad novel. This one was taken up by an agent, a halfhearted gesture by a friend of a friend, who sent the manuscript back after a year with a dreary gray Post-it note stuck to the front and one word scrawled over the agent's name and return address: *Sorry.* I heard from another writer that the local community college would hire just about anyone to teach freshman comp and before I knew it, I was responsible for teaching twenty adult Licensed Practical Nursing students expository writing. I surprised myself by liking this job. They hired me again for the next semester but the chair of the English department told me that if I wanted to continue teaching at the community college after that, I was going to have to get a master's degree.

In the afternoons, after my class was over, I sometimes visited Zip at the music store. One day, a jazz guitarist named Roy came in to pick up his guitar, which Zip had laid out before him on the work bench. Roy waited while Zip slowly spooled strings on the instrument; when he was finished, Zip looked up at me and said, "This is the guy I wanted you to meet."

Roy was handsome and he smiled and shook my hand and then said, "Is there some reason in particular Zip wanted us to meet?"

I'd begun to write short stories in which my life with Zip was pointedly not the subject so I looked away from Roy and said, in a very soft voice, that I had heard he'd published his stories in the

New Yorker and the *Atlantic Monthly* and that Zip knew that I wrote stories and Zip thought that I should talk to him. About writing stories.

He nodded briskly and said, "We can do that." Roy told me later that all he knew about me when he started reading my writing was that I was this mysterious woman who knew that guy at the record store and lived in a small town and wrote stories. He was intrigued.

Roy talked me through the whole application process. I applied to Syracuse University because I told myself I could commute and get my degree without having to leave Zip. Once I finished, I reasoned, I could keep teaching the occasional course at the Finger Lakes Community College to earn some money. I mailed the application the day before the deadline and when I dropped it in the mailbox in front of the post office, I told myself to forget about it, that this was a wish that was not going to come true, just like the bad novels had been wishes that I wrote for the wrong reasons and sent out with immature bravado.

A month later, I drove to the state park across the lake. Our town sat on the north edge of the same lake and wine country spread out to the south. The Senecas, who first lived on that land, said the Creator had reached down to the soft earth and, pleased with it, had pressed his palm flat into the hillside and then touched the earth deeply. He left the imprint of his fingers in long swaths that filled with rain from above and with water from below until the handprint was gone and in its place shimmered five brilliant dark lakes. On the eastern side of the lake lay the remains of the old Sampson naval training grounds, where sailors were schooled during the Second World War and train cars bearing German POWs rolled up to the barracks. By the time I lived there, most of Sampson was in ruins and had become a state park still laced with crumbling roads bearing names like Liberator Avenue or Stratojet Way.

I slowed down past the entrance and drove past the ruined hospital, with its half-demolished frame and its spigots and sinks and half-hijacked pipes hanging over green tile floors, and past the old prison, which was a hulk of brick with a rotting roof. I cut the engine at the spot where I could look out over the lake, over the moving water and out to the high sky and pretend to myself that I could see the street we lived on as it ran straight up the hill under old maples planted in perfect lines on either side, pretend that if I could see the street, I could see what was going to become of us. I got out of the car and walked down to the water and watched a hawk riding the air currents above the lake. I couldn't see our street. I could barely see our town. The Navy sonar station was a blocky blur in the middle of moving water, and clouds that were neither rain clouds nor snow clouds rolled up from the horizon.

"I have to get out of this town," I said. I hadn't expected to say anything out loud and when I heard the words, I shuddered. They were true. I let them hang in the air and then looked around to see if anyone might have heard. The place was deserted save for the hawk that was turning farther and farther away from me on each new up draught of air, so I said them out loud again, and then again, as if these words were a secret I could keep no longer.

WHEN I PULLED INTO the driveway, Zip was sitting on the steps leading to our front door, smoking with his cigarette held between his thumb and his forefinger. He stood up and walked toward me as I stepped from the car.

"Did Roy reach you?" he said.

I shook my head.

"He's been calling here all afternoon. You'd better call him. He said he had something to tell you and he has to talk to you right away."

So I WENT TO graduate school and they gave me a creative writing fellowship and then they asked me to stay and do the PhD program and they gave me fellowships for that, too. I no longer taught at the community college but set my sights on a faculty position at a four-year school. But in March, before I finished my master's, I sat on the edge of the bathtub and waited for the stick to stay the same or change color. Outside, the sun was coming up and the plum tree rattled in an early morning wind and scraped against the house. When I figured enough time had passed, I turned around and looked and it was blue. I read the back of the box. Blue was positive. Blue was yes. Blue was Chase, already beginning to shape the world.

SIX

||||||||||||

November finished and we passed into December. There came afternoons defined by a sinking of the light, by blue hooded twilights where the horizon was a mere memory of daylight. Chase didn't leave the hospital. One afternoon, he was asleep when I arrived, lying on his side with his back turned to the wall. I put my hand on his shoulder and said "Chase," but he didn't respond. His face was slack and pale. I picked up the fleece blanket that my mother had given him for his fifteenth birthday and covered him with it and then sat down on the desk and listened to him breathe. His hair was greasy and lank and he wore the same pants he'd been wearing all week, stained, torn out at the hems. It was obvious that no one was helping him stay clean.

I was glad to see him lying still. He hadn't been sleeping at night. The nurses were concerned about exhaustion. His weight had begun to slip, partly because he believed the food that was sent up from the hospital kitchen had been poisoned and he refused to eat it, partly from his relentless pacing. He also believed that the helicopters that landed on the roof were giant insects, the unit was a jail, he'd been sentenced to death, upstairs was a concentration camp, the dresser in his room was a control device for a nuclear bomb, and he was Zack de la Rocha.

Someone had taken a felt-tip marker and scribbled something that looked like an anarchy sign in the corner of the room where the bed had been shoved against the beige wall. It looked like Chase's handwriting. The spring before he'd been obsessed with the idea of anarchy, although I didn't think he had a clear idea what it meant. He and Melissa made a black flag painted with the anarchy symbol in white to hang in the corner of his room, like a banner, over his bed. I felt hollow when I saw the scribble on the wall, as if he'd tried to make his bare little hospital room seem more like home.

"I don't think he's going to wake up," someone said behind me. I turned toward the voice. Sam, the male nurse who was most often with Chase, stood in the doorway, where he watched me watch Chase.

"He's been sleeping for a while now," Sam said. "We had to give him Thorazine this morning, so he'll stay asleep for some time." He looked at me with an interested expression. "Maybe now is a good time to talk? There are just some questions, if you could answer—"

I followed him and we stood under the bright lights of the nurses' station. "Why Thorazine?" I said.

"Chase was pretty agitated and he got aggressive with a member of the staff," said Sam. "Something about Zack? Someone named Zack?"

"Zack de la Rocha," I said dully.

"That's it," said Sam. "Who is that, anyhow? Chase talks about him quite a bit."

"The lead singer of a band called Rage Against the Machine," I said. "Chase's favorite band."

"Does he know him? He says he knows him."

I shook my head.

"Yeah," Sam said. "He was talking about a concert, about how he had to go on stage." He looked at me and smiled, as if to show that this was nothing to be alarmed about, and shook his head at the wonderment of it all. "Chase is pretty amazing," he said.

"I know," I said, and swallowed.

"Well, look," said Sam. He cleared his throat. "We keep noticing that Chase can't do things like take a shower or brush his teeth. Did he do these things at home without supervision?"

"He had to be taught how to use the shower. We had a checklist on a laminated card so he'd know what to do first, and second, and third," I said. "Things like: Turn on the Water. Wet Your Body. Open the Shampoo."

Sam's expression never wavered. Friendly, cheerful, utterly unreadable. He spoke mildly, as if Chase were someone who had passed from this country into some other on an interesting trip. "What kinds of things can we do here?" he asked.

"I would think the same things would work here."

"Huh," said Sam. He paused. "What about a haircut?" he said. "There's a guy who works weekend shifts who cuts hair on the side. We don't have a hospital barber but we thought maybe it'd be good to give Chase a haircut. With your permission."

"That's fine," I said.

"And his nails?" said Sam. "How does he keep up with his nails?"

"You have to cut them for him," I said.

"We aren't allowed to keep nail clippers here," said Sam. "Too dangerous." He thought for a minute. "If you brought some in, we could do it when you had them with you. And then you could take them away again."

I nodded.

"And maybe," said Sam, "you could bring some more clothes? Some pants and socks and boxers? He keeps losing his."

"Okay," I said. "But someone needs to help him keep up with his belongings. Otherwise everything will disappear."

"We've got most of his clothes in a locker now," said Sam. "He's just allowed two changes in his dresser drawer. This will probably help him keep track a little better, right?"

I looked away and then back at Sam. "Chase cannot look after his own belongings," I said. "He needs help with that. Just like he needs help with the shower and with brushing his teeth. It's part of the autism," I said.

"We don't see many kids with autism here," said Sam. He smiled at me, as if to show he meant no malice. "Truthfully," he said, "we don't see many kids like Chase here. He's pretty unique." He paused and gazed at me, his expression still blank and friendly. "Some of us wonder if Chase is autistic at all."

I wanted to say, Join the club. Instead, I watched a boy in the dayroom bent over his knees, a mangled paperback trembling in his hands. "You don't see many kids like Chase here or you don't see any kids like Chase here?" I said at last.

Sam smiled again and then looked a little more serious. "Chase's symptoms are so severe," he said. His voice remained surprisingly cheerful even as he shook his head. "He's not exactly run-of-the-mill," he said. "But I'm sure they've told you that."

The first resident assigned to Chase, Dr. Lopez, had rotated off the unit in three weeks. At our last meeting, during the last week of November, she wore tight black trousers and a snug pink wrap-top with a deep neckline; a gold cross nestled in her cleavage. Her breasts erupted from her navy blue lace bra.

"My plan is for Chase to be home by Christmas," she said.

"Do you think that's possible?" I said.

She nodded vigorously and her glittering curls bounced on her shoulders. "I don't see any reason why Chase won't be ready to go home by the holidays," she said brightly. "And even if he isn't ready to go home to stay, maybe he can go home just for the day.

You could pick him up on a pass and then bring him back that night."

She'd borrowed the social worker's office so we could meet off the unit. For the two weeks prior to this meeting, Chase had been insisting that his real mother had been kidnapped by terrorists and was being held hostage and that's why she never came to visit. He had been demanding that I be arrested. He'd kick me if he could, or hit me, although the staff usually stopped him in time.

"We'll have to see," I said slowly. "If he still thinks I'm not his mother, it might be hard."

"Isn't that getting better?" she said. She looked at her notes and then back at me. "I thought I heard that was getting better."

After Dr. Lopez rotated out, Chase's second resident was a tall, earnest young woman who wore plaid skirts under her long white coat, and nylons, and flat shoes. She gave me the name for Chase's conviction that an imposter had replaced his mother.

"It's called Capgras syndrome," she explained. "You commonly see it in psychotic patients. It usually happens with someone close, like a spouse, but it can also be a parent, or a brother or a sister."

"Will he ever recognize me?" I asked.

She shrugged. "That depends on how severely psychotic he is. If he stays psychotic, he might not."

"But what do you think?"

"I think his prognosis is very, very poor." The excitement in her voice gave emphasis to the second *very* and she paused to find a more neutral tone. "He's been acutely psychotic for quite a while now and his psychosis is very severe. He isn't responding to the drugs. In patients like these, recovery is very rare."

As the weeks passed, I found that the residents were, without exception, young, green, callow, unformed. In studiedly neutral voices, they eagerly painted the bleakest possible picture of the outcome. I'm sure they only meant to tell me the truth. I'm sure that they did not intend to drain hope. But I grew tired of young doctors who, in their enthusiasms and interests, wanted to be the first to let me in on their opinion of this very interesting case. By the time the third resident appeared, I called Dr. B, the attending, and asked if I might, from that point forward, speak only to him.

AT CHRISTMAS, I BROUGHT Chase a shopping bag full of gifts: a chocolate Santa, a Rage Against the Machine CD, two comic books, and three long-sleeved shirts that I picked out for him because he looked thin and cold. His hands shook as he opened the gifts. He undid the paper and it fell to the floor by his feet and he lay the box on the table in front of him until I said, "Look, let's open it," and then he struggled to pry it open and I said, "Let me help you." He stared at the white tissue paper and I lifted the shirt out and showed it to him. He looked away. Pam came over and looked at the things I'd brought and told me that he could keep the shirts but everything else had to go back home. He looked on without expression as I gathered his things and re-packed them in the shopping bag. His face darkened. I wondered if he thought I had just given him presents only to take them away again and I explained again that I'd bring chocolate every time I visited and his other things would be waiting for him at home. He looked at me and said, "Is my room still there?"

"Of course your room is still there," I said. "All of your things are there. Just like before."

He stood up and swung his arms and swung his arms and I gave the nurses the three shirts so they could inventory them and told Chase he'd be able to wear one in just a minute, if he wanted, one of his new shirts, wouldn't that be cool. I told him how much we missed him at home and that things just weren't the same without him and he stood before me and didn't speak except to the space beside him, in a tone so low I could not make out what he was saying. He walked away from me but at the last minute turned his sad face toward me as I walked out the door with the bag.

Later that afternoon, Haley and I drove to a friend's house for dinner. Black pines lined the road on both sides, with even darker forest behind. Haley rode beside me and the car felt empty with just the two of us. I hadn't expected this. I hadn't known that Chase would go into the hospital and not get better. Before this, I had understood in the way of someone taking in news from afar that there were limits to the things that medicine can offer; I had not yet understood that in the way that one does when medicine begins to fail someone you love. I drove and longed for snow and for all the Christmases of years past, when Chase had been the first one down the stairs on Christmas morning, when it had been cold and Zip and I had bundled Chase and Haley into their snowsuits and boots and walked them along snowy streets on Christmas Eve to tire them out before bed, when Chase had stayed awake for a long time listening for the bells of Santa's sleigh and he and Haley had lain in their beds and talked to one another through the heating vents until they fell asleep. Now Haley rode quietly beside me, her small face turned toward the dark trees.

WE RODE THE HOSPITAL shuttle from the parking deck to Neurosciences and my sister held a Christmas present for Chase in her lap. She told me about a friend of hers, a woman who was a pediatric psych nurse, who told her that Chase would definitely get better, that the new medicines were miracle workers, that there was hope to be had. I nodded and led her through Neurosciences to the elevators, and then up to Five South. When we came through the door, Chase was pacing up and down in the dayroom next to the artificial Christmas tree. He turned toward us just as he turned toward anyone who came through the front door and he scowled when he saw me and then walked up to me and tried to kick me. Pam told him to stop and suggested we visit in the classroom, where Chase sat at the long table in the middle of the room and stared at us without speaking or spoke only in the words he made under his breath and tapped his leg and tapped his leg and tapped his leg. When we left the unit after the visit, my sister said nothing, and we rode the shuttle back to the car in silence.

THE FIRST MEDICATION didn't work. It seemed to make him worse and worse again, as if whatever hold he had on this place, on us, on himself, loosened and dislodged and came away, like a ship breaking its lines in a swift storm. He told me his name was Zack. He told me his name was David. He told me his name was God. He told me he was the Grim Reaper. He paced for hours, from his room to the front door, back and forth, although his fear of the profilers, the nailers, the executioner, the giant insects landing on the roof of the hospital upstairs, the concentration camps, the death cells, would drive him back to his room. He spoke darkly of the FBI and of his own death. I stopped at the nurses' station when I came in and asked how he was doing. Pam or Judy or Sam always spoke in careful tones. He's had a bad morning. He's had a rough day. He says he lives in the white circle of executioners in the sky. Where does he get this religious imagery? Did you teach him hellfire and brimstone? He never stops talking about the angel of death.

HE BEGAN TO TIME TRAVEL. He told me that he was twenty-nine years old, that he grew up a long time ago. I asked him if he remembered our house, with its purple door and the lilies he'd picked out to plant under the crepe myrtle when we made the garden out front.

"It burned down," he said.

"No, Chase," I said. "That's not true. Our house is still there. I was there this morning."

"That's a past life," he said. "I live in the future now."

He leaned away from me and his mouth moved and moved and moved, but no words came out. His left hand tapped his thigh in complicated syncopation, a beat only he could understand.

AT LUNCHTIME, I OFFERED to open his Boost for him.

"No!" he screamed and kicked hard at the table and then kicked harder until he'd kicked me. "You get out!" he screamed. "You get out!"

"Chase," said Pam. "Don't do that, Chase. That's not nice."

I stood up. "It's okay," I said. I looked around, shocked by the strength with which Chase had lashed out.

"Maybe it'd be better to come back tomorrow," Pam said. "He's had a rough morning."

I walked past the nurses' station. One of them tried to comfort me. "It's the illness that makes him do that," she said. "He doesn't really want to kick you. You understand."

SEVEN

It's only when I looked back on it that I saw things you might call identifiable signs. Instead of choosing someone, I let someone who loved me choose me. When Zip talked about me, he lingered over the details from the years we were friends: the way I looked one night at a party, dressed in a long, slinky, black halter dress with my shoulders bare and my dark hair framing my face. He told me that during the years we were apart, he used to look up at the moon and remember that I was under the same moon, that we were still connected because the moon shed its light on both of us. He wrote songs for me and when he played those songs, no matter where he was, he played them to me. Even when the band had fallen apart and the Trapdoors were playing cover tunes at some dive bar, I'd walk in the room and he would begin to sing "I Saw Her Standing There" and wink at me from the stage.

But there were signs. His misunderstanding about the engagement ring was the misunderstanding of someone who'd arrived on this planet from the moon. When the utility company turned the electricity off in his apartment for nonpayment of the bill, instead of having the lights turned back on, he said he refused to play their game, that they just wanted to see how much they could rip him off, and he lived in the dark and called himself an Urban Camper. He told me the reason he'd quit school was that there was no more money: his father had taken out student loans in his name to sink into the family business and refused to repay them and there was nothing left. He growled at me when I suggested talking to the financial-aid office about other things that could be done. When he moved out of his Keuka Street apartment into our new place, I found a letter written two years before but never sent. Addressed to his mother, it described how he had just met the girl he was going to marry. It wasn't me.

At that moment I could have understood that Zip wanted someone to marry and it didn't have anything to do with me but I was a sleepwalker in my own life when we courted, and I wanted someone to marry me as much as Zip wanted to marry someone. I set the letter down and walked into the kitchen, where Zip sat at the table, leafing through a pile of his drawings. There were beautifully rendered portraits of people he knew and he stopped at one and lifted it out and turned it around and said, "Look. This is the one I did of you." He'd used my photograph in my college yearbook as his model and when I saw the drawing, I saw myself, only now I was beautiful.

When we moved in together, he began to use the name Art Byrd, casually at first, and then with some regularity. Mail came addressed to Art Byrd. He used the name Art Byrd when he talked to the people at the record company. We had silly nicknames for each other, the way people in love always do, Bunny and Bird, and he left little cartoons of the adventures of Bunny and Bird on the kitchen table for me in place of grocery lists or notes about where he'd gone when he went out. When I asked him about Art Byrd, Zip said it just made sense to him to append Art to Bird—he was an artist, after all, wasn't he?—and then change the spelling so Byrd looked more like a name. He told me it didn't mean anything, but there were just some people he preferred never learn where he was. He cast it as a matter of privacy so I didn't recognize the fluttering wing of paranoia. Still, something in me closed a little whenever I saw that name, as if I knew something wasn't right.

He told me that when he was growing up, he felt like an alien left in the wrong family. He told me that when he was little, his parents could not keep up with him or catch him and that's how he ended up being hit by a bus. He rode his tricycle down a flight of stairs. When he said what he felt like saying, and his mother washed his mouth out with soap, he let her and just when she had the bar of soap to his lips, he bit the soap in half and tried to eat it instead. He told me his parents were endlessly frustrated with him, and that he learned things he liked and ignored things he didn't. His report cards were a punch-work of A's and F's. He told me he could fix any engine on earth. He told me that he'd spent a year or two in high school racing at some backwoods Jersey track and practically the first car he bought was a white Aston Martin, a convertible, and he used to race that car whenever he had a chance. He'd had to learn how to fix engines because of the racing. When I bought my first car, an old Buick, he popped the hood and stared down at the coils and carburetor and plugs and pins and belts and said that some newfangled mechanics must have come up with this engine and he preferred not to touch it—he didn't have a clue how it worked.

He wanted less and less to do with people and began to ask me to turn down invitations to parties. When he refused to go out at night and sat silently reading the same book over and over again, he told me it was because he was around people and on his feet all day and just didn't want to do anything when he got home. I began to plan activities for us so I wouldn't be cooped up all the time, drives around the lake, trips to junk shops to buy furniture I'd remake into something we could use, walks in the woods to look for birds. We could drive to Montezuma Wildlife Refuge

easily from where we lived and walk a three-mile trail through
the open pasture and forest and then ease the car slowly along the
road on the embankment above the wetlands, watching great blue
herons and vast flocks of Brant geese during the flyway months.
I kept a list of all the birds we saw and Zip walked with me and
made sure I checked things off: the American bittern, the green
heron, the night heron, the common yellowthroat.

CHASE WAS BORN on a Tuesday in late November, just shy
of Thanksgiving. After labor failed, they draped me and anesthe-
tized me and angled mirrors so I could see the moment when the
doctor, after a pull and a tug and a twist and a twist again, lifted
Chase free of the cord; I watched the doctor turn him through the
cord wrapped around his neck and shoulder the way you might
untangle the knot of a necktie. He was bluish pink and did not cry
but squeezed his eyes shut and said "Ack." They cleaned him up
and brought him to me and I reached up to him and he cracked
his eyes open and looked at me, his eyes glittery dark crescents
under the brilliant lamps of the OR. I swore he could recognize
me. "Hey Chase," I said. "It's good to see you. Hey Chase. Hey."

My master's thesis was due in two weeks and my feminist lit
professors gave me a one-week extension on my final seminar paper
because I'd had a C-section. They had explained to me when I was
pregnant that they otherwise expected me to be back in class right
after the birth. "This is what we did," one said. "This is what you
have to be prepared to do." When I announced the pregnancy,
one of them had called me into her office and asked me if I had
thought at all about not having this baby. "In terms of your ca-
reer," she said, "this is not the best timing."

We put Chase in a baby carriage in the kitchen and Zip set
my typewriter up at the kitchen table and I sat in a chair with a

pillow across my incision and retyped the pages of my stories on the special formatted paper the graduate school demanded for the submission of theses and dissertations. When I got tired, I lay on the sofa with Chase on my stomach and felt his weight and his wiggles. At night, Zip typed what I could not, working slowly, because these were not his words, and he did not know the endings.

I spent the winter reading and holding Chase in my arms. I loved his weight in my lap and I loved the way he gazed up at me and grinned his gummy toothless grin. I loved the way he kicked his feet when he lay nestled in blankets in his baby seat, and I loved the way he cried and peed and puked and pooped, the way he grinned at me, as if we had some special secret. I carried him around in a Snugli and walked him in his carriage and all the while, I felt the conviction that no matter what happened, I would never let anything bad happen to him, that I would stand between him and everything painful in the world.

In the summer, when my exams were over, I took him to the lake and dipped his toes in the water and held him so he could see the schools of minnows that sometimes came right up to the shore, slim fish darting like silver needles as they turned and turned and turned again in the clear, shallow water.

When Chase was thirteen months old, his pediatrician sent a social worker and an occupational therapist from the local cerebral palsy agency to our house to observe Chase once a month for six months. Everyone agreed that something might be wrong but no one knew what that something might be. Chase had kept his Moro reflex, that exaggerated startle response that newborns have in the first weeks of life, and he had not hit his developmental benchmarks. At his first birthday, when the doctor told me that Chase had global developmental delay, he said that this was probably completely normal, that some kids just reach things more slowly than others, that we'd just keep an eye on things, see what happened. He didn't seem alarmed so I was not alarmed. We didn't have the Internet in those days so I could not start reading every online article I could find about global developmental delay. I didn't even go to the library. The pediatrician asked me if anyone in my family had ever been labeled *slow* and I told him I didn't think so, unless maybe my cousin, whom I vaguely remembered the adults talking about as if he might be a half-wit when I was a girl. But he'd grown up just fine, had graduated from college, had gone to work in an executive position with a telecommunications company — surely this couldn't be what the pediatrician meant.

The social worker had a degree in psychology, runs in her baggy brown stockings, battered shoes so down at the heels that there were barely any heels left, and wild, thin black hair that stood quill-like away from her pale gray scalp. I thought she looked like an escaped mental patient. She checked to see if there was Appropriate Mother-Infant Bonding. Check. The occupational therapist had me sit tailor-style on the floor behind Chase, ready to catch him should he tumble to one side when she rolled a red and white ball to him. He was supposed to acknowledge the ball and reach for it. Half a Check. They both tried to get him to wave bye-bye. No Check. They asked me if he had any words yet and I mentioned his love for the sound *ba-ba-ba-ba-ba* which had begun when he was seven months old and continued without variation. No Check.

The whole thing took about an hour and when they were through we stood in a shaft of dusty sunlight by my front door while I held Chase on my hip and he beamed and beamed and they explained that they thought the pediatrician was right, there was something a little bit off, but they couldn't say what. They said they'd be back next month. They said tracking Chase this way gave us the greatest chance of figuring out what, if anything, was wrong, and the greatest chance of knowing what to do about it.

At the end of six months, after six visits, six assessments of Appropriate Mother-Infant Bonding, six rolls of the red and white ball, six times playing with blocks that Chase was supposed to use to build a tower but which he generally ignored, after six times looking at picture books where Chase failed to say *kitty* when he saw the picture of the cat, after six afternoons where the visits dredged up in me the terrible fear that something might really be wrong with Chase, although I couldn't see what—after six months of this, the social worker and the occupational therapist made their report. They explained that something was wrong but they didn't know its name.

Chase's pediatrician frowned as he read the report and said in a way that made me realize that he felt the opposite, "This is helpful, don't you think?" He waited for me to say something but all I said was, "What do we do now?"

Mostly we waited and played with Chase. Zip worked at the music store and I finished my classes and worked on my dissertation. When Chase was eighteen months old, we took him to London for part of one summer. Zip and Chase went to different playgrounds in the city while I did research at the British Library. When we went to museums on weekends, the Italian tourists were horrified that we kept Chase in a harness attached to a leash whenever he was not in his stroller, but Chase never walked, except finally, one day, just before we got on the plane, he got up and ran, and from that point forward was nothing but a blur, hurtling from one dangerous thing to the next; he ignored our cries of *stop!* so much that I had him tested to see if he might be deaf.

He loved the steps in the children's gallery at the Museum of Natural History in South Kensington that lit up in colors when he stepped on them and years later insisted that he remembered these. He loved the steps at the Tower of London, too, and the sewer grates, and then wouldn't look at anything but steps or sewer grates, even when we went to the zoo in Regent's Park, which we left with me in tears and Zip carrying Chase, who thrashed and screamed and twisted and bent and beat his heels against his father's thighs and arched his back and flailed and tried to get away. We'd made the mistake of trying to interest him in a display of bears, rather than a drain at the bottom of a set of steps.

CHASE SAT ON THE paper-covered table at the pediatrician's office and pulled at the paper and grinned when it crinkled and crackled. He looked me in the eye and did it again. I said, "Chase, please." He swung around and dropped his legs over the side and began tapping the heels of his sneakers together, so the lights embedded in the rubber would flash red and red and red.

The pediatrician sat on a rolling stool and watched him.

"We can see that Chase isn't developing in a typical way," he said. "That's clear by now, right?" His voice sounded almost pleading.

I wasn't so sure. At three, Chase was still a package of mysteries to us but I thought that was because we were new parents and neither of us had spent time around babies or toddlers. The very act of pinning a diaper in place had seemed to us to be a great achievement. And nothing about Chase seemed wrong, no matter what people told us. He smiled and he seemed happy.

"Yes," said Zip. He sighed and crossed his arms over his chest. "Okay."

I thought about his day-care teachers, who kept sending notes about Chase's inability to do the things the other kids did. I watched him kick his feet and then jump down and try to leave the room. Zip lifted him into the air and Chase struggled against him and, when he could not break free, began to turn and try to push himself away from his father with both hands, with the soles of his feet.

"All right," I said. "Yes."

"Good," said the doctor. "We're agreed. Chase will go up to the Developmental Disabilities Clinic at Strong Children's Hospital in Rochester. No one is saying Chase is developmentally disabled. He's such an odd mix of things that it's hard to say what's going on. But they've got whole teams of people who do nothing but look at children like Chase. They are the best people to help us figure this out."

As we headed for the door, the pediatrician stopped us. "I can't tell you what the outcome might be," he said. "I can only tell you that Chase is healthy and he has some skills and he keeps acquiring new ones. Even if he isn't quite on the time line, he's not losing skills. That's the thing we really worry about," he said. "When we see a child disintegrate, that's when we know we've got something very serious going on."

WE TRIED TO STAY in the room with Chase when they began the tests but the team felt we distracted him and so directed us to sit in chairs behind a one-way mirror. We could watch Chase but Chase couldn't see us. The team psychologist asked him to sit at a low brown wood table and manipulate some shapes. The idea was to place the shapes in the right spots on the board, a square into a square, a triangle into a triangle, a circle into a circle. The psychologist sat next to Chase and said cheerful and encouraging things and every time he tried one of the shapes on the board, I leaned forward and whispered under my breath, "Come on, Chase. You can do this, Chase."

A week later, when we returned, the clinic's pediatrician showed us all of the places where Chase didn't test the way a three-year-old should. In some places, he didn't even test the way a one-year-old should. They'd given up trying to determine his IQ; there was so much scatter on the test that it was impossible to interpret the results. His attention seemed to be severely impaired. He lacked skills that a three-year-old should have—dressing himself and brushing his teeth, for example—but he knew the alphabet and he knew his numbers and he liked to talk. The doctor told us it was simply not possible to say what was wrong. He preferred to think that whatever it was would make itself clear in time. Certainly, Chase had very interesting features of ADHD and Tourette's syndrome, and pervasive developmental disorder or PDD (the autistic syndromes), all overlapping as if they made up an unusual diagram at whose very center we found Chase. But no one thing stood out, no one thing made itself manifest. And he didn't want us to raise a syndrome. He wanted us to raise our child. He told us to go home and enjoy Chase and he'd see us back in six months.

EIGHT

‖‖‖‖‖‖‖‖‖‖‖‖‖‖‖‖‖‖‖‖‖‖‖‖

One Saturday morning, after Chase had been on Five South for three months, I took Haley to her first riding lesson. On our way to the barn, we passed stands of dark pines and cold pastures and a cow barn with a long slope of firm mud that leveled off in a brackish black pond. It was winter and the trees were still bare but, in time, dogwoods would bloom white against the black trees, and redbuds would purple the sides of the road.

The barn sat down in a hollow between two fields, just down the road from a country church and across the way from a ranch house where, the year before, a man had killed his daughter, his daughter's best friend, and her two-year-old boy. Fences lined the driveway and a splotchy gray pony grazed in the pasture beside the barn. A riding ring lay in front of the barn. The lesson before Haley's was coming to an end and the three girls on the ponies in the ring had turned them to the center and sat gingerly patting the ponies' shoulders. One reached forward and rubbed the mane between her pony's ears and then swung her leg over the saddle and climbed down. Just across the field, two turkey vultures turned circles in the bright blue sky.

I walked beside Haley to the tack room, where she picked out a helmet and put it on. She wouldn't let me check the chinstrap but told me it was fine. The other girls in the beginner lesson were already mounted up when we got back to the ring. The woman who owned the barn stood in the center and held the reins of a palomino pony named Ed. His mane fell over his eyes and he stood with his head down, swishing his pale blond tail and shifting his weight from hoof to hoof.

Haley walked into the ring and I followed her. She stopped and stood still. She looked at the pony. She didn't move.

"Just go over and mount up," I said.

She pressed against my leg a little and then turned away.

"No, thank you," she said.

The others moved out from the center of the ring and began to plod along the rail. Their ponies walked with their heads down; the girls had loose reins on them and the ponies walked slowly and blinked in the sunlight.

"Haley," I said. "You've been looking forward to this."

She watched her pony.

"Are you getting on?" said the woman who owned the barn.

"I'll go with you," I said. "Come on."

Haley shrank against me.

"Haley," I said. "Look. Just get on."

She moved as if to walk back to the gate. I stepped in front of her and leaned down and looked her in the eye.

"Listen," I said. "I have never in your life told you that you have to do something, no if, ands, or buts, but this is different. You have to get on that pony."

She shook her head.

"Haley," I said. "If you don't get on that pony, you are going to go home and hate yourself, not because you were scared but because you gave up and didn't try. You aren't going to be able to live with that. You can get down if you don't like it and you never have to get on a horse again, but you have to get up there and try." I straightened a little bit. "Don't let your fear get the best of you," I said.

She wouldn't look at me but eased off my leg and cautiously

walked over to Ed. She carefully stepped up on the mounting block and the instructor showed her how to gather her reins in her left hand, put her left foot in the stirrup, and swing her right leg over the saddle. Then she was up, and even without her command Ed trudged over and got in line behind the other two ponies and slowly the three girls circled the ring. The wind blew through the ponies' tails and rustled in last year's leaves. After a while, a man came by with an armload of wood and started a fire in an old rusty barrel and we warmed our hands over the flames while the girls rode. Pieces of white ash spun up into the blue sky and heat hung like a quivering veil over the fire. Haley looked straight ahead and held herself still and Ed ambled along behind the other ponies and the woman told Haley to put her heels down and sit up straight. After a time, the girls turned their ponies and went the other way and Haley turned Ed. At the end of the lesson, she carefully lifted herself and put her leg over Ed's back and jumped down. She walked across the ring and her shoes made puffs of dust in the dirt as she walked.

"How was it?" I said.

She stood in front of me and looked at me in her grave, quiet way. "I want to do this again," she said.

"Really? You had fun?"

She nodded, solemn, swift.

"Okay," I said. "We can come next week."

"Hey Haley," yelled the woman who owned the barn. "Come get your horse. You've still got to put him away." Haley walked back to the center of the ring and the woman showed her how to hold Ed with her arm slung through the reins and then how to lead him back to the barn. She stepped away and Haley did what the woman had just done and took Ed by the bridle and tugged and then tugged harder and finally Ed moved out and Haley walked him back to the barn.

WE DROVE UP TO the local crafts store in the afternoons after school and Haley drifted up and down the bright white aisles and touched packages of tiny buttons shaped like flowers or decals in the shapes of seashells or patches with that obnoxious sunny yellow smiley face or pale green unicorns. She bought select items with the money she had earned petsitting the neighbor's dog. Gradually, she transformed her *Nightmare Before Christmas* hoodie into something that was more a work of folk art than a garment to wear. I stitched patches from her favorite bands onto a piece of polka-dot fabric and then stitched that to the back of the hoodie. Haley banded the arms of the sweatshirt with tiny daisy-shaped brads and took apart her leather bracelet and hammered the studs into the shoulders of the sweatshirt. Jack Skellington's face disappeared under patches of roses and smiley faces and pins of tiny mice and ladybugs. She never left the house without the sweatshirt, and each week its design grew more intricate and elaborate.

Everyone knew that she was Chase's sister. She sometimes protected herself, her shy mermaid heart, by posing like a street urchin in dark black clothing and tights ripped out at the knees. And she protected Chase by turning the focus of the world away from him and toward her crazy jeans, which she covered in quotes from Nirvana songs, or lines from poems that she thought were cool, or the name of her father's band, over and over again, in repeating lines, as if she could conjure him out of longing.

OVER TIME, WE SETTLED into a new routine. I drove Haley to school in the morning and she sat in the front seat, in the place Chase used to sit, and then I drove to work. At lunchtime I drove over to the unit and saw Chase, or had a grim discussion with one of the nurses or with Dr. B. The nurses tried to keep my spirits up but when that didn't work, they were simply kind to me.

After work, I came home earlier in the afternoon than I used to, as often as I could, walking through our front door at four thirty instead of five or five thirty or six. I didn't want Haley to be alone for too long after school. I wanted to check on her homework, check and make sure she was still across the room.

I developed an unreasonable and intense fear that something was going to happen to her. If she went to the movies with a friend and the friend's mom picked her up, I watched the clock until she came home and in between imagined car crashes and drunk drivers and irresponsible parents who somehow managed to abandon their children's friends on the side of the road. When the phone rang and Haley came around the corner and said, "Mom, Zoe's on the phone and she wants me to . . . " I had to take a deep breath and tell myself that this was perfectly normal, it was okay for an eleven-year-old to go out with her friends and her friends' parents to the mall or the movies. Sometimes I tried to intervene in my own terror by taking Haley and her friends places myself. When summer came, we drove down to the beach, past peeling country churches with signs out front promising visitations and salvations, through dusty green fields baked hot and dry, past vegetable stands and bungalows once painted pink or yellow, now faded. I watched Haley and her friend play along the edge of the surf and then the three of us went in to swim. If I saw Haley more than ten feet from shore, I stood near her on the far side of the surf and told myself to breathe and to relax, but still I watched her in the waves and thought of sharks and tidal waves and rip currents and drownings of all descriptions, where she would be swept from me, far away, out to sea.

When Chase went into the hospital, the CAP workers stopped coming, as did the occupational therapist and the speech therapist, all the regular after-school visitors to our house, and Haley came home alone to eat her snack and spread her homework out on the dining-room table. When Chase had been gone a long, long time, I finally cleaned up his room and packed all of his things away in boxes that were carefully labeled, in case he should ask for something, in case he ever came home. I'd walked by the room for months and refused to go inside, refused to touch anything. But then I repaired the walls he damaged when he stripped the wallpaper border off and repainted his room green because Chase had once told me he wanted a green room. I turned his bed into a daybed and set up an old farm table under the window as a desk and lined up a row of dictionaries, an atlas, an old globe, and told Haley she had a cool new spot to do her homework. I felt a kind of relief in setting Chase's room to rights, but she still preferred to do her homework on the dining-room table. One day, when I felt the stillness of our house was particularly sad, I asked Haley how she liked coming home to peace and quiet.

She shrugged. "I don't know."

"Is it better? Worse? No different? What?"

She thought about this. Then she said, "I liked it better before."

I treated such declarations as anagrams, messages to decode. Did she mean she liked it better when Chase was here — did she mean she missed her brother? Or did she mean that she liked it because there were people around, even if those people weren't me? Or did she mean that she disliked change, this one, or any other I might devise?

"I liked it when Chase and Melissa were here," she said simply, as if my questions were those of a moron. She looked around. "It's too quiet now," she said.

• • •

ONE WEDNESDAY IN EARLY February, I got to the unit, and Mac and Danny and Melissa were already in the dayroom. Chase circled them in his stocking feet, wearing his weird twisted grin. He had no idea who they were. Melissa had known Chase since he was ten. Mac had worked with Chase for the year before he got sick. Danny was the CAP worker who had come to work with Chase in October, a few weeks before I took him to the hospital. Each of them had called me and had wanted to come visit so one day I asked if I could add a few more family names to the list and the nurse paged through her notebook and found Chase's page and handed it to me, along with a black ballpoint pen that was chained to the desk like a pen in a bank or a post office, as if this were just a place like other ordinary places. I wrote down the names and then handed the page back to the nurse, who popped the rings on the binder and put the page back in place.

They bunched together in the middle of the dayroom and watched Chase as he made his wide circle around them, as he glared at them, as he glared suspiciously at me. "Not my mother," he told Pam. "My mother was kidnapped by terrorists."

I suggested that we all go into the unit's music room, where someone might play the keyboard, where they all might like to sing, and Chase fell in beside Mac and they all followed me down the hall and around the corner to the music room. After everyone was inside, Chase stood in the doorway and looked in at Mac and Danny and Melissa. They stood in a line in front of the treadmill, next to the electric keyboard. "Hey Chase," I said. "You remember Mac, right?"

Mac smiled and waved and said, "Yo Chase."

"And that's Danny."

Danny waved. "Hi Chase," he said.

"And Melissa?"

"Hey Chase," said Melissa. She flapped the ends of her scarf at him in a wave.

"Do you want to come in and hang out?" I said. "Chase?"

He stood in the doorway, tapping his palm against his thigh. Then he raised his hands to shoulder level, flat and palms down, and began firing lasers. He made laser noises as he fired and narrowed his eyes so he could get a better line on his target.

"Chase," I said. "Come on in and hang out."

Melissa plunked a couple of notes on the keyboard but it wasn't plugged in so all we heard was the sound of the key depressing and releasing, a soft thunk-a-thunk.

"Hey Chase," she said. "What bands are you listening to?"

No one on the unit was supposed to have a radio but the nurses discovered that music often calmed Chase when almost nothing else would, so they sometimes unplugged the portable stereo at the nurses' station and let him listen to it in his room. They said he would sing along when songs he knew came on the radio, and they were amazed at his ability to recall the lyrics.

Chase was saying something now, but it was under his breath and he turned to someone beside him who was invisible to the rest of us and muttered something and squinted again and fired more lasers at Melissa. Then his face twisted out of its weird expressionless grin and darkened and he slammed his fist against the door, and then he yelled that Melissa was raped and dead and he'd killed her. He pounded the door for emphasis and the door rattled on its hinges. Mac and Danny froze beside me.

Melissa took a step toward him. "That's not very nice, Chase," she said. Her voice was thin and neutral. "If you keep talking like that, I'm going to have to leave. I don't want to leave. But I'm not going to stay here if you talk to me like that."

"Not Melissa!" Chase said. "Not Melissa!"

"Chase," said Melissa. "I'm right here in front of you."

"Melissa is dead! Dead! Dead!" He shook his fists and then began to kick the door. Sam and another male nurse came up beside him and spoke to him and turned him from the doorway and led him away. We stood in silence. Pam looked into the room and said, "Visit's over."

We rode down in the elevator together.

"I'm sorry," I said. "It's hard to know how a visit's going to go."

Melissa looked at me. Her face was white. "Is he always like that?"

I shook my head. "It depends on the day," I said.

Mac shook his head. "I know you said he was sick," he said. "But I never thought he was going to be as bad as that."

When we got to the ground floor, Mac walked away quickly. Melissa turned to me and said, "I think I won't visit again for a little while. I'll try next month and see what that's like."

Danny and I stood in front of the hospital. It was a cold, rainy day and the driveway had filled up with gurgling, chuckling water. The hospital shuttle splashed along the curb as it pulled up to discharge passengers and we stepped back to avoid the spray. I told Danny that Chase's stay was going to be a lot longer than any of us had first imagined and Danny would probably be better off finding another client. He resisted a little when I told him. He liked Chase. He could see he was going through a bad time of it, but he was going to need a worker when he got out and he would like to be that person. If I thought it was the money, he wanted me to know that that was no problem. He didn't need this job to earn a living. He could get along just fine without it. He wanted to wait it out.

"I appreciate what you've said," I told him. "I do. I can't think of anyone I'd rather have as Chase's CAP worker. But you might have to wait a long time."

"I can wait," said Danny. He set his mouth. "I *want* to wait," he said.

A car rolled up to the curb in front of us and we jumped back. A little wake ran away from its tires and down the hill.

Danny turned his coat collar up. "I'll come again next week, if that's okay."

"I don't think that's a good idea," I said.

"I want to come," Danny said. "I want Chase to know me when he gets out."

"I think it's too far off in the distance to hold you to this," I said. "All you need to do is call the Autism Society and tell them you would like to work with someone else."

Danny shook his head at this suggestion. "I'd really rather not do that," he said. "I'd really like to wait for Chase."

"Look," I said sharply. "We're all 99 percent certain that he's not coming home. Okay? He won't need a CAP worker because he's not coming home."

Up to that point, I hadn't said this out loud but as soon as I did, I felt the weight of it, the truth.

Danny blanched. But after a moment he righted himself and said, "Well, if you're sure." He turned his wool hat in his hands. "I'm sorry about Chase," he said. "I wish things had turned out differently."

"I know," I said softly. "Me, too."

NINE

||||||||||||||||||||

Eventually, when Chase was four, I made a list of things that made his life difficult, as if these were things that could be quantified and fixed. The list was broken out into categories. Under *Fears,* I wrote: fear of the dark, fear of window fans, fear of loud sounds (walks around house with fingers in ears at all times), fear of spider webs, fear of the Lady Sword, a figure who came to him in the dark when he tried to sleep and meant him harm, and who I was terrified was his fantasy version of me, the mother who tried to discipline him out of his behaviors. Under *Preoccupations* I wrote: sirens, construction sites and equipment, railroads and trains. I noted Chase's unbearable sensitivity to sound and yet his paradoxical insistence on making noise: hooting, yelling, whining, weeping; I mentioned that even when given an answer, he repeated the same question over and over and over again: *Why is there a railroad crossing? Why is there a railroad crossing? Why is there a railroad crossing? Why is there track? Why is there track? Why is there track? Why is there track?* Under *Physical Symptoms,* I described an increase in eye-rolling and staring, a decrease in appetite, an increase in energy (if that could even be possible), moony behavior alternating with explosions of maniacal aggression, inability to sleep, inability to take no for an answer. I noted that his day-care teachers thought that he was worse, and we all heard him make unusual statements about intrusions by other children: *That little girl tried to take my truck* — but she was on the other side of the room; *Cassie hit me* — but Cassie was on the swings outside. *David can control me. He tells me what to do.*

The pediatrician at the Strong Clinic wrote letters to Chase's pediatrician in town and copied us: *His parents had a number of questions and concerns to share with me. They have identified some bruises on his temples which he does not remember sustaining, and they wonder if he is having nighttime unobserved seizure activity. He is still having nightly bedwetting. His behavior ranges from very subdued to explosive in an unpredictable way . . . He is more aggressive at home, more perseverative on a variety of topics such as construction projects, Halloween, and ghosts. He continues to enjoy lining things up . . . he has no identifiable tics, although he does chew his clothing . . .*

Later, even after seeing many different specialists, I wondered if by writing these words down and handing them over, I had turned Chase into a boy made up of lists and issues. When I drove my car across the rolling farmland of the Finger Lakes and watched the sky or gazed out the window as I wiped the kitchen table, I wondered if by naming things I had secured Chase's future, had whipped it up out of my own anxieties, had taken the normal and transformed it into the abnormal. I don't think this is uncommon. I think parents of disabled children hold themselves accountable and have a hard time reconciling the fact that nothing could have changed the outcome of their own helpless experience of being a parent to a fragile child.

But it made me blind to Zip, too. At night, after Chase finally went to bed and silence fell on the house, I went into my study to work and Zip sat down on the sofa and I heard him crack open a beer. He drank each night and often slept on the sofa after I went to bed. When I got up in the morning, I'd cover him up with a

blanket and watch him fall more deeply into sleep, at least until
Chase got up. I didn't like Zip's drinking, didn't like the way he
slurred his words or the way he walked like a man under whose
feet the world tilted unpredictably. At such times, I felt so much
anger that the whole world receded and I could not feel anything
else, could not see anything else, could not hear anything else. At
such times, I wondered why he did not help me more. I wondered
why everything—the job that earned our bread, the running of
the household, the arrangements of doctors' appointments, the
talks with insurance companies, the meals that we ate, the outings
that we made—fell to me. It did not occur to me that Zip could
not help me more, that he needed help himself. Instead, I'd stand
next to him and swallow again and again until my throat ached
from trying not to feel what I was feeling. By that time, Chase
would have come to the gate that we still kept at the door of his
room and would be calling out to me: "I want to get out! I want
to get out! Get out!"

During the summer, we spent our weekends swimming at a
beach across the lake and Chase floated a yellow plastic boat on
the waves that lapped and chortled against the shore. My dissertation defense was scheduled for August. I'd taught for the last
two years at the college in town and the chair had asked me to
come back a third time. The writing program was brand-new and
still in flux; it was unclear if the college would decide to make it
a permanent department or if it would remain a program or if it
would remain at all. Each time the chair invited me to teach, she
told me that this would be the year the college might take these
jobs and convert them to tenure-track jobs. She knew better than
to speak of this with certainty but she never failed to mention it,
either. Since the job market for English PhDs was the worst it had
been in twenty years, and since Zip had a job in town, and since I

loved this college because I'd done my undergraduate degree there, it made sense to me to try to stay where we were.

And I was pregnant again. Zip and I had talked about a second child and we wondered if this was a good idea. After Chase, did we really know what we were doing, what we might be getting ourselves into? We discussed this at some length and it seemed we'd made a decision. Chase was enough; Chase would be it. But Chase began to sing the alphabet song in the bathtub and made me laugh when one day he pointed to himself and said, "That's my penis, right? Right? My penis goes in the boat, right?" And stuck his penis through the donut hole in the center of the rubber tugboat that rode the water lapping against his waist. He rolled his eyes in exasperated pleasure when I used a blue cup to pour water over his shoulders and then said, "Give me the red boat." His voice was firm and clear and commanding. I lifted the boat up and said, "This boat?" He said, fiercely, as if there could be no mistaking his intent, "That boat, Mom. I need that boat."

I told myself that nobody knew what was wrong with Chase, if anything really was, and he would probably outgrow all of this, and then we'd regret not having a second child. I interpreted the pediatrician's words to mean that Chase had symptoms of things but didn't really have those things. The only thing I knew about autism, for example, was from the television drama *St. Elsewhere,* where one of the fictional doctors had an autistic son and Chase didn't act anything like the boy on TV. And no one had said he had autism, had they? They said he had things that looked like autism, that looked like PDD, that looked like Tourette's syndrome, that looked like ADHD, but no one said these things were what was wrong with him. His psychologist didn't think that he was hallucinating when he said that David controlled him or that a robot voice told him the rules; she thought that these things were

Chase's fantasies. She didn't think the Lady Sword was a ghost or a delusion. She was troubled by the fact that Chase felt threatened by children who were nowhere near him but she thought this was just part of his compulsive nature. We listened to the psychologist, who was the expert, after all.

And I had always wanted two children. I thought if we were going to do this, we should do it before I got too old. I'd be thirty-five on my next birthday and I knew the older you got, the more chances you had of delivering a baby who suffered from a really serious problem, like Down syndrome. Now that my dissertation was almost done, we were getting ready to start the next part of our lives. In my mind, this meant that I would teach at a good school and we would have a big house full of kids and our kids' friends and our friends and their kids and everyone's pets, and Zip would play music and do work that he liked, and I would write books, and a reporter from the *New York Times* would come to visit us to write a piece for their Home and Garden section because we were such fantastic artists and had done such fantastic things with the house. There was nothing in my actual life that suggested that any of this was possible. I taught and wrote and took care of Chase. Zip worked at a music store and said nothing at night. There weren't any jobs for people with brand-new PhDs in English and we lived in an apartment and didn't even own our own place. But I thought that all we had to do was work hard enough; with a little luck, things would turn out.

I never said it out loud but I also knew that I wanted to have a second child so that I could have some kind of experience as a parent that did not involve visiting doctors who said, "There's something wrong with your child but I can't tell you what."

THE TECHNICIAN HAD LOWERED the blinds to block the blazing afternoon sun and turned the monitor so I could see it.

In this dim room, I watched the screen, where blackness whirled into light and then went back to black. A fuzzy white boundary separated pale dark from something darker.

Zip stood over my shoulder. Together, we studied the blurry shapes popping in and out of focus on the ultrasound monitor, the blob that suddenly had fingers and then receded to a wiggly white line, the pear-shaped rump that zapped into blackness, the soft tender curve of the baby's skull. The technician took measurements and tiny boxes appeared on the screen and then tiny dots appeared between the boxes.

"There's your baby," she said. "Right there."

I tried to lift myself on my elbows and the technician put her hand on my shoulder to stop me. "I'll move the monitor," she said. "Stay right where you are." She turned and fiddled and turned back to me and said, "Can you see better now?"

"Is the baby okay?" I looked at the gray blurs and the dark shapes and tried to see some defect, some hole, some absence, as if vacancy could ever be visible, as if the thing that made Chase who he was would appear on this screen like a subtitle in a foreign film.

"Your baby has all its fingers and toes," said the technician. "See?" She rolled the wand over my belly and let the baby's limbs swim into focus again, its hands, its feet, and then its beating heart, and then its face.

"I think that's a perfect shot for a portrait. Hang on," she said.

"But is it okay?" I said.

"Look at that sweet face. Hold on just a sec more. There. I think I've got it."

I watched the screen while the technician pushed a button. Something whirred and the machine rolled out a snapshot. The technician peeled the paper from the face of the print and handed it to me.

"There's your baby," she said again. "Perfect in every way."

I held the picture and saw my daughter, a beautiful girl limned in white against an unknowable dark ground. I knew she was a girl even without being told. "Haley," I said. I held the photo up so Zip could see. "We should name her Haley," I said. "She really looks like a Haley to me."

WHEN SHE WAS BORN, I took advantage of the college's generous maternity leave policy and had the whole semester off. After my stitches healed, I took the kids for walks, tucking Haley into a fuzzy yellow and white snowsuit against the upstate New York cold. In her carriage, beneath a heavy wool blanket, just her eyes showed under her white knit hat. I bundled Chase in his blue snowpants, his blue snowjacket, his red boots, his red-striped knit cap, and the red knit mittens strung though his sleeves on a doubled piece of yarn. We made our way up Main Street toward the college, past the big old houses that had been built in the nineteenth century, when the town had prospered, some with terraces that looked out over the lake. This was the same walk Zip and I had taken with Chase before Haley was born, up the hill to the vista in front of the college where we could point out boats on the lake or ducks by the shore. Chase would run ahead and we would run after him. I would call "Stop Stop Stop!" but Chase would run and run. I could picture him running into the street or flying from the butte into thin air and then tumbling down to the railroad tracks. And so one day I yelled, "Red light!" And Chase stopped. He stood still and looked back at us, his father and me, who were at that point trying to decide whether or not we would support Chase if he insisted on joining the military at eighteen. This was part of a larger conversation we entered into from time to time, about the extent and reach of the ways in which we would support our children, especially if they chose to do things with which we disagreed. We spoke seriously, ridiculously, about such matters, as if we could control the future. Chase waited for us to come up beside him on the concrete sidewalk and scuffed the tip of his sneaker through some pebbles he'd found, and watched us. When we reached him, I said, "Green light!" He ran and ran until I called, "Red light!"

Now, with Haley in the carriage, I called "Red light" if Chase got too far ahead of us. He liked to stand on the bridge over the highway that cut around town and watch the cars speeding below, but I hated it when he did this, certain that he would slip and fall and plunge to his death. I'd already had a dream about standing on a high roof with Haley in my arms and in the dream I dropped her and watched her bounce down the shingles and roll to the gutter and then turn and look at me with a plain, inquiring expression — *How could you let go of me? How could you let me fall?* — before she slipped over the edge and fell away and away and away. I woke up with my heart pounding and had to get out of bed and go to her crib and see if she was all right.

Once we got to the college, there was a good view of the lake. They'd set up a couple of benches to honor some alums and you could see clear across to the state park. I cleared the snow off of one of the benches so Chase could scramble up and sit down, and I could sit down next to him. I kept one hand on Haley's carriage and asked Chase what he could see. There were dogs with bandannas on the snowy slope below us, a black Lab with a red bandanna and a yellow mutt with a blue bandanna and a white face and a tail that curled up like the tail on a husky. Their owners saw us and whistled to the dogs and the dogs galloped through the snow and slid to a stop at their owner's knees, sat up and sat perfectly still on their hind legs, their tails thumping, their ears perked forward, waiting for fun.

"What do you see, Chase?" I asked again.

"Dogs," he said. He began to sing to himself and tilted his head from side to side.

"What color dogs?"

"Black."

"And what else?"

"Brown."

He kicked his red plastic boot against the bench and kicked it again and again.

"Chase," I said.

He kept kicking.

"Stop that, Chase."

He kicked and kicked and kicked.

"If you're going to kick the bench, we aren't going to be able to sit on the bench."

He kicked.

"Do you want to go home right now?"

He kicked again and again and again. I looked at him. His face was blank, unsmiling, and it seemed that he could not hear me. I held my breath and tried to swallow my frustration. I counted to ten. I exhaled. Chase kicked the bench.

The dogs chased a Frisbee and the two men who were walking with them stopped, passing the joint they were smoking back and forth between them and the blue smoke drifted away in the cold air. I could smell it. They climbed up the chalky painted stairs to McStewart House, the very same residence hall where Zip had lived when he was an undergraduate, and whistled to the dogs; they bounded up the stairs after the men and crowded around their legs and then stood on the porch and shook themselves hard.

"Do you want to roll down the hill?" I said. "Chase?"

Haley squirmed in her carriage. She was awake. We couldn't stay here for long so I stood and said, "Come on, Chase. Let's go home."

"I'm going to roll."

"Okay," I said, "go ahead and roll."

He rolled down the hill enough times to fill his boots up with snow and while he rolled, I picked Haley up and held her in my arms, her bobbing head, her face against my shoulder, until Chase had enough of rolling down the snowy hill. I watched the sunlight glint on the rippling blue water and watched three dark figures make their way along the snowy tracks far below.

After we got home, I took Chase's boots off and peeled his wet socks from his feet and asked him to step out of his pants. When he was in warm, dry clothes and settled down with a cup of Goldfish in front of his *Mickey's Parrot* cartoon, I made peanut butter sandwiches for lunch and told myself that things were getting better. I almost never went out with Chase and Haley without Zip, but we had just gone out and come back and we'd made it okay. We were having a good day.

EVEN BEFORE SHE COULD WALK, Haley followed her brother around in a wheeled walker like she was a satellite and he was the sun. She smiled and smiled and smiled, huge goofy baby grins that stayed and stayed. Chase decided she needed a new name and began to call her Haley-Ball; Zip and I called her Haley-Bird and Zip spent hours flying her like a bird through the air while she laughed and laughed and cried, "Do it again!"

IN THE FALL, when dark fell early, when it wouldn't be long until snow covered the ground, I sat in the rocking chair in Haley's room and held her in my arms and held the book so she could see the pictures and said from memory, *Goodnight noises everywhere.* Her head was under my chin. She touched the pictures as I turned the pages. I felt her muscles go soft and still. We came to the end of the book but I didn't want to come to the end of this, so I started again. Bedtimes for Haley weren't always peaceful. Chase liked to get involved. There were things he needed to know: "Can I hold the baby? Can I hold the baby? Can I hold the baby?" And then he'd reach for her and try to pull her out of my arms and I'd stand up and say, "That's enough, you can hold the baby in the morning, remember?" Eventually Zip would come in and say, "I think *Mickey's Parrot* is on," and sure enough, Chase's favorite cartoon, the one where Mickey thinks an escaped killer has gotten into his house, would magically appear on TV.

On this night, it was just Haley and me. I could hear Chase laughing in the other room but, after a time, things got quiet. Haley's new hair was as soft as the fur on a tiny finger-puppet mouse I'd had when I was a child. I rocked her slowly and I felt her weight in my arms, that soft, warm sack of flour weight of a baby who's about to fall asleep, and I sang to her, a song about pretty horses I pulled from my memory.

When I put her in her crib, she sighed deeply and smiled up at me while I covered her with her blanket.

I was on the phone in the bedroom when Zip came into the room. "I think you'd better come here for a sec," he said.

"Hang on," I said to the person on the other end. "I'll be done in a minute," I told Zip.

"No," he said sharply. "You need to get off now."

Chase was propped on pillows on the sofa, staring fixedly at the ceiling, his pupils huge and black, his lips deep blue and foamy. He beat his chest rhythmically, involuntarily, with his arms. The rest of his body was stiff. He breathed slowly and deeply, slowly and deeply, and then he vomited.

"Call an ambulance," I said. A plate with a half-eaten hot dog rested on Chase's lap. Donald Duck was peeling potatoes for the army on TV. I kept saying Chase's name but he didn't respond. I could hear Zip on the phone, giving our address, and I could hear Donald spluttering and fussing, and I had Chase on my lap, in my arms, and he was warm and I thought he was breathing, and then the paramedics arrived and the street in front of our house was filled with whirling, spinning light and the neighbors came upstairs and asked if we needed anything, if there was anything they could do. The paramedics unfolded a gurney, dropping its wheels with a clatter, and took Chase from me and covered him with blankets and put an oxygen mask on him. They asked questions while they worked. "How old is the boy? What happened? Did you notice anything unusual? How long do you think he was out? What's his name? What's your name, son?" By then he had begun to stir and they told him to lie still, he was going to get to ride in the ambulance, how's that for being a lucky boy? They carried him down the two flights and out the front door into the cold, sharp night with a million stars over our heads. Inside the ambulance, the vehicle shook as we bounced over bumps and the only light came from the strobing orange light of the emergency spinners. One of the paramedics took Chase's temperature.

"It's 103.7," said the paramedic. "He looks postictal." He was a young man with bright brown curls and he told me he had a boy himself at home, just about Chase's age. He blew up a latex glove and tied it off like a balloon. He drew a face on it and danced it through the air in front of Chase, who stared at it from under his plastic mask.

"What is that," I said. "Post—?"

"Postictal," said the paramedic. "That's the state you're in after you have a seizure. Does he have seizures?"

"No," I said. "Never."

"Sometimes kids get them when they run a high temp," he said. "It's nothing to worry about." He looked at Chase. "Want us to turn on the siren?"

He turned his head slowly from side to side, no, no.

Chase slept at the ER, lying in bed between two green drapes in a row of beds divided by curtains. In the considered opinion of the ER doctor, Chase had not had a seizure. We were to take him home and give him fluids and let him rest. He didn't think anything had really happened but if it had, it was probably a febrile seizure, brought on by whatever was making Chase's temperature go up. But he had no idea what might be causing *that*. His thought was that this was something best handled by Chase's pediatrician. Still, he really wanted to emphasize that this had not been a seizure, not to his way of thinking, anyway, and we had nothing to worry about. Yet to make ourselves feel completely at ease, we should follow up with the pediatrician in the morning. Just in case.

Chase's pediatrician dispatched us to the EEG lab. We were to show up at the hospital, where Chase would be sedated with chloral hydrate and hooked up to the recorder by electrodes glued to his scalp; they'd get a reading while he was sedated, which would emulate sleep, and then they'd get a reading when the drug started to wear off. The tech talked to him about trains while she fixed a paper-covered tray with a cup with a pill in it and a glass of juice.

"You like orange juice?" she asked Chase. "I got you some orange juice. You just need to take some medicine and then we'll get started."

He nodded and swallowed the pill. He'd been taking pills for a while. He knew how.

The tech went to work on Chase's head. "This'll be a little

cold," she said but the first time she touched the glue to his scalp, he jerked away. "Ow," he said.

"Chase," I said. "Come on. That's just glue."

Zip showed up in the doorway. "The car's parked," he said. "Hey buddy."

The tech touched his scalp with the glue and pressed another electrode in place. Chase stood up and tried to pull the electrode off.

"Sit down," I said. My voice sounded sharp. I took a deep breath and started over. I told him the test wouldn't take long and when we got home we'd have supper with Haley. Haley was over at Karen's house right now, waiting for us. All we had to do was finish up here and go see her. We might even get to see the horse named Chicken, who often sauntered down the field and put his head over the fence.

The tech worked faster now, slapping electrodes in place and rapidly arranging the red and blue wires so they wouldn't hang in Chase's face. He pulled at the wires and pulled some that were already in place out and then twisted and shrieked and tried to stand up. Zip squatted before him with his hands on Chase's knees and said, "It's okay, it's okay, it's okay."

"He'll be okay once the medicine works," the tech said, but she sounded doubtful and this was understandable because the medicine didn't seem to be doing what it was supposed to do. Chase grew more anxious and the more anxious he became, the more he squalled and screamed and shrieked and moaned. He pulled unendingly at the electrodes, pulling them out as fast as the tech could put them on. He tried to roll off of the chair onto the floor. He howled. He kicked. The tech stepped back. Chase jumped up and knocked over the chair. He ran across the big beige room. Zip was right behind him and wrapped his arms around Chase's waist and then picked him up and carried him, struggling and thrashing, back to the chair. But he wouldn't sit down. He fell to the floor to avoid his father's grip and tried to get up and run away. Zip picked him up and sat down on the chair with Chase bucking like a pony in his lap. They both fell off the chair.

"I don't think we'll be able to do this test today," the tech said. "Not unless you can calm him down."

But there was no calming Chase down. The more time passed, the more frenzied he became. Zip carried him out to the car and I buckled him into the backseat. A block from the hospital, he unbuckled his seat belt and opened the door. Zip slammed to a stop. I crawled into the backseat and practically sat on Chase to keep him from pitching himself out of the car. He rolled wildly from side to side and screamed and reached for the door. We parked in front of our building and Zip came around to the back of the car and opened the door behind the driver and I snapped, "Not that side. Not into traffic. Come around the other way." He opened the other door and I lifted Chase up and out into his arms. He beat his heels against his father's thighs and thrashed and fought and slammed himself against his father, but eventually we got him upstairs.

THE NEXT WEEK, the nurse at Chase's day-care center called to tell me that Chase had had some difficulty at naptime. He had gotten up and seemed dazed and confused and tried to find his way to the bathroom. They helped him but he kept doing this, maybe five times in the course of an hour.

"It never seemed like he knew where he was or who we were," the nurse said. The teachers had called her down to the room to see this, and it wasn't something that looked right to her at all.

FIVE DAYS LATER, another call. Chase was lying on his mat when his body went stiff and he began to pound himself rhythmically in the chest. He didn't respond when they called his name. Afterward, he slept for the rest of the afternoon.

"It was definitely a seizure," the nurse said. "No doubt about it."

WE TOOK HIM TO a neurologist who thought he might have a seizure disorder. She made an appointment for him at the hospital in Clifton Springs to have an EEG while sedated with Nembutal; they could do an MRI at the same time. She seemed concerned because Chase couldn't hop on his left foot and had switched hand dominance. He had been doing everything with his left hand, but now seemed to prefer his right. We brought him to the hospital one morning and watched while Chase slid into the tube. But things went wrong and the test failed.

SO HIS DOCTOR AT the Strong Clinic ordered the EEG and MRI and told us Chase would have general anesthesia at the hospital in Rochester. I was on break from teaching so didn't have to get someone to cover my classes, but Zip had to take off work, and I had to make arrangements for Haley, who I worried about with a worry that was with me like breath. I watched her closely, waiting for something to emerge, and she looked back at me with her thoughtful gaze and then grinned and giggled as if I were playing some sort of game whose rules only I understood and pushed off in her infant walker and scooted wildly across the floor.

I told myself she was safe at her day-care center and safe with Karen if we ended up having to stay late in Rochester. Karen worked in the infant room at the day-care center. She knew how to make a cake in the shape of Barney the Dinosaur. She'd come from Wyoming and she missed the West and talked all the time about how good it would be to get back home to Laramie, where you could walk fences for miles and never see another living soul. She was a big woman with big hands and a big round face and she kept herself busy. One night a week, she came over and stayed with the kids while Zip and I had an evening out. We went to the movies and sat in the dark and then found a place to have dinner afterward. We didn't speak. When we got home, she always said, "Did you have fun?" And I'd look glumly at my feet and say, "Yup." Once I found a twenty-dollar bill in the parking lot of the movie theater.

This time, I wanted us to be ready for the hospital. This time, I found a miniature toy operating room with tiny figures in green gowns and masks, and lamps on tall, skinny poles, and a patient with removable plastic bandages shaped to fit snugly on his head or arm or leg. I set the figures up on the kitchen table and showed Chase what it was like to go into the hospital. I showed him the Mommy and Daddy figures who would sit outside while the Chase figure lay on the table and the figures in the green gowns and masks took pictures of the inside of his head. I told him he'd be asleep and never even remember that part but his daddy and I wouldn't sleep. We'd be right there waiting for him and we'd see him as soon as he woke up.

We drove up to Rochester in the early morning. Snow lay on the fields and black creeks cut through the snow and hawks turned lazy circles high overhead. Every so often, the highway crossed a gorge where a river gleamed dully below.

We checked in at the ambulatory surgery center at Strong and then an aide of some sort escorted us to a waiting room outside of the MRI center. "It won't be long," she said.

I sat in a blue chair in that dim room with Chase on my lap.

Zip sat next to me. We didn't say much. After a while, I opened the book I'd brought along and began the familiar rhythm of *Go, Dog, Go!* Chase looked away from me at anyone who came into the room. When the double doors opened and someone said, "Chase?" I stood up and carried him toward the nurse. I followed her down another hallway and told Chase that everything would be all right, we'd see him again before he knew it. He rode in my arms and by now was crying. The nurse stopped in front of another door and it opened and a man in a mask stepped forward.

"I'll take that big guy," he said and lifted him out of my arms but not before Chase cried "No, no," and dug his fingers so hard into the back of my hand he cut me deeply with his nails. I went back to the waiting room and swabbed my hand with a tissue and then held a little square of tissue over the wound until it stopped bleeding.

The MRI was normal. The EEG was not. But it wasn't abnormal enough for them to say, This boy has a seizure disorder. His doctor ordered Tegretol. Chase became violent and threw a table at a group of children at day care. We stopped the Tegretol.

I USED TO THINK I knew when Chase started having seizures and would describe, with great confidence, Chase's first grand mal, when he was five. The problem was that even though I thought everything I said was true, and would have sworn to it at the time, and learned to speak with great authority to doctors about what I had seen, much of what I said was true only insofar as it was truthfully my perception; medically, it was not entirely accurate. Chase's seizure at five was probably not a grand mal; it was probably a complex partial seizure. And I have no idea if it was his first. The neurologist who saw him in upstate New York was not convinced of a seizure disorder based on what she saw when he was five but she did allow as how failure to treat would let a seizure disorder "kindle," if a seizure disorder existed. She said this in a letter to our pediatrician but she didn't say it to us. Instead, she simply told us that medication was our choice and it could be dangerous but it could be helpful. She didn't tell us one way or another what we ought to do.

TEN

||||||||||||

It was hard to think about those early years now, about the seizures and the doctors who talked among themselves but didn't talk to us. It was hard to think of misdiagnosis but it came to mind again and again, usually when I visited Chase and he told me that his shower was a gas chamber or that his nurse had killed him the night before.

Dr. B called and asked to meet with me, so early one stormy afternoon I walked up to the hospital on water-puddled sidewalks and then stood in front of the nurses' station holding a dripping umbrella. The nurse took the umbrella from me when I signed in and told me it could be used as a weapon so they would keep it safe for me behind the nurses' station. I raised the hems of my pants and tried to shake them out a little, the way a dog shakes after a bath. Just then, Dr. B stepped out from behind the station and nodded me toward the unit library and then closed the door behind us.

"Did you see Chase today?" Dr. B asked.

"Not yet," I said. "I thought I would when we were through."

He nodded. Dr. B was a man of acutely realized impassivity; even the staff commented on how little he showed his emotions. He was young with something of the appearance of a Boy Scout and I felt sympathy for him because I imagined he must have had to endure comparisons to Doogie Howser.

"I'd like to add another drug to Chase's medications," he said. "It should help stabilize his mood and retard the constant pacing."

"All right," I said.

He studied me.

"The nurses will ask you to sign a consent form, just as they have asked before," he said.

"All right," I said. "I can sign it on my way out." I bit my lips.

Chase walked past us without looking into the library, head down, arms flailing, listing a little to one side as he always did.

"I met with the insurance review board this week," Dr. B said. "They've certified Chase's care again but they won't do that forever. Have you found a place for him?"

I shook my head. "We're looking but no one will take him."

"Have you tried the mental-health side of things?"

I nodded. "And the developmental-disabilities side. The private providers out in the community don't want him. He's too complicated and they don't have the staff and they keep telling me that they can't offer any programs that are worthwhile."

"Well," said Dr. B.

"I think they're doing everything they can," I said.

"I wanted to meet with you to find out how this side of things is progressing. We still have treatments to try and Chase will be able to stay as long as that's the case. But sometimes these things don't go as you'd like them to. I don't want you to be blindsided."

"I appreciate that," I said. "But I don't know what I can do when no one will take him."

Chase walked by the library again and caught sight of me. He stopped and stared darkly through the glass walls, saying things in words we could not understand, and I remembered a night in New York City, years before, when I was still young, and an old man in the clothes of the homeless stood with his face pressed to the restaurant window beneath which I sat with my date, having dinner, and the man screamed and pounded on the glass and pointed at me and cursed me and the other diners turned to look at him until the waiter came over and pulled the curtains over the man's face.

Chase raised his fist and pounded it weakly on the glass and the glass shivered and I began to stand up but then Pam came and carefully led Chase away.

I felt tears well and bit my lips again and again. I looked at Dr. B, who looked impassively at me.

"Can't you help him?" I said. "Please, can't you help him?" I wiped furiously at my eyes with the heels of my hands and then dug around in my purse for a tissue while Dr. B watched me without showing any emotion at all.

"I'm sorry," he said. "We're doing everything we can. In cases like these—"

"Cases like these?"

He nodded blandly while I wiped my eyes. "In cases like these," he said, "where the patient is experiencing a significant psychosis that is refractory to treatment, we work to get him out of it as quickly as we can. Chase is experiencing an acute psychosis that has resisted our efforts to bring him out of it."

"So it's common?" I said. "This sort of thing? You see this a lot?"

Dr. B blinked. His hands were folded carefully together in his lap. "I wouldn't say it's common," he said. "Usually one of the drugs will be effective. But there are some people who don't respond to anything."

"What's wrong with him? Do you know?"

"It's hard to say. His psychosis is very severe but he doesn't quite meet the diagnostic criteria for schizophrenia. Maybe schizoaffective disorder." He frowned. "You have to remember that we treat the symptoms, not the label, so it probably doesn't matter what we call it. Unfortunately for Chase, his symptoms have been hard to treat."

"But what does that mean?"

"You mean long-term?" he said.

I nodded.

He looked thoughtful. "The longer a patient remains psychotic," he said, "the worse the prognosis. We don't know why. Something about the processes that create the psychosis seems to cause irreversible harm. In the most severe cases, the person never really gets better but his symptoms might wax and wane some; at times, he might seem to be a little bit better, at some times he might seem a little bit worse."

"And Chase?"

"He's been psychotic for quite a while now and his symptoms are very severe. It's extremely unlikely that he will get better. I'm sorry."

I wept and Dr. B watched me weep and Chase walked past us again and looked sideways through the window glass but didn't try to stop, just looked in at us with his suspicious dark face, and then stalked off toward the other end of the unit. I swallowed and tried to keep from sobbing and Dr. B. sat motionless before me. I struggled and he sat without expression and I thought of all the ways I had been unable to protect Chase from this illness that stood outside the rules and categories prized by all the specialists we'd ever visited, the pediatricians, developmentalists, psychiatrists, neurologists, neurosurgeons, geneticists, cardiologists, psychologists, occupational therapists, behavioralists, speech therapists, autism experts, and social workers who shook their heads and said, "It's difficult to say how, exactly, but it's clear there's something different about your son." Hospitals are ideas as much as they are places and, as such, develop expectations; in our common mythology, the fact of their existence suggests that it's possible to achieve comfort, treatment, cure. If we're lucky, we carry these beliefs without really even knowing that we have them. If we're lucky, we'll have no reason to test them and so have no reason to expose them as merely partial, merely beliefs, not even to ourselves.

I wiped my eyes and blew my nose. "What is this going to do to his life?"

Dr. B looked blank. "What do you mean?"

"Does it affect his life expectancy, anything like that? Or will he live a long time just like this?"

"For reasons that you can imagine, people who suffer severe psychosis tend to die a little bit early," he said. "They don't take care of themselves. They don't have access to good medical care. They can't report symptoms to medical personnel."

"They wind up on the street," I said angrily. "They live in tunnels and under bridges." I furiously wiped more tears.

He nodded. "That's sometimes the case," he said. "But I don't think that's what will happen with Chase."

I grasped at thin straws, steering for something that felt like hope. "Why not?"

"I think," he said, "Chase will always be taken care of. He will always need twenty-four-hour, one-to-one institutional care." His voice was plain and matter-of-fact, without a hint of anything that would give away what he felt.

"But please," I said, with a fresh wave of tears. "Please. Can't you help him? Please?"

As CHASE GREW SICKER, I blamed myself in ways too uncountable to name. Somehow I had made a million wrong choices. I rehearsed these failings in my head and always came out on the short end of the stick. In every case, I was the parent. In every instance, I should have known better.

To bring Chase back so I could have another chance, so I would do better this time, so that things would be different—this was some of what I wanted when I said to Dr. B, "Please help him. Please."

I MET THE HOSPITAL social worker in her office. I sat across from her on the sofa and she swiveled her chair away from the folder on the desk and looked at me.

"What are your plans for Chase?" she said.

"What do you mean?"

"You aren't going to be able to bring him home. Where do you intend for him to live?"

"I thought he would come back to us," I said slowly. But even as I said this, I knew it wasn't true. The Chase that Haley and I knew wasn't coming home. I'd told the local area workers that. But I had to keep telling myself that, in order to make it stick, in order to get myself to believe it. On the one hand, here was Chase before me, so transformed by illness that he no longer knew me as his mother and, on the other hand, here was my dream of Chase, the boy who loved to dance and read comic books and who always, in my mind, had a future.

Now the social worker shook her head. "He's not coming home. That's not going to happen. You need to find a long-term-care facility that can take him, a place with the right program, a place that knows how to take care of someone like him."

It was very quiet. This was not like the rest of the hospital, not like the pediatric intensive-care unit, with its glass walls and humming, hulking machines, not like the pediatric postsurgical floor, where families used the microwave and the ice dispenser and got

Popsicles and ice cream out of the freezer and nurses banged the metal doors of the linen locker and called to each other about extra gowns or pillowcases and rolled hampers on hard plastic wheels up and down the linoleum floor and every night at eight thirty the man with the squeaky sandwich cart came by and I'd buy Chase a bag of chips.

When I didn't say anything, the social worker leaned forward and gave me a hard look. "He's fine here for now," she said, "but one of these days your insurance company is going to kick him out and you'd better have a place lined up when that happens."

"What about Chase's Medicaid program? Won't that kick in when the insurance company refuses to pay?"

"No," she said. "Absolutely not. Medicaid will follow the insurance company. In your case, I think the review board for your insurance company is the same as the review board for Medicaid."

"But they don't even know Chase," I said. "How can they make an informed decision?"

She shook her head. "It's the system. Every so often, Dr. B meets with the board and argues that Chase still requires this level of care. So far, he's been successful. But time is going to run out. You need to be prepared."

I looked at my hands in my lap and felt my mouth quiver. The social worker asked me what I wanted to do.

"I don't know," I said softly. I thought about holding Chase in my lap when he was a baby and I thought about holding Haley in my lap and I thought about the way I held them together and the way I held them apart and I thought about going home to a family that was now just two, and I thought about this illness that had no name but that had nevertheless left us diminished and uncertain and changed forever. Then I cleared my throat and asked her for the hospital's list of long-term-care facilities.

"We don't keep any lists like that," she said. "That's for you and the area mental-health unit to figure out. You'd better do it soon. There's no time to waste."

"This just seems unbelievably unfair. He needs care. How can they just kick him out?"

She shrugged. "They won't argue that he doesn't need care. What they're going to tell you is that he no longer needs this level of care. And then they'll pull the plug."

"Based on what?"

"They'll review his treatment and his prognosis and they'll listen to Dr. B's recommendations, but in the end, it'll be their decision. They don't need to meet him or to meet you," she said. "They'll have what they need in Chase's chart."

ELEVEN

||||||||||||||||||||||||||||||||||||

When Haley was two, the college closed the writing and rhetoric program where I'd been teaching and we moved to the Midwest. The word *Midwest* sounded to me like "failed test." I hadn't published enough and made enough of a name for myself to get a Big Job at a Big School so I took a job at a small liberal arts college in the middle of nowhere.

Our only other choice would have been for me to quit teaching and for us to live off of Zip's earnings at the music store. But he had no health insurance, no benefits of any kind, and I knew we could not afford Chase's medical bills on Zip's earnings alone.

So I took the job at the college and hoped for the best. I read *The Berenstain Bears' Moving Day* to Haley and Chase, over and over again, pointing out the new house, and the new rooms each child would have, and the way that the movers would move our furniture and our things so that when we got to the new house, everything would be there, waiting for us.

We left the Finger Lakes early one morning in August and headed west, toward Canada. The plan was to stop and eat lunch and show the kids Niagara Falls. The plan was to make this move a pleasure trip. I cried as we left town and then stopped, so Chase and Haley would not see. We made the Rainbow Bridge before noon and parked near Horseshoe Falls. We allowed ourselves to be carried to the lookout in front of the falls by a little shuttle bus, just another family among the tourists, and we took pictures of each other with crashing spume behind us and ate overpriced hamburgers at a stand across the street from the place where the Niagara River stops being a river and hurtles over cliffs to become a waterfall. It was gusty near the falls and I watched the kids eat and watched the stiff breeze ripple along the edge of the bright orange canvas awning that shuddered gaily in the wind.

After lunch, we crossed the flatlands of Canada near Hamilton, and in the late afternoon passed back into the States on a high bridge that took us into the air and then down. A huge sign hung like a banner across the roadway, welcoming us to the state. Chase climbed up on his knees and looked out the window so that he could get a better view of the boats passing far below, the water glittering under the afternoon sun, long shivering V's of silver behind the boats on the white-capped water.

"Chase," said Zip. "Sit down, Chase."

He grinned at us and turned around and sat down. "They have boats here, Mom," he said. "Can we go on a boat?"

"Maybe someday," I said. "Look. Do you see the lighthouse?"

"When can we go on a boat?" he said.

"Maybe after we're all moved in."

"And then we'll go on a boat, right? Right? Right?"

"Maybe," I said. "We'll see."

By nightfall, which comes late in the northern part of the Midwest in early August, we were headed north again. Chase and Haley slept in the back. Haley's head lolled against the side of her car seat; she rested her hands on the soft furry pelt of her stuffed giraffe. Chase's chin dropped forward onto his chest and every so often he would jerk upright but he did not wake up. Zip leaned forward in the dark, trying to find something on the radio, and I listened while he punched buttons up and down the dial. Nothing.

There were very few cars on the highway and the only lights were those that appeared on farms, where some enterprising dairyman had wired a single bright light to the peak of his barn, or had hung a security light over the farmyard between dark house and dark shed. Zip fiddled but all we heard was static, or the occasional weak voice of a late-night preacher, his voice calling to the faithful, a ghost of the airwaves out on the great flat plains in the middle of the country.

At ten, we drove into town past the oil refinery, the twin torches blazing in the darkness. Downtown was empty but there were fireworks over the Masonic Home, blooming flowers of sparks and screaming rockets that briefly lit up the sky and died. We found our new house and pulled into the driveway, our headlights sweeping across the previous owner's garden, the tomatoes and peppers and beans and pumpkins poking through a crazed jungle of tall, twisty weeds.

Inside, the house smelled like gas. We walked from room to room to open the windows and went to the neighbor's to call the gas company. I fixed sandwiches and chips and juice for the kids and let them eat their suppers tucked into the nest of blankets we made for them on the living room floor.

Just before we'd left the Finger Lakes, I'd met with Chase's pediatrician and asked him to tell me what was wrong with Chase. I had seen the MRI report, where the radiologist had written: *5-year-old male with pervasive developmental disorder*. It was the first time I'd seen those words when someone was talking about Chase and I'd asked Chase's doctor what they meant, but all he told me was that these were just descriptive words that helped the radiologist know what he was looking for, they were not a diagnosis, no one knew what to call the thing that might be wrong with Chase. In his opinion, I didn't need to worry about naming the thing. He had a philosophy, he said, of not telling parents the name of the thing that had come to live in their house because, he believed, the parents would focus on the thing and not the child. I found this statement bewildering; the name, it seemed to me, told me what I already knew: that my child was himself and this thing was part of who he was.

I told the pediatrician that I needed to know the words that had been entered into the medical record about Chase before we left town. We would change insurance companies with my new job and I needed to have the same information the insurance companies would have. I needed to know the words they knew.

"Autism," he said. "Atypical autism. That's what's in the record. That's what's been coded for the insurance companies." He suggested that I call a pediatrician in our new town and explore services that might be available for Chase. When I did, I was met with silence on the other end of the phone. Finally, the nurse said, "We don't have anything like that. We just don't have families with those needs here."

It's easy to say now that we would not have moved to the rural Midwest if we'd known that Chase had an autism diagnosis but I'm not so sure. His pediatrician had done his job well and I didn't see autism — even an unusual type of autism — when I saw Chase. I just saw Chase, who loved trains and dump trucks and riding his bike and who spun from room to room, who asked questions about everything he saw, the same questions over and over again, and stood on his bed and crowed like a rooster, giggling all the while.

WE COULD AFFORD THE house in the Midwest because the market was depressed and the house needed a lot of work. Chase's bedroom had a hole in the ceiling, where wires from an old light fixture snaked out from the darkness. The downstairs bedroom and bath were separated by a hole shaped like a doorway cut into the wall that you could step through into the bathroom; the previous owner had rented the upstairs bedrooms and kept the downstairs for himself, padlocking the two rooms so his renters couldn't get in. You could see a greasy crescent-shaped stain on the wall of the bedroom where he'd rested his scalp against the paint; it took Zip three coasts of Kilz to seal over the mark. The upstairs bath had a hole in the floor where the linoleum just dropped off to floor joists. The toilet had been salvaged; so had the bricks the last owner had laid along one side of the house to make a walkway through the enclosed garden. He'd dropped an old bathtub into the ground to make a pond and Zip spent one fall weekend digging and levering the thing out of the earth because I was afraid that Chase or Haley would fall in and drown. We lifted a half-rotted deer head out of the compost pile. We harvested the garden and then brush-hogged the backyard and raked up the stones and loose sticks and seeded and watered until we had grass where the kids could play. We put up a swing set, just a board on two large wooden tripods from which hung twin swings with a trapeze in between, and Chase and Haley could swing and tip up under the trees and fly back over the grass and tip up under the trees and fly forward, again and again. Forty-foot cedars lined the back of the yard and I planted daffodils and crocuses and snowdrops below their dark branches so that in the spring, we'd look out and see flowers across the grass, at the rim of darkness. We painted all of the rooms and pulled the old carpet up. We turned the downstairs bedroom into a study, with shelves that lined one wall, and made a desk by putting a slab of door on top of two file cabinets, so I could have a place to work.

The house held a hidden room in the basement and Zip had

planned to make it into a music room, a home studio, a place for
his guitars—he had nine—and his bass guitars—he had three—
and his four-track recording deck, and his electronic keyboards.
But the house sat in a part of town that tended to be wet and our
neighbors told us that someone did a geological survey one time
and they discovered a hidden river running below the earth. We
had a sump pump and every so often we'd hear the thing kick on
and send water spewing into the polyurethane pipe that drained
into the street. It was too wet to put instruments down there so
Zip took the cases and slid them into a long, wide closet under the
stairs, just off the study, and gradually his music room went black
with mold.

Every morning I got up and went to work at the college. I
took on an overload teaching assignment to make more money;
when I didn't have papers to grade or courses to prepare, I tried
to write something that would get us out of there. Our plan had
been that Zip would find work and Haley would go to day care
while Chase was in school and, in between, we'd work on the
house. But this part of the Midwest had taken a turn for the
worse and there were no jobs for Zip. It didn't take long before
Haley got mono at day care and we realized Chase needed someone at home after school. After that, I'd come home from work
and find the three of them in the driveway, Chase on his bike
and Haley in her racing car and Zip on a bike, wobbling in slow,
easy circles behind them.

Zip hung drywall in the doorway-shaped hole and then sanded
and primed and painted the room. He crawled into the space
below the eaves to figure out why water leaked into that corner
of the house. He redid the floor in the front foyer. I stripped the
wallpaper from the walls and he painted the dining room. We had
the counter in the kitchen replaced after we got a dishwasher.

One evening, when I came home from work, I found Zip doing laundry while Chase sat at the kitchen table and refused to do his homework. No one had started supper and as soon as Chase saw me, he jumped out of his chair and said, "Mom's home. I'm done now!"

Zip turned away from the washer and shoved a wad of damp towels into the dryer. "Chase," he said. But Chase was already gone; we could hear him on the stairs and then the sound of a racing car coming from his room.

"Hey," I said. I hung my briefcase on our old brass coat tree and slowly unrolled the scarf from around my neck and then took my winter coat—an old navy blue cashmere coat I'd bought in the East Village—and slipped my arms from the sleeves and shook the coat before I hung it up.

"I told him to sit there until he was done," Zip said. "I didn't tell him to sit there until you got home." He turned the dial on the dryer and slammed the door shut and pushed the start button. "Chase's teacher was here this afternoon," he said.

"Here? Why? Was I supposed to be here?"

He shook his head. "She just showed up at the back door."

"Why?"

"She said if we couldn't get him to do his homework, she was going to try. She sat at that table for an hour and tried to get him to do his work. But he didn't do much. He kept getting up and walking away. She told me he was going to have to focus more."

"That's original," I said.

Zip shook his head. "She said that he keeps telling her that kids are bothering him at recess but he doesn't play with anyone. And then she complained about his clothes and his appearance at school. She said he needed to come to school in better clothes."

"He chews all of his shirts," I said, "and then there are holes.

He wears clean shirts when he leaves here. I don't know what else we can do."

"And his hair," he said. "She said we need to wash it more often. And that he's always dirty. That he smells."

I leaned against the doorway. I could smell laundry soap and the heat from the dryer. I breathed in and out, and finally said, "What do you want for dinner?"

He shrugged. "I don't care." He brushed past me, out onto the back porch, and sat down on the second step from the bottom and took his cigarettes out. I couldn't understand how he could sit outside in the cold but I stepped out after him.

"I can make chili, if you want," I said.

He smoked and didn't say anything.

He faced away from me, out to the backyard. I'd pulled the car into the garage and you could see tire tracks in the snow pack, icy tracks so compressed they took the imprints of the treads and froze the patterns into place. The fact of the matter was that it was true: Chase did have an odd aroma, one that I noticed whenever I went into his room, whenever I stripped the sheets from his bed, whenever he stood next to me. Fresh from the bath, that aroma moved with him like an invisible cloud. Years later, I'd tell a geneticist about it, Chase's odd, off smell; I told her that Zip had it, too. Some days it was really strong, and some days it was barely there. Chase had had it for a long time but it wasn't something Zip had until after we were married. She took notes and nodded and I felt helpless because I couldn't produce the odor at that moment, so she'd know what it was. When Chase's third-grade teacher complained about it, I had even less ability to explain this to her; I didn't know then that genetic metabolic disorders are sometimes signaled by strange odors.

Chase also had dirty hair some of the time because by the time he was seven or eight, he no longer tolerated water in his eyes and thrashed and screamed in the bath when his hair was washed, and flung water everywhere, and howled as if we scalded him without care. Zip and I had to tackle the shampoo process together, one of us holding Chase down while the other sudsed and rinsed. Afterward, the bathroom would be flooded. We couldn't face this more than twice a week. And Chase chewed on his sleeves and the neckline of his shirts—all soft T-shirts or sweatshirts for he could not tolerate anything scratchy, anything with buttons—until the enzymes from his saliva had burned through the fabric. We could not afford to keep replacing things and when he'd chewed his cuffs down to shreds, I'd cut them off and sew hems in the short sleeves so he'd still be able to wear the shirt.

By third grade, it was clear that Chase did not like homework and would find any means possible to avoid it. Some days, he flung open the back door and simply ran away, down the alley behind our house, down the busiest street in town, across the bridge that arched over the scummy river, anywhere he could be free of us and of the things we expected him to do. In the winter of his eighth year, a psychologist told us to padlock him in his room to keep him from running away. I hated the lock but I hated the idea of Chase lost or gone or crushed beneath a truck even more, so Zip went to the hardware store and bought a lock that fit on the door like a plate on a hinge, with a loop for a padlock, which we planned to keep in the loop with a key in the lock at all times. He drilled the door frame and screwed the lock in place and Chase watched. Once he was inside his room and the lock was turned, he kicked until the wood was splintered and the door pulled away from its frame. The lock dangled from one edge and he was out again and running and running and running.

The smoke from Zip's cigarette curled upward in a blue stream.

I leaned one hip against the railing. A single star, so huge that it must have been a planet, hung on the horizon in front of me. "Like a diamond in the sky," I said softly. I watched Zip's back. He wore his old beret and his shoulder bones poked sharply through his cardigan sweater; he looked thin, suddenly, as if he'd lost a lot of weight fast. His hair was dirty. I couldn't remember the last time he'd bathed. He no longer slept in our room but had taken to sleeping on the sofa every night, telling me that he liked to stay up late and he knew I had to get up early. He slept in his clothes and then wore the clothes the next day, the same clothes night after night and day after day. Now he sat on the back porch in clothes he must have had on for a week and smoked and when the cigarette between his fingers was nearly down to the filter, he shook the pack and lit another. All around us, kitchen lights had come on, yellow squares and oblongs, the occasional shadow of a shape or hand, where someone prepared dinner.

"You're at home," I said at last. "I can help but you've got to keep the kids clean, at least. You've got to make sure their teachers don't think they're suffering from neglect."

"Yeah, right," he said.

"I can't do it from my office at school. If I were here, I would. But I can't. I'm at work."

"Blame it on me," he said. "You always do."

"That's not the point," I said. "That's not what this is about."

He sucked smoke into his lungs and looked out over the road that ran next to our house.

"Do you think you can do this?" I said.

"Whatever you say," he said. "You're the boss." His voice was filled with contempt.

"Please don't be like that," I said. "I'm just trying to figure out what to do. Do you agree that we can't have Chase's teacher showing up here for visits out of the blue? Do you know what that says?"

"That she doesn't know how to mind her own business?"

"Come on," I said. "That isn't going to help."

But he stopped talking and stood up and brushed the seat of his pants and slipped his cigarette pack into his shirt pocket. He opened the back door and walked away from me, into the house. I walked down into the driveway and took a deep breath and stared up at the big star. A gust of wind came across the snow and I felt dry, icy crystals hit my cheeks. The house suddenly felt like it was going to be too close, too hot, too airless for me so I stood under the new evening sky and let the wind blow snow dust against me.

When I went inside and up to Haley's room, I found her coloring in her Lion King coloring book. She wore her Lion King sweat suit, with the smiling lion faces printed on the front and the yarn fringe around her hood, like a mane. She picked this outfit every day and sometimes I had to slide her out of it when she was sleeping just to get it clean.

"Hey Haley," I said.

She looked up at me and smiled. "I have lions," she said. She pointed to Mufasa and Simba, regally ruling the rocks above a vast African plain. She'd colored the rocks a deep navy blue and the lions bright yellow but the plain was still coloring-book beige, its limits and undulations defined by thin, sharp lines of black ink.

"You want to go for a ride?"

She scrambled to her feet and I reached down and picked her up and held her. We could hear music coming from Chase's room and I settled Haley on my hip. "Or do you want to dance?" I said. And we swayed back and forth while Pete Seeger sang *A-bi-yo-yo, yo yoyo, yo yoyo.* Haley wrapped her arms around my neck and rested her head on my shoulder. I loved the way she held tightly to me, like a monkey, and I wanted to put her in the car and flee, but I could feel how tired she was; her head was heavy and her weight sagged against me.

"Come on, Haley-Bird. Let's go downstairs and make some dinner. Want some spaghetti?" I lifted her around the waist, hands on each side of her ribs and she spread her arms like wings and I swung her gently from side to side. When I flew her through the air like this, like a bird, she laughed and yelled at me to do it some more, her whole little body taut with pleasure and excitement.

ONE OF THE GUILTY secrets of those who care for someone with a disability is how angry we can become. I don't mean to suggest that we become purely angry at the person we love, although it can seem to take that form. I know I became furious with Zip and sometimes I was exhausted and irritated with Chase and just plain screeching mad that he could not seem to do one single thing that I asked him to do. But that isn't the kind of anger to which I refer, although that anger has brought me a good deal of shame and a good deal of grief, stemming, as it did, from an inability to understand truly rather than simply to know. I mean that we become angry at the disability itself. We feel the injustice of it, and see the ways in which that disability, that thing that belongs to someone else, which neither that person nor we would have chosen, has broken our lives open, too. It does not seem fair. And we are tired. And sometimes it feels unbearable always to be barred from the things you once enjoyed. Over time, it can become exceedingly difficult to live without a moment or two of privacy or to accomplish something mundane, like going to the grocery store without having every person in the world feel it is his or her prerogative to stare at your child. We struggle not to be angry, because it isn't helpful, not in that moment, but also because it's painful to be reminded that you live life at a remove you did not choose for yourself. But anger is an emotion. It comes.

TWELVE

||||||||||||||||||||||||||||||||||||||||

After we planted the lawn and the grass came up and we put up the swing set, we had a strange hot autumn day. A wind blew up from the south and carried before it pebbles from the edge of the road and scraps of old litter grown flat and blank from many days lying in the rain. This day was dry. High white clouds swept over us and I remembered what it was like to be a child and to lie on my back and watch the movement of the clouds and pretend their slow drift was the movement of the earth. The wind was hot and the sunshine on the grass was hot and I sat under the breezeway with my books and student papers on my knees. I thought I might work and for a while I did, but eventually Chase blasted through the back door, Haley right behind him, and Zip right behind her.

"Mom," said Chase. "Mom, Mom. We're going with Dad. Okay? Okay?"

Zip looked over to me and said, "You said we needed milk."

Haley wore a white tank top covered with pink flowers and blue and red and green plaid shorts and yellow rubber boots that came up to her knees. Her long hair blew around her shoulders and she pushed it back out of her eyes and grinned at me.

"Don't you want to stay here and play?" I asked her and she squinted at me and shook her head, no, no.

Zip let Chase ride in the front seat and buckled Haley up in back and got in behind the wheel and backed slowly and carefully in his grandmotherly fashion out of the driveway. As the car slid past me, Chase turned his face to the window and beamed at me.

I finished grading six papers before they returned, which meant they'd been gone more than an hour, even taking into account the number of times I stopped reading to look out at the trees, to listen to the wind roaring through the tops of the dark evergreens. It was rare to sit alone like this and I found myself distracted by small things, my concentration ready to drift at the slightest provocation. I considered the ivy growing under the apple tree by the back door and wondered if I ought to pull it up or leave it. I watched the children's swings move unbidden under the board. Then Zip pulled the car up and Chase flung open the front door and bolted for the house with a bag in his hands and banged the screen door behind him and Zip opened the back door and unbuckled Haley, and she stepped out and then around the car in her yellow boots and she had a bag in her hand, too, as did Zip.

"Did you get the milk?" I asked.

He stopped and hit himself in the forehead with the heel of his hand and grinned at me.

"I'll go," I said. "I don't mind."

"No," he said. "I'll go. I just have something to do first. Keep working."

"I might be about done for the day," I said. I stretched and let my stretching make my words come out slow and long, like a stifled groan. "I have lots to do but I can't seem to focus," I said. But I turned to my lap and took up my pen, which had rolled under the chair, and turned to the first sentence of the next student paper. The student had written something inscrutable and I studied the sentence for a moment, trying to ascertain its subject, first, and second, its validity. Both prospects seemed hopeless. I made a mark in the margin that looked like a question mark. And then a second question mark, since, after all, I had two questions in mind.

The kitchen windows were open behind me and I could hear the kids giggling inside and the rattling of thin plastic bags and the tearing of cardboard and then water running and Zip saying, "That's enough, Chase, you don't want to get too much in there."

"My turn, my turn," Haley said and Zip said, in the most tender voice you can imagine, "Okay, here you go."

Chase pressed his face against the screen as if it were a mask. "Mom," he said. "Oh, Mom."

"What, honey?"

"Chase," said Zip. "Come over here. Remember what I said?"

Chase giggled. "Bye, Mom," he said and the screen went flat.

"Got it?" Zip said.

"Yes." Haley's voice was small and clear.

"Okay," Zip said. "Wait one more sec while I do mine."

I turned back to the paper and underlined the second sentence, which was not a sentence at all, but a strange amalgam of words that connected in ways that were not obvious to me. I wrote "Frag?" hopefully, as if this might provide an explanation. The third sentence caused me to burst out laughing and then feel ineluctably sad: *After the publication of Bleak House, Charles Dickens became known for his sanitary hygiene.* I wrote "Really?" in the margin and rubbed my eyes and looked out across the backyard, where our neighbor's black and white cat picked its way through the flowerbed. I looked back at the paper and felt briefly hopeless, as if my teaching had come to this, which meant my teaching had come to nothing.

"Mom," said Chase. "Oh, Mom . . . "

I looked up. "What?"

And Zip yelled, "Fire!" and they all sprayed me. Chase had a big Super Soaker and Zip had a slightly smaller water gun, same type, and Haley had a water pistol of the sort I used to love when I was a girl.

I dropped my papers and threw a book on top of them and leapt to my feet. "Why, you, I ought to . . . !" I yelled. And then I ran after Chase and said, "Give me that!" He pulled away and I said, "Help me get your father," which appealed to him much more. He handed the gun over to me and I turned and ran after Zip, who was, by this time, hiding behind a tree in the side yard.

"I see you," I said. "Better give up now."

"You see me?" he yelled. "I see you!" And then a high-powered spray hit me in the chest. I screamed and took off for the backyard and then turned and fired at Zip, who pounded across the lawn behind me. I got him in the face and he stopped, so I got him again. Then he fired blindly and I screamed again and he got me, this time in the head, and my hair felt cool and wet against my scalp. Haley danced around her father's knees and he said, "Go on! Go get Mommy!" She ran up to me and squirted me until her pistol was empty.

"I need more," she said.

"Chase," I yelled. "Go help your sister!"

"I'll show you how to fill it," he said. He ran to the kitchen with Haley right behind him while Zip slowly advanced on me.

"Don't you dare," I said. "Don't you dare."

"Don't I dare what?" he said. "This?" He squirted me in the stomach.

"I'll get you," I said. "I swear."

Chase and Haley came back and Haley took aim at me.

"What're you doing?" I said. "Get your father!"

But before she could, he was across the lawn in three strides and had hooked me around my neck with his elbow and was spraying down my shirt while I screamed and screamed. I fell to my knees, which just gave Zip a better angle. I squirted ineffectively at him and then threw the water gun to Chase. "Get your father," I said damply from the ground and Chase said, "Whooooo!" and sprayed the back of Zip's shirt while he leaned over me and laughed for what felt like the last time.

THIRTEEN

Winter persisted and Chase stayed on at the hospital. I looked for a place that would take him when he got out but the mental-health facilities didn't want a kid with a developmental disability and the developmental-disability places didn't want a kid with a mental-health issue. In the state of North Carolina, you had to be one or the other; you were not allowed to be both.

Dr. B had no suggestions. He gave me another chance to talk about Chase's grim prognosis. He said he was sorry. When we were through, I stood blinking and damp-eyed in the doorway of Chase's room and watched him pace the length of the nurses' station, turn, pace back to his room, turn, and pace the length of the nurses' station again. His trousers sagged down around his hips, but he paid no attention until Sam stopped him and pointed out that he was about to lose his pants. Then Chase yanked at his waistband while he was walking, hiked his pants up until the hems reached flood height. He didn't look at anyone as he paced but he tapped his hand against his thighs and every so often fired his weapons.

A young medical student filled out paperwork behind the nurses' station and tried to enlist Chase in conversation as he passed. "Dude," he said. "Hey dude. Give me five. Dude."

Chase ignored him.

Dr. B glanced up from his own stack of papers and watched Chase for a few minutes. Then he turned back to his forms.

I swallowed the lump in my throat and became aware of a woman standing in front of the next doorway. She wore a short camel jumper and a blouse with a Peter Pan collar, white ankle socks with lacey cuffs, and black patent-leather Mary Janes. This was the sort of outfit you'd typically see on a third grader so I was surprised to see that the woman was over fifty. Her mouth was an astonishing shade of red, as if it were a cartoon version of a mouth. For a minute I wondered if she'd wandered in from the adult unit on the fourth floor but then I realized that every so often she'd turn to someone in the room behind her, say something, and someone — a girl, maybe it was her daughter — would make an unhappy and put-upon sound, and the woman in the child's outfit would turn and continue to survey the dayroom.

She watched Chase make his way along the length of the nurses' station. She said something to him as he passed but he didn't respond, didn't even bring her into focus so he could turn a laser on her.

She began to sidle toward me, her arms folded across her chest, still watching Chase.

"Quite a place they've got here," she said, her smile hard and unfriendly. Chase passed us and turned and passed us again. She watched him with open curiosity. "I guess it takes all kinds," she said, and then laughed a little. She looked at me and stuck out her hand. "I'm Shirley Powers," she said. "That's your son, isn't it? I've seen him here before."

I ignored her hand and didn't give her my name. This was not some sort of demented PTA meeting; this was a place, if ever there was a place in the world, where it was absolutely essential to respect everyone's privacy. My silence didn't stop her. She let her hand hang between us and then dropped it back to her side.

"He's quite a boy," she said.

Chase yanked his pants up again and I felt my heart twist.

"Oh, ho," said the woman insanely dressed like a seven-year-old child. "Look at that!"

I turned to her and leveled her with my most unfriendly look. "Would you excuse us, please?"

She stopped smiling. "All right," she said. And then she backed away.

As time passed, I came to see more and more parents on the unit. Sometimes I'd see the whole family gathered in the classroom, along with the doctor, the social worker, and the psychologist who ran the groups. The doctor did most of the talking while the patient stared at his or her knees. You had to wonder what became of these kids when they left the hospital, what their prospects were for happiness, what combination of hope and encouragement needed to obtain for something like a future to evolve, and just how heavy were the odds that were stacked against them. As I searched for a place for Chase, I learned that there were facilities across the state that would take some of these kids, the ones who'd been abused, the ones who'd pushed their luck way too far, the ones who couldn't live at home anymore, the ones who ran away but weren't able to keep running; these were locked, level-four facilities that housed violent kids who'd committed crimes—theft, rape, arson, murder—often after crimes had been committed against them. These were the only facilities in the state that had on-site medical and nursing care, round-the-clock staff who were awake all hours of the day and night, and programs of therapy throughout the day. The next step down, the level-three places, were less restrictive and functioned more like group homes, where no one who stayed on duty overnight stayed awake, and the kids who lived there were supposed to be independent enough to go to school during the day, look after their belongings, contribute to the household chores, perhaps hold a job. These facilities weren't locked and had a nurse who dropped by once a week and a doctor who came by once a month.

One level-four place called the Lighthouse said it took developmentally disabled kids but when I looked into it, I discovered that it was filled with children who had committed serious crimes and the expectation was that the developmentally disabled patient would be in that league, too. I talked to a woman I'd met through a program called TEACCH, which stood for Treatment and Education of Autistic and Related Communication-handicapped Children. Her autistic teenage daughter had had a psychotic episode and landed at the Lighthouse; she lasted ten days before they pulled her out for fear that she would be raped or killed.

Finally, Linda, the area mental-health-unit social worker who'd arranged for Chase's CAP services and now led the search for a place that might take Chase, found a level-three place that said it was especially designed to meet the needs of teens with both a developmental disability and a psychiatric illness. It was in Jacksonville, down on the coast, three hours away from Chapel Hill. I thought this was too far away but I said I would drive down and take a look.

Jacksonville is a military town, the home of Camp Lejeune. It has tattoo parlors and strip joints on every block, interspersed with burger places and pawnshops. The day I visited, its streetlights were swathed in patriotic bunting to cheer the soldiers who were getting ready to ship out to Iraq, or the families left behind of those who had already gone.

I followed the main street past a Wal-Mart and along the chain-link fences that bordered the base. The home was on a side street off the main drag, a modest one-story place with dingy pink shutters and three unassertive shrubs in front, where, the director was quick to mention, she had a lawn service come and mow the grass once a week, to preserve a homey feel. She showed me the main living areas, and the bedrooms that were mostly shared by two kids doubled up; some of them had creatively hung sheets to make dividing screens. Kids had TVs and computers and stereos but there were strict rules about the use of such items, as well as about the music they could listen to and the movies they could watch. No one was at home during the day but off at the residential service's day program, which was held in the main office; she mentioned that I'd seen that when I came in. I thought of the small windowless conference room where six kids who looked to be anywhere from eight to sixteen sat around a single rectangular table and worked on a coloring project while someone who looked like a high school student supervised them. None of the clients went to local schools, the director admitted, and they were always looking for fun things to do, but this being Jacksonville, there wasn't a lot that was local that would make a good outing. She mentioned band concerts in the town park in the summer but said they only went to those when they had the staff and it wasn't too hot. They didn't have a nurse to administer medication but there was an on-site staff person who kept an eye on that.

The director told me they didn't have any openings now but she was looking to expand the program. On our way back to the main office, she drove by a house that she planned to buy so I could see the possibilities there and said it might be ready in the next two or three months.

We sat in her office while she interviewed me about Chase, interrupting herself only to flip through the pages of his application for admission or write with intense concentration on a yellow legal pad.

Finally she looked up and said, "I've been twenty-five years in this business. I started out working for the Lighthouse, where they take some of the worst offenders and lock them up. They call that rehabilitation. I think they probably need a place like that. But I decided to go out on my own and start a business that I thought would meet a need that was going begging. Where were the residential facilities for children with things like PDD who also have some psychiatric disorder? Do you know how many of these kids are obsessive-compulsive? ADD? Manic-depressive? Do you have any idea the havoc this wreaks on a family? The parents are exhausted. The siblings are overlooked. They need to get these kids out of their homes but they don't deserve to be sent to a place like the Lighthouse. We've been up and running for nineteen months. We're all set up for Medicaid here. We take private insurance, if you have the kind of plan that will pay for this kind of care. Don't be surprised if yours doesn't. Most don't. I like to think of us as having a vision about the kinds of clients we can serve. I like to believe that we're small enough where we can still be flexible when we need to be, where we aren't too hidebound by our own rules. But I can tell you, just after looking at your son's application, that we aren't going to be able to take him here."

She paused. "I feel for you. I really do. But we don't have the kind of services he needs. We don't have the medical care, for one thing, or the security for another. We have a neurologist who we can call if we need to but to be perfectly honest with you, I don't know if he will have ever seen a case like Chase. He's older. He works with us as something of a favor because he and I go way back. We don't have the therapeutic day programs that Chase's going to need. We're going to have those someday but the plain truth is we haven't got them now. And we certainly don't have the staff for someone who isn't close to being fully independent, which most of our kids are. Your son is very complex and has very complex needs. But I don't need to tell you that. I think you know that already. We'll keep his application on file. But you can tell your social worker that we turned him down and she's going to have to keep looking. And to be honest, I don't think you're going to find anything. If I were you, I'd be worried. I feel like I have a pretty good idea of what's available in this state and I have no idea what you're going to do."

I DROVE HOME and the skies began to clear. It had rained all day, until water ran in flat undulating sheets across the county highways and the smell of the loamy fields rose up around the car. I listened to the thunk of the wipers and watched water drain along the edges of the windshield. The side yard had flooded the way it always did in a heavy rain and when I pulled into the driveway, I could see a light on in the kitchen. I imagined someone waiting for me inside, someone to make dinner and stroke my hair and tell me that everything was going to be all right. But the front door rattled vacantly when I opened it and the house was cold and dim.

ONE AFTERNOON JUST BEFORE spring, I came up to Five South to see Chase. He walked past me in hard pushing strides, turned, and marched back the other way.

"Hey Chase," I said, but he just glared at me, let loose a few lasers, and walked away. He was tapping his hand against his leg. When he came to a ceiling vent, he stopped and squinted up at it. The hospital had the heat on and if you stood under the vents, you could hear the sound of the blowers. Chase listened for a minute and then began tapping again. Then he paused and turned to Pam, who was entering information into a spreadsheet on the nursing station computer. He leaned over the counter so she could hear him.

"Why is that woman here?" he said, and waved in my general direction. His voice was loud and agitated and angry. "I don't know who she is."

"That's your mother, Chase," said Pam, in the mildest voice imaginable. "She's here to visit with you."

"My mother was kidnapped by terrorists," said Chase. "That is not my mother." He looked at me. "You are not my mother," he yelled.

"Chase, you know that's your mother," said Pam. "You know her. You know she comes to visit you." She looked over at me to see if I could hear this exchange and I shrugged to let her know I could. She gave me a sad, drowning look in return. I didn't blame her. After a while, none of us knew what to say or do.

You would think I would have been used to this by now. Chase almost always did the same things when I saw him: he fired lasers, he tapped his hand against his leg, he made words but no sounds and moved his mouth constantly, he told anyone who would listen that I was not his mother. But each time I came up to the unit, I came with the hope that this day would be different. Maybe the drug would have taken effect. Maybe the psychosis would have lifted on its own accord. Maybe Chase would look across the room and see me and know who I was.

Dr. B came through the front door, saw me, and said, "Good. You're here. I wanted to try and catch you."

I followed him into the library. We didn't sit down.

"Chase has not responded well to this drug," he said. "In certain ways, I think it has activated his symptoms. And Chase has not responded well to the other drugs we've tried. I had high hopes for all of them, especially those in the newer classes of antipsychotics. They are often very effective in difficult cases and you get good results right away. But we have not had that outcome with Chase."

He paused. "I'd like you to consider a trial of Clozaril. It's a relatively new antipsychotic and it has been extraordinarily effective in some very difficult cases. But it has some nasty side effects so you need to be fully informed before you give your consent." He held a sheaf of paper out to me. "I'd like you to read this and let me know what you think. Once you've read, we can talk more. I don't want you to rush into this. You need to take your time and make sure you're comfortable with the decision."

Just outside the door, the hospital teacher piled a stack of books on the counter next to the sink in the dayroom. Catherine was close to my age. Whenever we spoke, she tried to give me optimistic accounts of Chase's time in class. She said things like, Today Chase Sat for Three Minutes While I Read to Him. Or, Today Chase Made an Incoherent Comment When the Other Students Were Discussing Current Events but Perhaps This Is Evidence That He Wishes to Communicate. She waved at me through the glass and I looked over Dr. B's shoulder and smiled in return. She crossed the floor to the doorway in three steps and said, "If this is a good time, I'd like to speak with you."

Dr. B gave her a calm look. "We'll be just a minute," he said.

"I'll wait," said Catherine.

He gestured at me with the sheaf of papers again and I took the pages from him and glanced down.

Patient Information: Clozaril. Pronounced: KLOH-zah-ril. Generic Name: Clozapine

"What kind of side effects?" I asked.

His expression never changed. "Some are mild," he said. "Things like drooling, sedation, constipation, dizziness, weight gain. We worry the most about a kind of very serious disorder of the white blood cells, but that's rare and we do blood work every week to monitor the patient." He paused and gave me a level look. "It's called agranulocytosis. It's very serious. It can be fatal. Researchers were unaware of the risk when this drug first came onto the market and a number of patients died. It was pulled back and then reintroduced with a national registry of users. Very, very few patients develop this disorder now, and almost no one dies of it anymore. In some ways, Clozaril is the gold standard for the treatment of all psychotic patients, but its use is reserved for those who are the most seriously ill and who have failed at trials of at least three traditional antipsychotics." He stopped and rubbed his nose and then started again. "Chase has been on five different antipsychotics since November," he said. "He has not responded to treatment. He is eligible for this drug. We will draw blood every week and watch for the precipitous drop in white blood cells that signals the onset of the blood disorder. Hopefully, that will never happen and he'll respond and do well. We will discontinue the drug immediately at the first sign of trouble."

I rolled the papers into a baton as he spoke. Chase strode by the library, his gaze trained on something beyond the walls, the ceiling, the floor. He tapped his leg and muttered and disappeared from view. In another minute I saw one of the nurses start down the hall after him. "Chase," he called. "Chase. We need to come back to the dayroom." I walked over to the doorway and saw Chase standing in the room of one of the boys who'd come in over the weekend. Everyone on the unit had turned toward Chase when the nurse began calling his name, each head angled in the same direction, each face still and watchful. The kids in the dayroom fell silent.

Chase was talking in a loud voice. "Hey man," he said. "Hey man, hey man. I'm Zack. Zack. Zack. You wanna join a band, man? Hey. What do you play?" Beyond him, I could see the boy in the room, standing still, in the way of someone afraid.

The nurse touched Chase's arm. "Let's leave David alone now," he said. "There you go. Turn this way. Chase. Turn this way."

He curled one hand around Chase's arm and used the other to apply pressure in the center of his back, like a door swinging on a pivot, until Chase turned and allowed himself to be walked back past the nurses' station through the dayroom and past the classrooms to his own room. He kept talking, loudly calling for the arrest of those who were holding him here, in this jail, against his will, until he'd crossed into his room and could stand at the windows and begin to press buttons.

I watched him and twisted the papers in my hands. Then I turned back to the library.

"You need to be comfortable with this decision," said Dr. B softly. "It involves some risk." He waited. When I didn't say anything, he said, "Clozaril is an excellent drug with a strong track record among the most severely ill patients. If you plan to try it, this is the very safest, most controlled setting in which to try it." He paused. "But you need to be sure," he said at last. "Read the patient information and then give me a call."

"Is there anything else we could try?" I asked.

He shook his head. "No," he said. "No. I'm sorry. This is what's left."

CATHERINE STOPPED ME AS soon as I left the library.

"I need to talk with you about end-of-grade tests," she said. "While it's early to be talking about this, it's not as early as you think. He's in eighth grade. He's going to need to take the end-of-year writing test and that's supposed to be administered in March. This is the end of February."

I stared at her.

"Then we have the regular end-of-grade tests," she said. "Those come in May. If Chase is still here, we need to make arrangements for him to take them."

"You're joking," I said. "Right?"

"No," she said. "I'm not joking. He's on the hospital school census and we need to make arrangements for him to meet state requirements."

"How's he doing in class?" I asked.

"Well," she said. "To be truthful, I honestly don't know. He doesn't seem to be able to read. Did he ever read?"

"At the ninth-grade level," I said.

She shook her head. "I don't think he can read at all now. Here," she said, and flipped open one of the folders. "This is an example of his writing. This is what he produced when he first got here. He hasn't written anything for a long while now." She handed me a sheet of paper that had a few lines of the same sort of inscrutable symbols Chase had written on the walls of his room.

"It's not language, you see," said Catherine. "You can tell that it's not any sort of language at all."

"Isn't there some form of medical exemption?" I asked.

Catherine shook her head. "No," she said. "He's enrolled in the hospital school, as we're required to do by law, and therefore, by law, he must take the end-of-grade exams."

"But he's not on this planet," I said. "He's incoherent 100 percent of the time. He doesn't know who he is. He doesn't know who I am. He doesn't know where he is. He's hallucinating." I took a breath. "Are you telling me that there is no exemption whatsoever? What if he'd been in a coma for the last six months and was still in a coma? Would he have to take the end-of-grades while he was in a coma?"

Catherine sighed. "Unfortunately," she said, "yes. The law does not provide for exemptions, exceptions, just because you have a medical situation."

"You're aware of how insane that sounds," I said.

She flushed. "Yes," she said, "but it's the law."

FOURTEEN

In the second grade, Chase became obsessed with tornadoes. He read everything in the local library about tornadoes and Zip bought him a video that showed twisters touching down and barns flying into splinters, garage doors floating like stiff paper through the dusky air. The narrator of the video spoke in firm, somber tones: *Tornadoes form when warm Gulf air meets the cooler air that comes down onto the plains states from the Rocky Mountains to create supercells, giant thunderheads that, when conditions are right, spawn the funnel clouds we call twisters . . .* Chase watched this video over and over and over again, each time with the rapt attention and pleasure of someone who has waited for the film for a long time. He wanted to chase tornadoes just like storm chasers do and one afternoon, as black clouds churned and rolled in the west and wind began to bend the tops of the cedars, I heard a weather alert for big thunderstorms on the radio. I told Chase to go get in the car. We were going to chase this storm.

I was relieved when Chase developed an interest in the weather. It seemed much healthier than his interest in the Lady Sword who came to him at night or the children in his class who were trying to attack him or the ghost that lived in our house.

Now Chase buckled up and we pulled out of the driveway as the first raindrops began to falter against the roof. Zip and Haley waved from the back porch. We drove west out of our town, out onto the long flat highway toward the thunderstorms. I kept to the open highway where it cut through sugar-beet fields and fields of feed corn, out across the flat straight plains of the Midwest, where the sky was a line just above the horizon and the thunderheads bellied out like sails and billowed darkly, and white laundry on backyard clotheslines behind farmhouses whipped into the gusts of wind and stood straight out on poles and then the poles came down and the sheets and towels and bleached white shirts and socks flapped and blew away. It began to rain, slowly at first and then more urgently, until it was hard to see. Trees bent and shuddered. Branches came down around us and skidded across the road. I eased over onto the shoulder and flicked the flashers on and hoped I wasn't about to put the car in a drainage ditch. We listened to the rain pound the roof and hood and then came hail the size of peas, skittering and flying across the hood of the car and over our heads and rattling into the crispy dry grass along the edge of the highway.

As soon as we turned onto the country highway and the rain slashed down in earnest, I knew I'd made a big mistake. I'd seen plenty of Midwestern thunderstorms by that time and knew they were fierce; we'd outrun one coming home from Lake Michigan the summer before and I'd never seen a sky turn such an eerie shade of purplish green, as if everything above us was bruised inside the clouds. The darkness came on fast and we drove east on Route 46 at five in the afternoon in light that looked like midnight. Now I turned the windshield wipers to high and the rain sluiced in gray sheets over the glass and Chase stared out the window and said, "Look at that, Mom! Look at that!" Then he turned to me. "Why are we stopping?"

"I can't see to drive, sweetie," I said. "There's too much rain."

"No," he said. "We should go."

"We just need to wait until the rain eases up a little. I can't really see the road to drive."

"No," said Chase. "We need to go."

"Keep still," I said, forcing myself to keep my voice light. I suddenly realized the very real possibility that Chase might try to get out of the car. I could see him twirling away from me down the road, no longer safe, suddenly lost, gone for good. Thunder crashed overhead and dazzling lightning fissured across the sky.

"We can see really well from here," I said. "It's really great. Look up. Watch the sky."

Chase leaned forward and turned his face up to the clouds. "Look at all that rain," he said, marveling. "Wow, Mom," he said. "Would you look at that?" He reached for the door handle. "Let's get out," he said.

"No," I said sharply. "Sit down. I'll turn this car around right now."

He gave me a look but he let go of the door handle and looked out the window. "There's rain," he said, "and there's lightning, right?" And I said, "Yes, and listen for the thunder." The sky blackened above us and the light around us was dim and watery and the car shivered a little in the wind and Chase said, "The warm air meets the cold air in the upper atmosphere and begins to turn together until a huge funnel is formed and that's when we have a twister." He rose up on his knees until he could look out the car's rear window but he could see nothing but rain sluicing down. The hail had passed and the wind had settled a little and, after a time, the rain began to let up and I said it was time to drive home. "Maybe we'll see a twister on the way," I said.

When we pulled into the driveway, Zip was sitting on the back steps, smoking a cigarette. "Dad, Dad!" said Chase as he burst from the car. "We went storm chasing! It was cool!"

WHEN CHASE BROUGHT the sign-up sheet for the science fair home, it seemed only right that we channel all of his interest in storms into a project. I asked him if he wanted to make a tornado for the fair.

He dismissed me with a glance. "That," he said, "is not possible."

"Of course it's possible," I said. "Want to see how? Want to be the master of your own tornado?"

"Mom," he said. He looked very serious. "I have to tell you."

"What?" I said. I was taking dishes out of the dishwasher and wiping them dry before I put them away. I knew what was coming.

"*Tornadoes form when warm Gulf air meets the cooler air that comes down onto the plains states from the Rocky Mountains to create supercells, giant thunderheads that, when conditions are right, spawn the funnel clouds we call twisters,*" Chase intoned. "You can't make a tornado at home, Mom," he said. "Do you see any Gulf air around here?" He looked around as if waiting for something to appear. "We don't have mountains here," he said.

"I know, Chase. We don't live in Kansas. I am not the Wicked Witch of the West. But I know how to make a tornado at home."

We lived in the rural Midwest so we didn't have the critical part handy. Chase's aunt sent it and the day her package arrived — a small brown envelope sealed with everyday packing tape — I fetched it from the foyer, where the mailman shoved our mail through the mail slot, where Zip got junk mail addressed to Art Byrd, and tossed it to Chase. "Here's your tornado," I said.

"Where?" he said. He turned the envelope over in his hands and shook it and then held it out to me. "Open it," he said.

"Come on," I said. "Come into the kitchen."

We cut the envelope open and Chase looked at the black tornado tube that my sister had picked up at her local fancy toy shop. If you fill a single two-liter plastic soda bottle most of the way with water, and use the tube to screw that bottle to a second two-liter plastic soda bottle, and then upend the bottles so the one with the water in it is on top, and you rotate the bottle in quick little swirls, pretty soon, a perfect tornado will form. It's just the whirl of water as it's sucked down a drain — another of Chase's early preoccupations — but it looks exactly like a twister.

At the last minute, before we screwed the two tubes together in a final and absolute way, Chase decided the water alone looked too plain. He added a little glitter of the sort you find in snow globes and a tiny black and white plastic Holstein he'd robbed from his farm animals set. When you activated the tornado, the cow flew through sparkly water. The glittering twister stood out in sharp relief against the empty air inside the bottle, just the way a tornado stands out in sharp relief against the sky.

"Wow, Chase," I said. "That's very cool." I put my arm around his shoulders and hugged him and he leaned his head against me and I allowed myself to feel hope. I liked to tell myself that Chase might have a bumpy childhood but once he was through it, everything was going to be fine. His face was bright when he looked at the tornado in the tube and he spent the rest of the afternoon tilting and twirling the bottle to make the twister appear and I watched him while I finished the dishes and started dinner and the worry in my stomach eased up a little. Chase was a smart boy. He was going to be fine. That tornado proved it.

They held the science fair under the greenish florescent lights of the cafeteria and Chase's simple tornado, with his complicated yet perfect descriptions of weather systems, seemed small in comparison to the real working batteries that caused lightbulbs to flash white and then off with the flip of a switch or the baking-soda volcanoes made of cornstarch clay that erupted in fantastic displays when someone poured a half cup of white vinegar into the caldera. Chase carefully stood his poster board on the easel stand we'd devised and stood his tornado in the center of the table. The binder with all of his notes in it rested to one side. Whenever anyone approached the table, he'd crow, "Want to see a real tornado?" If the visitor stopped, Chase carefully rotated the bottle and activated the tornado. But not many people stopped to explore his display—nothing exploded here, nothing flashed. He was wearing a New York Yankees baseball shirt and I noticed that his rat-tail had grown so long that perhaps we ought to think about cutting it. But Chase loved having the long tendril curling down his back. He thought it made him cool.

The judges were high school science teachers, drafted for the occasion. They moved around the room, clipboards in hand, and wore yellow ribbons pinned to their lapels that said *Judge*. I noticed that they stood for a long time before the volcanoes and asked many questions of the children who had made them. One finally made his way to Chase's exhibit. He read the poster board and he picked up the binder with the facts that Chase had amassed about tornadoes and flipped through the pages. He noted that Chase had supplied a bibliography.

"All right, young man," he said. "What do you know about tornadoes?"

"*Tornadoes form when warm Gulf air meets the cooler air that comes down onto the plains states from the Rocky Mountains to create supercells, giant thunderheads that, when conditions are right, spawn the funnel clouds we call twisters,*" Chase said.

"That's fine," said the judge, holding up one hand. "Now your sign says you have a tornado here. Show me what you can do."

Chase lifted the bottle and carefully upended it so the water would be on top and then, just as carefully, rotated the top bottle very slowly, until the water picked up internal velocity and the whirlpool effect began. The tornado glittered under the cafeteria lights and the cow spun with the centrifugal force of the funnel cloud, turning and rollicking, spun out to the outer limits and held in place at the same time. The judge didn't say anything but watched the cow fly through the air with a great solemnity. He didn't write any notes on his clipboard. When all of the water drained out into the lower bottle and the cow fell unceremoniously to the drain, the judge squatted down so he'd be more or less Chase's height and all I could see was a messy tangle of gray curls knotted over the back of the judge's skull like a hat.

"Did you make this tornado?"

"Yes," said Chase. "I rule tornadoes."

The judge smiled. "It seems that you do," he said. "Where did you get the idea for the cow?"

"*The Wizard of Oz,*" Chase said. "There's a cow when Dorothy goes up in the twister."

The judge chuckled. "I remember that," he said.

"It says *moo,*" said Chase, grinning and ducking his head. "Do you want to see it again?"

"One time will do it for me," said the judge. And then he reached into his jacket pocket and pulled out a blue ribbon that said *First Prize* and pinned it to Chase's poster board. "You keep at it and you'll be a great scientist one day."

FOR HALEY'S THIRD BIRTHDAY, we bought a Fisher-Price racing car, black with yellow trim and a red seat. The day after her birthday, she took it out into the driveway and pushed the pedals and ten minutes later had figured out how to steer left and then right and make the car turn. Zip took her for walks. She drove the car and he rode behind her on his bicycle, riding so slowly that he couldn't keep the front wheel straight and had to stop and put his feet down so he wouldn't lose his balance. They made a beautiful picture, Haley in her car, her arms resting on the steering wheel when she came to a stop, and Zip, his long hair falling softly around his shoulders, the breeze lifting it, his hand pushing it out of his face, just the way he had years ago when I saw him walking across the parking lot to the bus.

And yet, if he looked at me across the dinner table or looked up when he was done with the dishes, I didn't see him at all. His expression was blank and dark and he sat on the back porch and smoked. He didn't believe there was anything wrong. He couldn't understand why I was unhappy. I asked him to talk to me. He said he could not. He said it was as if he knew what he wanted to say but he could not get it out, that somewhere between his brain and his mouth, he lost the ability to say anything at all. It took him ten minutes to tell me that. I waited to see if he would come inside but when he did not, I wandered into the living room and read a book for class and felt the house shudder with loneliness. And beyond the loneliness was a kind of anger that had no limits: I worked hard and supported us and then I came home and still had to plan meals, cook dinner, clean the house, and organize the kids' rooms, and plan for their clothing purchases, and organize birthdays and holidays, and track the school calendar, and look after the pets, and handle the household bills, and arrange for sitters and doctor's appointments and dentist's appointments, and for refills on Chase's medication, and for the monthly drives to the state university, where he was seen by a child psychiatrist.

We went to see a marriage counselor. I sat on the sofa but Zip sat across from me in a chair upholstered in cloth the color of eggplant, under a reading lamp that cast a shadow on his face. The marriage counselor thought we were there because I was angry about housework. She asked us to talk about our home responsibilities. She gave us an assignment: for our next session, we were to bring in lists of everything we did to manage the house and the family. The next week, I pulled mine from my bag: it was two pages long. Zip didn't have one. He said he had forgotten to do it. He said he'd have it next time. He said he always remembered things but for some reason had forgotten this. He sat in his purple chair and felt very distant from me, and I realized he was baffled. He didn't understand why we were there.

After the session, the therapist asked to see me alone for a few minutes. She told me she could not help us. Zip was beyond her reach.

"He needs psychiatric assessment," she said. "It's like he's not there, it's like there's no one home. Do you understand what I'm telling you? He's not being passive-aggressive. He isn't there. I'm afraid he has a serious psychiatric illness and he needs treatment. At the very least, he needs to be seen by someone. I'll give you a referral."

"What?" I said.

She repeated herself. "This kind of thing can be shocking," she said. "It's hard on the families. But he needs to see a psychiatrist. He needs an evaluation."

Outside, Zip leaned against our car and smoked. When he saw me, he opened the passenger-side door and sat down. I realized I was always driving, always planning, always saying how things were going to be. He was quiet on the ride home and it didn't surprise me when he refused to seek medical treatment.

ONE MORNING, CHASE and Haley and I raked until we'd raked every leaf we could find into a giant pile; all around us, you could hear other rakes moving swiftly and steadily across lawns and the air was full of the smell of leaf fires burning but, unlike our neighbors, we didn't seek to make short work of our chore. Instead, we wanted to make the biggest leaf pile anyone had ever seen, a colossus of a leaf pile, the Empire State Building of leaf piles. Chase had been asking about it all morning. When we were through, we had a sizable accomplishment; the thing mounded to four feet in the center. Chase dropped his rake and grabbed Haley's hand and said, "Let's jump!" And he and Haley walked backward until they were at the perfect spot to get a running start and I counted them down and at *one* they ran and leapt into the leaves, and threw leaves into the air, and began rolling and swimming until they were completely submerged and only their two faces came up through the leaves, like divers emerging from some beautiful shadowy deep, and they lay on their backs, swimmers, my family, floating in the giant pile, grinning at me.

WINTER FELT PARTICULARLY DARK that year. A raw wet wind blew in from the west and we had little snow, just dark days where the sky lowered over our heads and ice made glassy patches on the back steps and Zip stood outside in his old coat and smoked and smoked. At night the stars hung above us, distant and not much gazed upon; it was too cold to stand in the yard and look for Orion's Belt or Cassiopeia. We went to sleep at night with the wind and we woke in the morning with the wind and in between, the wind blew.

One cold midwestern morning, the snow that had fallen over-night drifted softly against the trees. A woodpecker drilled against the neighbors' dead silver maple. I stood at the foot of my bed and folded laundry and listened to the woodpecker and felt a draft through the old window. I heard Chase's voice, clear, high-pitched, arguing, and then his father's lower voice, flat, sonorous, but it too rose in pitch, and then someone ran and someone else ran after him, and there came a terrible thumping from the kitchen. By the time I got downstairs, Chase was on the floor between Zip's legs, held up only by his father's hands around his neck, and Zip was shaking him as hard as he could. I shouted Zip's name but there was no answer.

Chase's arms were limp, his hands batting weakly against the floor.

"Stop it, stop it, you'll kill him," I shrieked but my own voice was only so much sound from a far distance; it did nothing, stopped no one. And then I pushed Zip as hard as I could and he fell to the floor and I stood over Chase and screamed at Zip to get out. When he was in the driveway, staring away from us into the snowy backyard and reaching for his cigarettes, I locked the doors.

I got the marriage counselor on the phone and with my heart pounding and my breath heaving explained what had happened and asked her what she thought I should do.

She was a white-haired, rosy-cheeked German woman in her early sixties, who wore stretchy activewear — pants and warm-up jackets — with small animals appliquéd on the front. Often, she was just finishing a little nibble of something when I saw her, and she'd lick the last of it, whatever it was, from her fingers before she wheezed out her standard opening, which was, "Now, let us begin."

"Did you strike your spouse?" she asked.

"Yes," I said. "I'm sorry but he was trying to kill our son."

"And where is he now?"

I looked out the cold kitchen windows. I couldn't see Zip. Snow lay heavily on the black branches of the evergreens at the rear of the yard, weighing them down until the branches were bowed and touching the ground. "I don't know," I said. "He was in the driveway. Now he's gone."

"You must never, ever strike your spouse," she said firmly.

"He was trying to kill our son," I repeated.

"That is of no matter," she said. "I want you to make a contract with me right now, that you will never, ever strike your spouse again. We must have these ground rules straight."

"Look," I said. "You don't believe me."

"It doesn't matter whether or not I believe you," she said. Her voice sounded singsongy, irritatingly mild and friendly. "We must agree."

"Fine," I said. "Fine. I'll never strike my spouse again."

"If you feel that you or the children are in physical danger, call the sheriff," she said.

"My son would be dead by the time they got here," I said.

She ignored me. "And where is your spouse now?"

I looked out the windows in the front and the back, I unlocked the doors, I settled Chase in front of the TV with a Thomas the Tank Engine video, I checked on Haley. After a while, I stood on the front steps and waited while my slippers filled up with snow, studying the footsteps that led away from me down the street.

IN EARLY SPRING, I came home from work and found Chase twirling on the swing in the backyard. It was a cold day but the ground had begun to thaw and great patches of bare mud erupted where there used to be ice. The snowdrops were up; we'd have daffodils in another month. Chase wore his blue down jacket with the red and yellow chevrons and a hat pulled down over his ears. He sat on the swing and with his toes pushed off against the packed dirt until he'd wound the chains into a tight braid and then he pushed off again and the swing twirled while the chains spun apart. Thin clouds stood in a high, frail line over the evergreens at the back of our yard. I stood on the back porch and watched him and then crunched over the cold grass toward him and he looked at me and said, "No Mommy! No Mommy! No Mommy!" I stopped and waited and then took a step forward and he kicked in my direction and began to scream.

I stepped back and breathed and then turned and walked back to the porch.

Chase pushed off from the ground again with his toes and turned and turned and turned until he'd turned the swing's chains tight. Then he lifted his feet and let go of the ground and again let the swing spin free. He was talking to himself.

I put my briefcase and the stack of books I needed to read that weekend down on the back steps and began to cross the lawn.

"Chase," I called. "Hey Chase."

He spun and didn't lift his head.

The ground was squishy underfoot and water spread out under each of my steps as if each footfall pressed a saturated sponge. I realized I was probably ruining the only pair of decent shoes I had to wear to work. The blue tarp our neighbors spread over their stacked firewood had come undone and rattled a little bit in the breeze and the trees creaked the way they do in early spring.

"Hey Chase," I said.

This time he looked up. "No!" he roared. "No you!"

"What?"

He began to kick in my direction. "No you! No you! No!" His voice rose in pitch and he flailed his arms. "Stay away!" he commanded. "You stay away!"

Inside, I would find a note from his teacher that explained that Chase was sure that a girl who walked home down the same streets that Chase walked along had poisoned him. Apparently, she kept poison pellets in a jar of marbles. Attached to the note was a disciplinary action form; Chase had been sent to the principal's office for fighting with a boy who, he claimed, had punched him in the eye and caused him to go blind. But I didn't know this yet.

"Chase, honey," I said.

He raised his little fists at me. "Stay away! Stay away! Stay away!"

I stepped back over the wet ground and crossed the driveway and sat heavily on the back steps. Inside, Zip had made coffee and was getting ready to go to work. He'd taken a job at a big-box store and now worked nights on the loading dock. I still had dinner to make and Haley needed a bath. Chase needed a bath, too. The steps were cold but not uncomfortable and I buttoned my coat up to my throat. Zip opened the door behind me.

"He's been on that swing since he came home from school," he said. "He won't come inside."

"Where's Haley?"

"She's watching *The Lion King*."

"Is she okay?"

He nodded.

The weekend before, Zip had called me to the front yard. We'd set to raking the last of winter out of the garden and he'd discovered a dead mouse curled up on the sidewalk. I poked it with my rake and looked at Zip, waiting to see what meaning this mouse had for him.

He picked it up with a shovel and flipped it into the storm drain in the street. When he came back, he leaned against the shovel and looked at me intently. "You know what that is, don't you?"

I shook my head.

"It's a signal. Our enemies are very near now."

"Come off it," I said.

He reached over and held my arm. "You'll see," he said, in a low voice. And then he let me go and moved off around the corner of the house.

Now Chase twirled on the swing and, when the spin ran out, twisted the chains so he could twirl again. Zip stood behind me and watched and, when I didn't move, went back to his coffee. I waited for a while, watching Chase turn and turn and turn, and then picked up my things and went inside. I gave Haley a hug and a kiss and changed into jeans and found a heavy sweater and pulled that on, and pulled on an old pair of mittens. I found a wool hat that Zip's mother had sent me for Christmas one year and I took a blanket from the linen closet. I put the blanket on the steps so I would not be cold and I sat down and I watched Chase, watched him turn and spin and twist and unwind and twist again. He seemed tireless, relentless. He saw me sit down and he shouted, "You stay there! You stay there!"

Our neighbor pulled her car into her driveway and waved to me. "Nice evening," she called and I nodded. She picked up her mail and went through her back door. A little while later, I could see her watching me through her kitchen window while I walked up and down in the driveway and Chase said the same thing over and over and over again, and twirled in the yard. The sun had gone down and the sky turned cobalt blue; the last of the shimmering pink light glowed behind the trees but soon that would be gone, too. Zip came out and wordlessly walked down the road to catch his ride. Haley was alone inside.

The breeze picked up the leaves and blew them rattling across the lawn and then the last of the brown leaves rattled, too, in the trees. I sat there for a long time, as the sky grew darker in the way of northern skies, which dim before they darken, and the light grows low across buildings and trees, and watched Chase spin and spin and spin and spin and spin. A line of geese came overhead just at dusk and I could hear the terrible wild rustling of their wings as they flew low and otherwise silently into the dark. After a while, I stood up and walked up and down in the driveway. When the first stars were out in a vivid dark blue sky, I went inside. I watched the clock and counted down: two minutes, three minutes, four minutes. I didn't turn on the outside light and I kept the lights in the kitchen low, so he would have a hard time seeing me. Finally, when six minutes had passed, I turned on the yard light and stepped out on the back porch and yelled, "Chase! Chase! It's dinnertime!" Chase sat on the swing and hung his head in his lap and scuffed his toes along the dirt. He was saying something under his breath and I crossed the yard and came up quietly and he looked up at me and his eyes sparkled and he rocked back on his heels and pushed the swing a little bit forward and then swung back by pushing gently from his toes and I said, "It's time to come inside now."

He stood and looked at me and said, "Peter Parker was known to everyone by that other name Spider-Man and that was how he hunted for the diabolical men of evil who cast a corrupt taint on our fair city."

I reached down and took his hand. We walked back to the house, where the warm light of the kitchen made the windows look like home.

"Go wash your hands," I said. "I'm making hamburgers and French fries for dinner."

That night, when the dishes were done, and Chase watched TV, and Haley sat at the kitchen table and drew pictures of mermaids and girls with wings who knew how to fly, I thought about Chase on the swing. His language seemed different. He generally spoke in complex sentences and expressed sophisticated ideas. He had a

detailed understanding of the complex web of political relation-
ships that defined parts of the *Star Wars* stories, for example. In
November, he'd written a report about penguins: *The penguins live
in Antartica. The penguins line up on the frozen ice shelf. They push
one of the smaller ones in and see if it comes out . . . alive! Leopard
seals and orcas live in the water and wait, stalking them. Rookeries
are built in the breeding season. The adult penguins feed the young
penguins, ready for the same lifecycle their parents had.*

But that night, when I got close enough to Chase to hear what
he was saying, it was only the same thing, again and again: *Peter
Parker was known to everyone by that other name Spider-Man and
that was how he hunted for the diabolical men of evil who cast a
corrupt taint on our fair city. Peter Parker was known to everyone
by that other name Spider-Man and that was how he hunted for the
diabolical men of evil who cast a corrupt taint on our fair city.*

I felt hopeless. I saw something in Chase I'd never seen before, a
strangeness and a dislocation, as if he had slipped from our world,
and I worried that his horror at my approach could be turned outward as assault or inward as injury. For the first time, I was afraid.
And so I decided to quit writing, quit teaching, quit the Midwest,
quit that house, quit that marriage, and move to a place where
there would be help for Chase, where he could have a better life. I
didn't care what happened anymore, as long as it stopped happening to Chase and Haley.

FIFTEEN

|||||||||||||||||||||||||||||||||||||||

Dr. LJ visited Chase in the hospital. He had been Chase's doctor for a long time and he wanted to figure out what had gone wrong. At first, he talked to Chase by the windows that looked down over the steamy vents of the heating system, but when Chase couldn't stand still, he walked beside him as he paced and matched him step for step. Sometimes he was able to elicit from Chase something that seemed like a lucid response, or something that approached the borderlands of the coherent, but by far the greatest percentage of time, he could make no sense of anything Chase said. It puzzled him and worried him. In some ways, he thought the psychosis was just like Chase's psychotic stuff from the past, except more extreme this time, as if he'd tipped over into an area where he could no longer monitor his thoughts and everything that was on his mind came out without regard for meaning or coherence. He linked this to Chase's bipolar disorder. But he could also see why others saw classic hallucinations and delusions in Chase. Still, he thought that we were chasing our tails with the trials of antipsychotics, heading down the wrong path. And he couldn't account for the role that seizures might be playing in all of this, but he thought they probably had some hand in it, no matter what the last EEG said. Then he told me that it might well be schizoaffective disorder, a real true full-blown case of it, a stew of psychosis and manic symptoms that was as notoriously difficult to treat as it was rare to find a person who really had it.

But Dr. B disagreed. By February, he'd decided Chase had schizophrenia. He said Chase's symptoms were not classic and in some ways didn't meet the exact criteria for the diagnosis, but in his view, this was the best available diagnosis, or at least the most capacious, the one, like autism, that gave the most room to accommodate the whole of Chase's clinical presentation. He reminded me that there wasn't one kind of schizophrenia but many and, in fact, the field guide to psychiatric illnesses—the *Diagnostic and Statistical Manual of Mental Disorders,* or *DSM-IV*—provided a taxonomy of schizophrenia that detailed five different forms, each listed as a subtype: the paranoid, the catatonic, the disorganized, the undifferentiated, the residual. I studied the symptom lists. I could see that Chase fit. I could see that Chase did not fit. I could see that it was almost impossible to know what to do about this. The *DSM-IV* made clear that pervasive developmental disorder or other autistic disorders would need to be ruled out before schizophrenia could be ruled in; those diagnoses could not exist in the same person.

And yet, in Chase, Dr. B was sure they did.

In March, I gave consent to try the Clozaril and Chase worked up to a therapeutic dose, as if this was something he merely needed to practice, like sinking baskets or tying his shoes. At every visit, I came prepared for a miracle. There was no change. Chase did not know me. He retreated from me and told the staff I was a crack addict and a prostitute. He was filthy when I saw him. Sam told me that he didn't want to get into the shower, that when this was suggested to him, he'd cower and bellow, "No, no, I know what happens in there—sex parades!" I tried to imagine the terror of being undressed in a small tiled cubicle in a place that you were convinced was a concentration camp. I tried to remember how much history Chase had had in school and if he'd heard about the gas chambers and if he remembered how they worked. It seemed

likely that he had not lost any of this. He fled from strangers on
the unit, but every so often, he'd approach someone and scream
that the person was a murderer.

ONE DAY IN MARCH, Linda called me and said that she'd
called the social worker at the PATH unit at Murdoch Center and
told her about Chase and the social worker was willing for us to
come and visit. We could take a look at the place and if we liked
it, we could submit an application. And once PATH had the application, a unit psychologist and a manager would come to see
Chase and make a determination about his eligibility for treatment
there. Linda was plainly surprised by this turn of events. She told
me that she'd known about PATH, which stands for Partners in
Autism Treatment and Habilitation — but from what she knew
they wouldn't take a child with a psychiatric diagnosis. Still, when
the PATH social worker heard about Chase, she agreed to see us.

Murdoch Center was in Butner, a small town north of us by
some forty-five minutes, where North Carolina collected its institutions: its federal prison, its state prison, its youth prison, its
school for troubled children, its local branch of the Army National
Guard, its state psychiatric hospital, its mental retardation center.
The mayor of the town was the state's secretary of Health and
Human Services. To get to Butner, you had to take Interstate 85
past Durham and then north as if you were heading for the Virginia border. You couldn't see much from the highway: a couple of
strip malls barricaded behind the concrete walls of a construction
site, orange barrels, signs warning about traffic shifts, and then the
land spread out and flattened and the towns and malls dropped
away. Next to the short causeway over Falls Lake, an eagle's nest
crowned a telephone pole sunk in water like something suffering a permanent flood, and everywhere you looked, the thin hard

light of the lake reflected up to the bright sky. There was a place that gave airplane rides in a couple of old biplanes and sometimes the planes would come in over the highway and bump down in a grassy field. After that, the margins of highway were a blur of dark trees, cedars and pines, whose branches brushed the ground and made an impenetrable shield, and you couldn't see anything else.

Before it was a town filled with incarcerated people, Butner had been Camp Butner, a military training facility for soldiers preparing to fight World War II. When the war was over and the army no longer needed its buildings or parade fields, the state bought the acreage and turned the prison for German and Italian POWs—where, I imagine, frightened men far from home had stared out into the vast blank landscape and tried to see America in it—into the federal prison. Murdoch Center was begun in an old army barracks, but in those days it was known as the Colony and then as the Butner Training School. It was intended to serve all sixteen counties of central North Carolina. It grew apace, for just after the war anyone with the slightest hint of cognitive impairment was rounded up and sent away, after admonitions to the family that this was for the best. New buildings were opened in 1957 and residents were assigned to them until 120 or more people lived in cottages that today serve 25 or fewer. They lived in open rooms, where cots were lined up across the floor, and a few staff members watched the residents lie on these narrow beds. With the reforms of the 1960s and 1970s, many residents were moved out to group homes and other community facilities, and the Butner Training School became the Murdoch School, and then Murdoch Center.

With the exception of two units—PATH and BART—Murdoch became a mental-retardation center charged with providing care for the most severely impaired. After the 1970s, only the most profoundly disabled remained, and among those were included the medically fragile, and then the young men on the BART unit, and the boys on PATH. PATH followed BART, which stands for Behaviorally Advanced Residential Treatment, into existence and was set aside for the care of boys with incapacitating autism who required intense behavioral interventions. BART came into existence almost by accident, after the state office for developmental disabilities discovered that a handful of clients were being housed in facilities outside of the state, sometimes at a cost of half a million dollars per person a year. Murdoch Center was asked to write a proposal for a ten- to twelve-bed unit that would make it possible to care for these individuals in state. They were all young men. They'd all failed at other treatment plans or places. Some of them, after repeated run-ins with the law, had developed criminal records, not because they were hardened delinquents, but because they could not understand that the things they chose to do or loved to do or wanted to do, the exposing of themselves in public, the noncompliance when a police officer told them to move along, the disruptive behaviors in movie houses and restaurants that they clung to even in the face of security guards and law enforcement officers, were things that would invariably land them before a judge. All of them had a deep and abiding innocence about the consequences of their own actions, even in the face of the strongest possible admonitions to cease and desist. BART is the only locked unit at Murdoch today, existing, as it does, to help young men with histories of walking away or running away from other placements, almost by accident, with a thorough lack of intention, because their complex disabilities, a stew of symptoms and gaps in skills, make it impossible for these young men to understand that if they wander off they will be lost and in harm's way.

Both BART and PATH are housed in the same cottage, one unit at either end. In between are common spaces: a nursing station, conference rooms, classrooms for each unit, dining rooms where the boys learn to cook and empty the dishwasher and set the table. Out front, a stone sculpture stands as a solitary sentry by the front door. At first glance, it looks only like a block of granite, its sharp angles cut as if by accident or indifference, but then it reveals the face of a human being as if a soul were struggling to rise and emerge from the stone, as if the stone held a person who both sought the protection of the stone, like armor, like love, and hungered to be shed of it, this thing that sets him apart.

LINDA AND I STOOD in front of the PATH cottage and talked until the PATH social worker, a cheerful woman named Tania, came out to meet us. Sunlight glinted on Linda's black sunglasses. On the wide lawn beside the cottage, a blond man wearing a fleecy green pullover and a pair of heavy blue cotton gloves and gray sweatpants slowly kicked a black and white soccer ball between two horseshoe pits. He listened intently to a disc player, the headphones strapped to his head with an extra strap that buckled under his chin. I watched him while Linda talked. He looked happy and calm. A breeze blew up and ruffled his hair and a man in a clean white T-shirt stepped through the front door and called, "Paulie, Paulie," until the young man with the soccer ball stopped and turned and looked at him. Then he saw us and began to walk toward the sidewalk. "Hey!" he said in big bright voice. "Hey! Do you like Aerosmith?"

Then the man in the bright white shirt called to him again and Paulie stopped and turned back toward the cottage and followed him inside. He walked with his head turned in our direction so he could watch us until the door closed behind him.

"I've got the application with me," Linda was saying and held up her briefcase to show me. "It's probably the biggest application I've ever filled out. They ask for so much. But we're ready."

She paused and the wind blew her hair away from her face. "It's a long shot," she said. "Right now, there are 140 children on the waiting list for PATH."

"How many?" I said.

"I think it's 140," she said. "Something close to that. Maybe a little bit over. They make decisions based on who has the greatest need. Someone who's locked up in a hospital is going to be seen as having greater need than someone who's at home."

"How many live here now?" I asked.

"Eight boys in permanent beds, two more in respite beds. And then there's the PATH group home. That just opened. I think they take girls and I think they've got another four beds there."

"That's it?"

She nodded. "But it's a two-year program," she said, "so the kids have to leave."

"And then what?"

"And then we're back to something like this," she said. "Trying to find a place that will take your child that is also a place where it's in the best interests of your child to be."

Tania opened the door and looked out at us and waved her hand to get our attention. "I'm sorry," she called. "I don't mean to keep you waiting. I'll be right there." She wore bright pink pants and a white sweater dusted with pink polka dots. Her lipstick matched her pants, and her hair was cut short; she'd moussed it so it stuck up in little tufts.

The wind scuffled across the parking lot and rattled the bushes planted along the front of the building. Neither of us said anything and then Linda said, "To be honest, I don't know why they've agreed to let us look at PATH. I don't think Chase is eligible. The kids there are much younger and they're nonverbal and I'm not sure it's the right place for him at all." She looked at me. "But they do take kids with autism, and they do take difficult kids, and they've said that we can visit, so maybe it's the right thing to do."

"How long is the wait?" I asked. "If they put him on the list?"

Linda looked away from me. "I don't know," she said. "Someone told me they thought there was going to be an opening here in the next couple of months, but I don't know where Chase will be on the list. Someone might be ahead of him. There are children who've been waiting for years." Her voice grew softer. "Really," she said, "I don't even know if Chase will be on that list. They have a review board. They will have to decide."

Inside, it smelled like disinfectant and vegetable soup. Tania turned us toward the PATH unit. The floors gleamed and cheerful paintings of sailboats and children with dogs or bunches of balloons hung behind sheets of acrylic that had been screwed into the cement-block walls. Tania threw open the doors of the classroom and the dining room, the kitchen and the dayroom, and I walked inside of each and looked around and made approving comments. Boxy sofas covered in easy-care vinyl stood under the windows but there were soft fleece throws and colorful pillows covered in durable fabric. Each child had his own room, and each was outfitted to look like home. You could see the things that parents brought to make their children's lives better—television sets, or rugs imprinted with designs.

I walked behind Tania and she pointed out the facility's features and described the programs that were intended to lead to higher levels of function, if not to independence. We passed children in the hall, each boy accompanied by an adult, and some of the children looked at us as we walked by and some of them did not. I

smiled at the boys who looked at us but they did not respond. As I
looked around, I tried to imagine which one of these boys could be
Chase's friend. Even as I did that, I wasn't thinking of the Chase
who stalked the halls of the hospital and muttered about death and
Zack de la Rocha; I thought about Chase as he had been, the way I
hoped he'd be again. If the boy Chase had been before he got sick
came to live at PATH, he would be made miserable by his room-
mates, for they wore their disabilities openly and were not aware
of the way others saw them. The old Chase tried desperately to
conceal his differences, studied cool like it was a book of common
prayer. He wouldn't like it here.

Tania led us out to the playground and she spoke in a cheerful voice about how the kids loved to play basketball or swing
on the swings. She waved toward a hilltop and said there was a
gymnasium on its far side where the boys went to play on Special
Olympics teams, if they were interested, or just to shoot baskets, if
they were not. There was a swimming pool and a building called
the Munchroom, where boys who'd earned enough points could
trade their red and yellow and blue tickets for cans of soda and
candy bars.

Two boys who could not have been older than eight or nine sat
on the swings and listed to one side and stared past us, their feet
pressed hard into the dirt below the swing set, and each pressed
and released, pressed and released just enough to move the swing
a little bit forward and then feel it fall back. A couple of staff
members sat at a picnic table and I watched while a woman helped
a boy draw a picture. She held her hand gently over his and he
watched intently while she moved his hand, crayon caught between his fingers, across the paper until a long green line appeared,
and then another, and another. The boy made some sounds that
weren't words and smiled at the paper. He sat pressed close to the
woman but he didn't look at her or at us.

We stood there and watched the boys drifting on the swings or the boys tossing two different plastic basketballs at a Little Tikes basketball hoop or the boy making many lines with his green crayon, each line different than the last, but each also the same, a line where none had been before, guided into place by the hand of his aide. The boys didn't talk to each other or to us. They made sounds and sometimes laughed but no one had words. I felt my throat close, wrenched by the idea that I would consider this place for Chase. Chase had never been this low-functioning. He had some trouble communicating. He had some impulse-control issues. He couldn't care for himself or do his schoolwork. He couldn't stop moving. He'd been grossly psychotic for five months and he was not getting better. But he was Chase. He loved rock-and-roll and spaghetti and meatballs and pets. He wanted friends and to learn how to drive a car. He did not belong here.

At the same time, there didn't seem to be any other place for Chase in the whole state.

The aide who'd been holding the boy's hand gently let it drop to the paper, where it lay without movement, and he stared at it as if it were a thing apart from him. She turned her wrist so she could check her watch, and then stood up and announced that it was time to go inside. Tania explained that all the boys were on a strict schedule. We watched them file through a door held open by an aide and disappear into the dayroom. When they were gone, Tania took us to a conference room where we sat around a long table and she explained the population that the PATH unit served. She wanted to know if we had questions. I shook my head woodenly. She asked if we had Chase's application with us. Linda reached down and unsnapped her briefcase and pulled out a thick stack of papers and handed it over. Tania explained that the review board would probably meet in April and before they did, they would send the team to see Chase in the hospital. She flipped through the first few pages of the application as she talked and then something caught her eye and she stopped talking and began to read. We waited silently. In the room next door, a boy made loud cries and I could hear someone talking to him and the sound of furniture as it slid across the slick floor. Tania looked up.

"Don't mind that," she said. "Some of our little fellas can get very wound up. It's normal. It's natural."

She glanced back at the page in front of her and then looked at me.

"Chase is fifteen?" She calculated for a minute. "Really almost fifteen and a half," she said. "Is that right?"

I nodded.

"You know that kids age out of here at sixteen?" she said. "He would not be able to stay the full two years. We might not be able to get him to where we'd like him to be in one year, and this seems like he might age out before a space comes available."

She looked at the page again and this time she didn't look at me when she spoke.

"He's psychotic?"

"Yes," I said.

"How psychotic?"

"He hasn't really responded well to treatment," I said, "so he's been in the hospital."

Tania nodded. "What I meant to ask was this: does the psychosis substantially interfere with his daily functioning?" She smiled at me encouragingly. "We've had other kids who had a little bit of trouble in that direction, nothing very serious, most of them didn't really even need medication for this but we've had some that did. But we've been successful with them, pretty much across the board. Their psychoses, if you want to call it that, really didn't get in the way of the things they had to do, day to day. This program is very goal directed, very intensive. It would be hard for someone who isn't really . . . " she stopped and searched for the right word. "It would be hard for someone with a more significant level of psychotic symptoms," she said at last.

No one said anything. I watched three boys walk past our window on their way to the PATH unit van, each with his aide, each held by the hand.

"Chase is psychotic," I said at last. "I think a doctor would describe his symptoms as severe. Significant. Something like that." I stopped and watched Tania lick her index finger and turn more pages in the application.

"Do you think we shouldn't apply?" I said finally.

Tania looked up. "Oh, no," she said. She shook her head and her tufts of hair bounced a little. "That's not what I'm saying at all," she said. "That decision is entirely up to the review board and I have no say in any of this whatsoever. Not one bit. All I can tell you is that we're going to process Chase's application and Jim and Sandy are going to come and see Chase in the hospital and we'll probably get that set up in the next couple of weeks. I just want to give you some things to think about is all. I just want to be sure you have the whole picture and know what this place is all about. This can be a big decision for a family."

I nodded and looked away. She stopped flipping through Chase's application and sat quietly next to Linda. Not long after that, we all stood up and said good-bye and Tania walked with us as far as the front door, where she told me to be sure and call if I had any questions.

SIXTEEN

|||||||||||||||||||||||||||||||||||||

When Chase and Haley and I left the Midwest for North Carolina, we fled like a family escaping a haunted house. We packed up the truck and we packed up the car and Zip agreed to drive the truck south along the interstate behind us, and then over the mountains into Virginia and then North Carolina, where I'd learned there were programs that might help Chase. The kids and I climbed into my old blue car and even though it was four in the afternoon, I said, "Let's go. We can make Ohio before dark." I wanted to put miles and miles between us and that small town, miles and miles between us and the dead marriage, miles and miles between us and the family that failed, and the only way to do that was to get moving. So I drove hard and fast and got us out of there. I didn't even want to look in my rearview mirror, in case whatever it was had made good time and was gaining on us. But it wasn't some ghost that packed itself up in the box of children's books in the truck that followed us. It was a nameless thing, this thing that was whatever was wrong with Zip and Chase, the thing that was milder in Zip that had bloomed in Chase. I didn't realize what it was I was trying to run from then because I hadn't yet seen it at its worst, I hadn't seen Chase at sixteen. When I ran from the Midwest, I thought if I took the kids south and we started over, I could leave what we'd been through behind.

We drove until six and then pulled over at the hotel just over the border in Ohio where I'd reserved a room for us. Zip waited, idling the truck engine, while I went into the office and got a key. The place smelled damp and boggy and I didn't feel optimistic about the room. When I opened the door and Chase and Haley pushed past me and threw themselves on the bed, I smelled stale smoke and something dank and wet and, below that, the faint aroma of urine.

"Come with me," I snapped. "Don't touch anything. We aren't staying."

I put the kids back in the car and buckled them up and told Chase to please, please, just sit still, and I locked the car doors and walked across the dark parking lot to the truck, where Zip leaned and smoked. He turned to look at me as I approached and I called, "Can you drive some more?"

"What?" he said. He flicked the cigarette into the drainage ditch beside the parking lot. A damp breeze blew his dark hair across his face. Across the street, a Big Boy and a Dunkin' Donuts began to glow brighter in the dusk.

"I want to get out of here," I said. "The room's disgusting. Besides. We can make another three or four hours before we stop. The kids will sleep. We can get them McDonald's and keep going."

"Fine by me," he said.

I could tell he wasn't going to argue with anything I said on this trip. I might have said, *Let's take the kids and drive off a cliff,* and he would have smoked and stared and then said, *Fine by me.*

We drove in formation, the truck lumbering along behind my car. Haley's head drooped and nodded until she fell asleep with her giraffe in her lap. Chase sat strapped into his seat and banged his cars together, again and again and again. We played music and he sang along with Bono, his voice high and clear, with a pitch so true it reminded me of Zip, when he'd sung with the Strangers, when the other guys teased him and called him Broadway Zip.

We passed through an enormous flat land, with a huge dark blue sky the color of the blue of a Maxfield Parrish painting. And then the color began to fade with the light and I told Chase to be on the lookout for stars. He saw an airplane moving along the horizon and he said, "There's one."

"That's right," I said. "Watch for some more."

Chase twisted against the door, peering up at the sky, his small face bright with expectation. "I see stars, Mom," he said. "I can see lots of stars."

"That's good, Chase," I said. "Why don't you count them?"

He began, "One, two, three . . . "

"Why don't you count them to yourself?" I said. "Inside your head?"

He was quiet for a minute and then I heard a tiny whisper as he counted the lights on barns and the headlights on cars that drove along the roads parallel to the big interstate. I glanced again and again in the rearview mirror. Zip followed us with the truck but I couldn't see into the cab at all; just the dark of the windshield.

It took us three days to drive to Chapel Hill. This meant that we had to spend two nights on the road: the first night, when we had gone as far as we could go, the second night at a planned stop in West Virginia. We rolled in road-weary from careening through the mountain passes, where the road swept in big undulating spirals around and down steep hillsides and then along big grass ramps built by highway crews for runaway trucks.

I'd rented a room at a Holiday Inn Express near Charleston, and before we checked in, I pulled in next to a drive-through window and picked up white paper sacks full of burgers and fries and shakes. At the hotel, I signed in with the clerk and Zip pulled around to our room, parking the truck near a strip of grass. Then we went upstairs and crowded together in our one hotel room as if we had not already lost one another, as if Zip did not have a ticket to fly back to his apartment in the Midwest when the week was out. We ate our hamburgers and lay down on the beds and spent our last night listening to each other breathe in the dark.

We drove into Chapel Hill on an August day when the temperature topped out at 104 and unloaded the truck into a second-floor apartment I couldn't really afford. At the end of the week, we drove Zip to the airport, where he kissed each of us in turn and then walked down the Jetway to the plane. In those days, you could still go to the gate and we stood at the glass and waited until the plane took off. Chase and Haley swore they could see their father at the window, right up until the moment the jet lifted into the sky, but I wasn't looking. I stood there, alone with the kids, and wondered what it is you do when you have finally gotten away.

Our apartment was in a brand-new complex that stood raw and sterile and freshly painted yellow under a high bright sky. We had three bedrooms, two bathrooms, a view of the pool. On the third day I drove the kids to their new school and we got out of the car and looked into the classrooms through the dusty windows while cicadas buzzed in the trees over our heads.

"See," I said. "This is a good school. This is going to be great."

I'd come south for a weekend and rented the apartment in a hurry. Then I had driven around and taken pictures of the places the kids would see when we lived here. Our new front door. Their new school. The pool at the apartment complex. A grocery store. I ran out of ideas after that, not knowing what they would miss the most from the Midwest, what they would most want to see in their new home in the South, but I had the pictures developed at a one-hour place and then slid them into photo albums I'd picked up, one for Chase, one for Haley. I labeled each one, *We Move to North Carolina!*

On the plane trip home, I had these photo albums tucked into my carry-on bag. I hoisted the bag into the overhead and settled into my seat. Two rows in front of me and across the aisle to my left, a child screamed and screamed and thrashed and kicked the backs of the seats and flung himself from side to side. His mother wept and two flight attendants called to a third and together they looked at the child and I heard one of them say, "We might have to ask you to get off the plane." This brought fresh tears from the woman who was the child's mother but who stared helplessly at the child—it was a boy, about three, his face purple with rage he couldn't express—and could not reach him. I watched the boy and saw Chase, thrashing at birthday parties and on school outings, in grocery stores and on our kitchen floor. I thought of all the people who had not helped Chase. I looked at the woman and saw myself, helpless, hopeless. Then I stood up and walked up to the flight attendant and she grudgingly took her attention from the boy and turned to me with an annoyed expression.

"Do you have a blanket?" I said.

"If you would just take your seat," she said, but I interrupted.

"Not for me," I said. "For the boy." I nodded at the child. "If you can drape a blanket over him so that he can't see anything, he might settle down. Just lightly. Don't tuck it in. He has to feel free."

The flight attendants let the child thrash while one of them fetched a blanket. They gave the blanket to the dark-haired mother, who stood up and shook it from its wrappings and looked at me.

"Over his head," I said. "Just lightly. He has to be able to breathe."

She leaned over her son and spread the blanket over him, as if she had found him lying on his side in bed with no covers, but then gently spread the blanket over his head until he was completely covered. The surprise of darkness stopped his screams. A few minutes later, he lay still on the seats. His mother carefully lifted the edge of the blanket and slipped the boy a stuffed bear. When we were ready for takeoff, the boy sat wrapped in his blanket, some of it still shielding his face. He looked exhausted and old.

Later, the flight attendant asked me how I knew what to do. She explained the mother had brought her son to North Carolina for evaluation and she was just learning what was going to be needed. I felt foolish casting myself as some kind of expert when I was not that, when all I had was years with Chase.

"I was just thinking about that little boy," I said. "Everything seemed to be too much for him."

"Well," said the flight attendant. "We would never have tried that blanket trick. I'm going to have to remember that."

During the snack service, she brought me extra packs of pretzels and I slipped them into my purse, thinking how much the tiny bags would amuse Chase and Haley. And then I closed my eyes and thought again of the way a sheet of glass stands between the disabled and the rest of us, so that we see the disability alone and react to that, if we react to anything at all, if we do not turn our faces away. We do not see the person who is just like us, struggling inside.

I WAS SURPRISED by the persistent heat of September but decided to take advantage of it. One day, three weeks after the start of school, I packed up the car and buckled Chase and Haley into their seats and in the early morning drove east to the beach, past Raleigh and on into rural North Carolina, past the flat fields that flooded when it rained and disappeared under water during hurricanes, until all that was left of towns and farms were rooftops pitching up out of the water. But there was no rain on that sunny morning and we drove past cornfields and cotton fields and fields full of a tall broad-leafed plant that I suddenly realized must be tobacco, and then I recognized the high tobacco sheds whose tin roofs flashed white hot in the morning sun. Chase was about to turn eleven, Haley was almost seven, and I was without work. Chase had pulled a knife on me the night before, in the kitchen, threatening to kill me or kill himself. I didn't know it but that would be the refrain of the fall that still stretched out unknown before me: Chase would cry for the knife that would allow him to cut the pain out of his chest. This time, the first time, I went through the kitchen and took all the knives and scissors and anything else that looked sharp and put them in the drawer of my dresser, under a pile of sweaters I expected never to wear again, and checked the calendar; our first appointment with TEACCH was still two weeks away.

I drove fast and watched the fields and tobacco barns slide by. We pulled off for gas and cold drinks at a country store. Men lined up on stools at a lunch counter in the back of the place while another man pushed piles of greasy yellow eggs around on a griddle. Back on the road, we passed signs for boiled peanuts and fireworks. The highway fell off into a two-lane and then we came up and over a bridge and there we were. We could see the ocean behind the beach houses and a long line of low dunes and a big sign that said WELCOME TO ATLANTIC BEACH and, right next to that the hotel where I'd booked a room. As soon as we got out of the car, I had Chase and Haley walk across the hot parking lot and stand next to the sign and then took their picture so they would have a souvenir of their first North Carolina beach trip, so I'd have something that said we were a normal family, doing the things that normal families do. I had had enough of extremes by then. I had long before learned that it wasn't necessary to go looking for trouble, that trouble had a way of finding me. I joked with friends that I'd been born under a bad star and they laughed but they didn't know that part of me really believed this.

We spread our blankets and towels in the clean white sand just above the high-water line, where crispy seaweed coiled like hair, ornamented with stones and broken shells and shells still intact and bits of wood gone pale and gray from the pounding currents of the surf. I stroked sunblock into Chase's skin, moving over his back and his shoulders and then palming the lotion in my hand as I made long strokes down his arms and rubbed the lotion on his chest. He giggled and stood still while I covered his legs and the tops of his feet and the tops of his ears and then spread the lotion over his nose and his cheeks.

"You look like a raccoon in reverse," I said and smiled.

"Can I go?"

"Wait a minute," I said. "I have to do Haley, too."

While I smoothed lotion onto Haley's skin, Chase pulled his blue boogie board from the edge of the blanket and flipped it up in the air and flipped sand over the blanket, and over my legs, where I now rubbed a slippery-slide of sunblock.

"Chase," I said, and used my warning voice. "Be careful."

"Can I go?" he said again and danced up and down on the sand next to the beach towels and kicked sand into the basket where I'd packed peanut butter and jelly sandwiches for lunch.

"Hang on," I said. I stood up. "Haley. Haley. Are you coming?"

She got to her feet and I fastened the cord to her boogie board around her wrist and then told Chase to stand still so I could do the same for him. He jiggled in the sand and laughed and when

I closed the Velcro around his wrist, he ran down the beach to the water's edge and waded knee-deep into the surf. He turned around and looked back at me and by that time I was in the water up to my calves, expecting the sharp shock of the cold water of the northern lakes.

"Wow," I said. "It's almost like bathwater."

Chase plunged through the waves and I yelled, "Not too far, Chase. Don't go too far." And he slid and dove through the waves like a sleek animal at last in his element but he didn't go too far. He dragged his board behind him and as soon as he was out past the surf, he fell chest first onto it and paddled about.

Haley leaned belly first onto her board and tipped off. She tried again and again.

"Here," I said. "Wait. Use it like a paddleboard." And I held the board while she grabbed the board's prow and then hauled herself up so that only her legs dangled in the water.

"Now kick," I said. I held the sides of the board. "Kick kick kick," I said. Holding her board on each side and stepping carefully through the low waves, I navigated our way out past the breakers, where Haley could float in deep blue water that rolled but did not crash.

"There," I said. I dipped myself in whole and then fell back and floated so I could stare up at the sky. A biplane chugged by dragging an advertisement for a swimsuit sale and even that felt miraculous on this day.

"Look up," I said. "See the plane?"

Haley looked up and lost her grip on the board. She went under and came up, her golden hair wet now and sleek against her head. She spluttered and clung to the board, her mouth drawn into a wide grin but she wasn't laughing. She turned her head hard from side to side and opened her eyes, and blinked and blinked, as if she had forgotten where she was.

"Come on," I said. "Try again. You've got to keep trying."

I held the board again and Haley hoisted herself on and Chase came up beside us and bounced up and down. "Did you see me?" he said. "Did you see me ride that wave? Man! It was cool! Watch me! I'm going again!"

He plunged away through the water and threw himself belly first on his boogie board just at the point where the waves began to rise before their big fall and then the wave took him and propelled him toward the shore and when he came to a stop he stumbled up and out of the white foam and looked back at me and raised his hand over his head in a victory salute and yipped, "Whoo-hoo!"

Haley balanced on her board next to me.

"Did you see Chase?" I said. "Did you see what Chase did?"

She nodded and started to slip off her board, so I grabbed her and lifted her back into place.

"Do you want to do that?"

"No, thank you," she said.

We floated around for a while and Chase rode his board. When Haley got tired of her board, she dragged it up onto the beach and abandoned it next to our blanket. I rubbed her down with a towel and then draped it over her shoulders and gave her a juice box to drink. But this wasn't a northern beach, where children need to be wrapped up as soon as they get wet; this was a southern beach and she dropped the towel and finished her drink and then ran back to the surf. I followed and the two of us waded again out through the churning waves until we could float and paddle in relative calm. Chase stayed in the surf, riding his board, as if he had some wildness in him that only the breaking waves could match.

WHEN WE HAD PULLED into the hotel parking lot, Chase
had spotted the amusement park across the road. Jungle Land.
A trio of African animals—an elephant, a giraffe, an enormous
gorilla—each as tall as a small house, stood out front. As soon as
he was done pounding himself through the surf, he made a play for
us to spend our evening there. Haley chimed in. Our hotel room
faced the ocean and had a balcony where we could sit outside and
listen to the waves breaking on the beach but we could see Jungle
Land every time we left our room to go to the restaurant or to our
car. I figured Jungle Land was inevitable through proximity, that
we raised the desire for Jungle Land every time Jungle Land came
into view, and that, in some ways, Jungle Land probably didn't
even exist outside of Chase's desire to visit it; it was a mirage of
childhood and who was I to argue?

We bought admission tickets that gave us access to everything
and rode a miniature train done up in festive colors that took us
all around Jungle Land, past every ride, so Chase and Haley could
decide where to go first. They settled on bumper cars. From there,
we made our way to miniature golf. The rides were small and on
the mild side. We rode a roller coaster where the track was shaped
like a deep saucer that had been partially melted in a microwave;
it didn't rise more than twelve feet in the air; the thrill came from
the way the track stood you nearly on your side as you whirled
around its spiral, swooping low and then straightening out and
rising again only to fall once more.

Haley took my hand and dragged me toward a ride where a
central pole supported a kind of steel disc from which hung swings
on long chains; when the ride got going, the swings would fly up
and out, just like the cow in Chase's tornado. Haley loved her
swing in our backyard in the Midwest and I had often watched
her tipping up into the sunlight that spread across the lawn and

then flying backward into the shadow under our neighbor's maple trees. The evening had taken on an elegiac tone for me, as if I could, by swooping through the air on rides and good intention alone, make up for the fact that Zip was gone and we were, the three of us, firmly on our own and far away from anything that felt like home.

"Please," she said. "Mom, please?"

"Yes," I said, "you bet. Let's go."

Chase wanted to ride the train again so we settled him in the first car, which loaded and unloaded its passengers at the foot of the big swings. The workers on the ride buckled Haley into her swing. I stood off to the side to watch. The swings were little wooden frames into which each rider was firmly strapped. The ride began with a hum and then the typical carnival music; lights under the steel disc bloomed, bright red and green and yellow. Haley hung onto the chains of her swing and gradually she was lifted higher and higher and turned faster and faster until she flew through the night well above my head. My stomach flopped when I saw this but I held onto the rail and watched and thought, hang on hang on hang on, don't fall don't fall don't fall. It was as if I had become so accustomed to catastrophe that I assumed catastrophe was a given, something that would appear with regularity, like mail, and with unchangeable finality, like weather.

It had been growing dark for a while and at first I thought this was merely what night at a North Carolina beach looked like: dense and close, the sky bereft of stars. But it suddenly seemed too dark for the time of day, which was not much past seven, and almost as soon as I realized that, the first drops plopped down around us, heavy and hard in the manner of rain that's about to turn into a real downpour. I turned around and looked for Chase and saw the train heading straight for the station. I crossed the pavement and leaned down and unbuckled him as soon as his train car pulled up to the discharge zone.

"Come on," I said. "We have to get your sister."

"It's raining."

"I know that," I said. "Come on, Chase. Let's go get Haley."

By this time the rain had begun to pelt down and the workers had stopped the swing ride and all the others had gotten off and run for cover but Haley dangled too high above the pavement to get down. A woman ran up to her and began to fiddle with her belt; she stepped aside when I got there and said, "I just wanted to help." I thanked her but thought of how Haley had looked, hanging there under the dim steel disc alone in the rain and I lifted her out and we ran for cover in the Jungle Land Saloon. But there were too many people and we stood under the droopy ledge on which the sign was nailed and continued to get wet so I took Chase and Haley by the hands and ran for our hotel room. Rain blew in sheets across the road and a line of cars climbed up out of the Jungle Land parking lot. Ahead of us, the sea had turned oily and black and the sky dark and flat. The wind picked up and thunder boomed over us and lightning flashed and flamed back into darkness.

Chase and Haley loved this. This was better than any ride. The hotel's restaurant had closed for the night so, after I gave the kids warm showers and dried them off and got them into clean, dry clothes, we made a picnic out of peanut butter crackers from the vending machine, and bags of corn chips and potato chips, and Snickers bars, and cans of lemonade. Chase stood at the sliding door in front of our balcony and watched the storm out over the ocean. He counted the time between thunder and lightning and tried to guess how far away the storm was and notified us when he had lost sight of the lights of a ship at sea. It rained until midnight, a steady, driving, thunderous rain, and the world fell away from us; we were just three in our cocoon on a rainy night at the beach, safe and whole and sound. I lay in the middle of the bed, with Chase's head resting on one shoulder and Haley's on the other, and I imagined a future defined by this moment, as if we had found a way to leave all of our troubles behind.

THE NEXT AFTERNOON, WHILE we were swimming, Chase's face froze in place, the surf churning around him, his eyes rolling up until the whites showed. His eyelids fluttered and his lips twitched and his jaw clenched and unclenched subtly, surely, muscles tightening and releasing, tightening and releasing.

"Chase!" I yelled. "Chase! Chase!" I called his name, and again, and then again, and again. He didn't answer. I slipped my arms under his shoulders and pulled him from the surf and then took him by the arm and pulled him up to the beach blanket where Haley was drinking a Capri Sun. We sat there, both of us breathing heavily and Chase shivered and I put a towel around his shoulders and no one argued when I said it was getting late and probably time to think about driving home.

AFTER WE GOT BACK to Chapel Hill, I took Chase to a neurologist and described the length of the episode. It had not been the first that day but it had been the longest of the day and the only one in the water, the only one that really terrified me. Then I described what Chase's teachers had reported from school. He'd spent two weeks in the fifth grade at his new school in a regular classroom — after all, he'd spent his elementary school years in regular classrooms when we lived in the Midwest — but by the end of the second week, the school had called and demanded that I come in and observe Chase in class and talk about an alternative placement. I'd visited the class on a rainy day. When I came in with my dripping umbrella and tried to stand quietly in the back of the room, the other fifth graders turned in their seats and some-one said loudly, "Who's that lady?" Chase never looked my way. He didn't look anybody's way. He had a worksheet on his desk but he didn't look at that, nor did he look at the blackboard or the teacher or out the window. He just looked away, his face expressionless and staring.

When he was moved to the special ed room, which was really a cheerful trailer out behind the school, his teacher called me up to describe times when Chase would stare off into space and drool, or his speech would become slow and slurred, or his eyelids would appear heavy as he stared. It was hard to teach Chase because of this. Sometimes, she said, his elbows would almost slip off the table. Sometimes, she said, he could be redirected through repeated questions, but sometimes he could not. These things happened a lot, she said, and she wanted to know what I planned to do about it.

The neurologist was a tall man with a long face. He listened carefully. He noted that children with autism often have behaviors that might look like seizures when they are not seizures. He explained how behaviors could look like medical conditions. He mused aloud on this theme for a time. Wasn't it possible that what I had seen was not a seizure at all but perhaps merely a new twist in the way Chase's autism made itself known? Could I recall other times when this behavior had happened, but when Chase clearly was also aware of his surroundings? He told me that he himself had seen any number of cases when parents and teachers had insisted that a child was having seizures when really what he was having were staring spells. "The children," he said, "were playing a new game. The staring was a kind of self-stimulation behavior that met the child's internal needs."

I explained again that this was not a behavior, that Chase was not a behavior, that if Chase had autism, it was a kind of autism so odd that everyone called it atypical. I kept my voice even. I wanted this neurologist to understand that I understood his theory but I had one of my own.

"Perhaps the best way for us to be confident that Chase is engaging in self-stimulation behaviors is a negative EEG," the neurologist suggested at last. He looked at me sorrowfully, as if I had forced him to order this test against his will. His nurse came in a few minutes later with a small device that looked like an oversized Walkman, a handful of blue and red wires, a couple of straps, and a roll of white gauze. She asked about school and Chase's favorite subject while she pulled on her latex gloves and vigorously went after various points on his skull with a cotton ball saturated with rubbing alcohol. His hair stood on end in little tufts and she glued an electrode at the base of each tuft. He flinched every single time the glue hit his skin. I reminded him that it was just glue and couldn't hurt him and said things like, "Hang in there, buddy," or "Almost done." I promised him a stop at a fast-food restaurant, his choice, for lunch.

When all of the electrodes were in place, the nurse hung the recording device around his shoulder and pinned the straps to his shirt. Then she bundled the wires and ran a piece of tape around them and wrapped his head in white gauze, around and around the sides in a cap that eventually covered his whole skull, and then down and under his chin and around his neck, to hold the whole thing in place. He looked like he'd had a terrible accident. But he smiled and reached up and patted the gauze gingerly, as if he expected something to hurt. "I don't have to go to school today, right?" he said. "Nope," I said. "Not tomorrow, either." People gave Chase's headgear frank appraisal when we rode the shuttle back to our car, but they'd quickly compose their faces into attitudes of general sympathy and concern if I caught their eyes.

I'd been told to press the button on the machine whenever Chase showed signs of the behavior I'd described. All that afternoon and the next day, we read stories and listened to music and ran Chase's wooden train around an elaborate track it took us two hours to build. I pushed the button eight or ten times but wasn't always sure; sometimes, I thought I should have pushed it when I didn't, and sometimes I pushed it when I wasn't sure I should, to make up for the times I didn't push it when I thought I should have. The difficulty came in trying simply to record what could be nothing more than a fleeting expression on Chase's face, to make a swift and certain determination that *this* was a seizure while *that* was merely a moment of boredom or thoughtfulness or sleepiness.

It was peaceful in Chase's room. Our neighbors in the apartments around us were off at work. I'd dropped the blinds against the relentlessly sunny days of North Carolina, so it was cool and dim. When we tired of books, we talked about how things were going to be in the future. I was going to get a job and then we would buy a house and we'd have a pretty good life, with good food on the table and trips to the movies or museums. We could go to the beach or maybe drive out to the mountains to see snow. Chase wanted to play baseball and I said that was surely something he could do, once we got a little more settled. He asked about his dad, when was his dad going to send the birthday present he'd promised, why hadn't it come yet? I reminded him that his birthday wasn't until November and changed the subject.

Our conversations weren't your average conversations. Chase never stopped talking or asking questions. He didn't give up on the thing that was most in his head. You could pull him off the subject and then be blindsided by the same questions three minutes later.

When he played with his trains, he repeated long stretches of story line from his Thomas the Tank Engine videos. "Percy doesn't like James when James is cheeky," he'd say and then push the train along the track until it came to the water tower. That first fall in North Carolina he was stuck on Spider-Man and I drew comics for him that featured pictures of Chase with his pal Spider-Man as Chase learned to wait patiently for the school bus, not to talk to strangers, or how to brush his teeth. In these comics, Spider-Man always said encouraging things and the last panel would feature Spider-Man with his arm around Chase's shoulders.

When Haley came home from school that day, we met her at the bus and Haley stared at Chase's white gauze hat and said, "What's that thing on Chase's head?"

"He's having a test," I said. "The doctor wants to see how Chase's brain works."

She touched the top of her own head. "Does it hurt?"

"Not a bit," I said. "Chase's fine."

It only took a few days for the EEG report to come back. The long-faced neurologist called me up with the news. He almost couldn't believe it himself. Why, he would have staked his reputation on a different outcome. All in all, it was the darndest thing. Chase was having seizures night and day. Petit mals, if he was any judge of things. He needed to be on an anticonvulsant. If I'd give him the name and number of a pharmacy, he'd call in a prescription. "We'll give him the best drug for this sort of thing," he said. "That'll fix him right up." And then if he could see him back in three months?

That was when I knew without any doubt that Chase had seizures. Before that, he'd had episodes that looked like seizures, that might have been seizures, that a neurologist in up-state New York had failed to tell us were seizures. The signs were subtle: staring and eye-rolling, or moments of eyelid fluttering, or instances of chewing that seemed involuntary, automatic, his face motionless except for the grinding motion of his jaw. Everyone we consulted told us they couldn't be sure.

So I had no idea when they'd begun and could only think of the years they had gone undetected, untreated.

By the time we'd lived in Chapel Hill for a year and Chase was almost twelve, he still had these little seizures but he'd also graduated to the kind of seizure most people are familiar with, the big one, the tonic-clonic or grand mal, the Mount Vesuvius of seizures, complete with a crash to the ground, loss of consciousness, whole body convulsions, a long period afterward of dazed confusion. Other times, he'd simply fall to the ground, lose consciousness, and his arms would jerk; this was the funneled whirl of a complex partial seizure. Many people with petit mal or absence seizures go on to develop grand mal seizures but the neurologist who first diagnosed Chase's seizures hadn't felt any need to mention this, perhaps because it was impossible to predict, perhaps because there was no way to know which child would be the child in which seizures would take hold and bloom.

That neurologist also led me to believe that epilepsy just wasn't that serious. He taught me to be casual, dismissive. Seizures looked worse than they were. Seizures were scary but you could get used to them. They didn't hurt the person who had them although sometimes he could be hurt when he fell and that was really the thing you had to watch for. But nothing in Chase's brain would be fried, for example, and nothing would go wrong. People with epilepsy could lead normal lives if their seizures were well controlled.

When the teachers at the middle school called me at work and said Chase was having petit mal seizures that wouldn't stop and they'd called the ambulance, I felt irritated at their overreaction and asked them why they'd called an ambulance. I patiently explained that the seizures couldn't hurt Chase and they should just let him rest someplace quiet and did they really think an ambulance was necessary? Did they really think I needed to come get him? It wasn't like this was something new. It wasn't like anyone could really do anything about this. Yes, I'd call his neurologist and let him know. Perhaps we could change the dosage on his meds.

I would call and leave a message for the neurologist, who would call me back hours later or sometimes the next day. "We can increase the dose," he'd say. "Is that what you want to do?"

He asked this as if it ought to be my decision, as if I knew anything about seizures, as if I knew the options and could make a reasonable decision. Sometimes he'd suggest that we try a different medication but by the time we got to his office for an appointment, that suggestion had evaporated. Sometimes he'd ask if Chase had ever had an MRI and I'd tell him yes, once, when he was five. The neurologist would look thoughtful and say, "Maybe we ought to do another." But we didn't.

One day, when Chase was thirteen, the school called an ambulance when he was seizing and the teacher put the EMT guy on the phone with me. "Do you want me to take him to the hospital?" he asked. "It looks like he's been seizing — petit mals, I guess — for quite awhile now, maybe thirty minutes, according to his teachers. Do you think he needs to go to the hospital?"

"Is he in any danger?" I asked.

The EMT guy sounded surprised. "He's been seizing a long time," he repeated.

"But it's just petit mals?" I said.

"I think so," said the EMT guy.

"Then I think we should just let him rest until he gets through it," I said.

No one said the words *status epilepticus* to me, but they do appear in Chase's medical record. Later, when I learned what *status epilepticus* was, the very dangerous constant seizing that can lead to death, I stupidly thought it only applied to someone having a grand mal seizure. I didn't understand that it also applied to petit mals and felt relieved, quite wrongly, that Chase had never experienced that.

SEVENTEEN

||||||||||||||||||||||||||||||||||||||||||||||||||||

In April, Chase had been in the hospital on the acute-care stabilization unit for five months. He wasn't anywhere close to being stable and the staff told me that he held the record for longest stay. It was a dubious honor. When Dr. B and Dr. LJ couldn't agree on what to call what was wrong with him, we called a famous autism expert at Yale University to consult on Chase's case.

He told us he'd read the files with great interest. In his years of practice, he'd seen maybe two kids who looked like Chase. One was a twelve-year-old girl with an undiagnosed seizure disorder. Her symptoms cleared when her seizures were treated. "But," he said, "I see that Chase has already been treated with anticonvulsants." Dr. B and I both nodded and then Dr. B said, "Yes." He leaned forward a little when he said this, as if he were afraid the speakerphone wouldn't pick him up.

We sat in Dr. B's second-floor office, where a narrow window overlooked the hospital driveway.

"The other case," the famous man said, "was a boy of fifteen who became severely psychotic and stayed that way for about eighteen months. Then the psychosis just lifted. His parents started him on Clozaril and that may have helped but it was hard to know for sure."

"Is he better now?" I asked.

"He still believes he's Jesus in the Garden of Gethsemane," he said. "He does some minor carpentry work for his father's construction company. His psychosis has largely abated but he isn't entirely lucid all of the time."

"He lives at home?"

"Yes. It's extraordinarily difficult for the family but I think they manage. His mother doesn't work so she's able to be with him when he needs to be at home, on the days he can't work."

"Are you aware of any facilities that might be able to help with a child like that?" I asked.

There was a long silence. Across the miles, I could hear the man shifting in his chair. At last he said, "I think that will be very difficult to find. It's the great challenge for families, no matter where they are. Finding services. Getting the help they need. I wish I had better news for you."

"Do you have any thoughts about what we might try with Chase?" Dr. B leaned forward again as he said this. His office lacked decoration save for the framed portrait he kept of himself standing with his arm slung over the shoulders of a pretty woman; she held hands with a pretty little girl. All three of them were dressed in white clothes. When he leaned toward the speakerphone, I could see the portrait clearly.

"Clozaril, if you haven't already," said the famous man.

"We've just begun that," said Dr. B.

"It might be well worth your while to do some video EEG studies," said the Yale doctor. "Fully evaluate what might be going on with his seizure disorder. I don't know that this is going to be the cause but it would be worthwhile to explore this."

"Anything else?" said Dr. B.

I heard the man's chair creaking again. "I think those would be my avenues of choice," he replied. He paused. "Sometimes," he said, "there are no explanations. Sometimes psychosis merely descends like a curse from God." He cleared his throat. "If anyone tells you that he knows how this is going to turn out, don't believe him. Chase is a population of one. No one has any studies on which to base predictions. No one has any idea how things are going to go for him."

"Thank you," I said. My voice sounded dull and flat.

"I'd like to know how this progresses," said the famous man. "From time to time, I'd like to hear how things are going."

"I'll be glad to let you know," I said.

"We'll stay in touch," said Dr. B.

When we hung up, we sat without speaking. Dr. B looked out the window and then looked at me. "That was helpful, if merely to confirm that we're on the right track," he said.

I nodded. "What about video EEG studies?" I said. "Are those a possibility?"

Dr. B sat in his chair in absolute stillness, absolute neutrality. "I don't think so," he said.

"Why not?"

"When Chase came in we did an ambulatory EEG that was completely unremarkable. No findings of any kind. Based on that test, further EEG testing is unwarranted." He paused. "Even if it were warranted, how would we do it? He'd have to go to the sleep studies clinic for a week. How would Chase manage at the sleep studies clinic for a week? He couldn't do it. And we don't have the staff to send with him to maintain him for twenty-four hours a day there for the week he would need."

"What about a portable unit of some kind?"

Dr. B looked away from me. Then he looked back. "Too expensive," he said, "given that I don't believe it's warranted at all."

It was a gray day, without wind. When I crossed to my car I

wondered how long the weather would hold. From the top of the parking deck, I could see into the hazy distance in the east, where clouds flattened in a great bluish wash along the horizon in advance of rain. Behind me lay the hospital and the campus and the libraries and many people who knew a great many things but no one who knew anything conclusively about Chase.

Years later, Dr. LJ described Chase's psychosis and his loss of skills as a crossing of the Rubicon and I understood him to mean that this time in the hospital marked an irretrievable final action, from which much return was unlikely. In this, he seemed to be in agreement with Dr. B, even if the two of them could not agree on how to name the thing that caused that river to be crossed.

FRIENDS WHO BELIEVED intensely in alternative therapies offered me cures. In each offering, kindly intended I have no doubt, I felt nothing more than an accusation, as if I had failed to do enough, as if I had caused this in Chase and now must find a way to cause him to be restored. The theories were boundless: his nutrition was bad and he needed a different diet; he had leaky gut syndrome, like everyone with autism and schizophrenia; I was the dupe of the big drug companies, who didn't want me to know about cures; he should eat no dairy, no wheat, no sugar; he should eat macrobiotic foods, fast for a month, take Chinese herbs, do acupuncture, have a massage; he should seek a shaman for soul retrieval. He needed yoga, a course in drumming, a faith healer, and for me to accept that he had chosen this path for himself.

ON A COLD AFTERNOON in April, when the sky outside the hospital was the color of dirty snow, the PATH unit's advance team paid Chase a visit. The weather felt northern and familiar and unlike a spring day in Chapel Hill. The insurance company was getting edgy. Its representative felt that five months was too long for a teenage boy to require acute care and said so fairly regularly. No one from the insurance company came by to see Chase or make an assessment based on physical findings but instead held hearings where Dr. B argued that Chase was still acutely psychotic, still in need of stabilization, still in every way conceivable eligible for care. I could often tell when Dr. B had had one of these conversations, for he'd walk over to Five South from his office and stand at the nurses' station and watch Chase for a long time.

Jim, the PATH psychologist, was a man close to my age; he'd cut his gray hair in a stylish fashion and wore a button-down shirt with his pressed jeans. When he shook my hand, his manner was easy and evenhanded, as if he'd just happened to stop in to see Chase, and there was nothing odd to be seen here, nothing unusual in Chase's situation. Sandy was the unit manager. From where we sat in the library, we could see part of the dayroom. I watched Sam, the male nurse assigned to Chase, and Dr. B step from behind the nurses' station with their clipboards in hand and walk over to Chase. He wore his dark gray hoodie and his dirty black parachute pants and his hair fell down over his eyes. Sam put his hand on Chase's arm and Chase looked at Sam and then looked over at us and took a step toward us but Dr. B. said something and Sam patted Chase on the arm and Chase stopped and stared over at us before moving off down the hallway toward his room.

We reviewed Chase's history, with reports from Dr. B. and the nursing staff, and from Catherine, who was able to talk about all of the ways in which Chase was unable to do anything at the hospital school. I pointed Chase out to Jim and Sandy. They watched as he walked by the window. He tapped his hand against his leg. His eyes were sunken and dark and he stopped outside the window to squint at the ceiling and recoil a little. There was an air vent there and he stared at it and then lifted his hand and cupped it next to his eyes. We could hear the hissing sound even with the door closed. Then he walked on.

"That was interesting," said Jim mildly.

"Lasers," I said.

"I assume he's on medication?" Jim looked at Dr. B.

Dr. B nodded. "We switched him to Clozaril about a month ago." He looked down at the folder in front of him. "He's just now at a therapeutic dose. He seems to be tolerating the drug well."

"How effective is the medication?"

"Chase has been on the unit for as long as he has been because he has been refractory to treatment," said Dr. B. "We pursued trials of five other antipsychotics before introducing the Clozaril. It might be too soon to tell but we think it's having a beneficial effect. His levels of agitation have decreased somewhat, and his paranoia has subsided to some degree, and the staff reports moments of lucidity during the day."

Sam said he had heard Chase singing in his room and when he brought the radio in so Chase could sing some more, Chase had talked with him for a minute or two about U2 before he slid back into talk about the death cells on the sixth floor.

"And this represents a gain?" Jim asked.

Chase walked by the window again. This time, he stopped and leveled us with a weird look that was both distant and prying.

"I think the staff feels these things demonstrate improvement," Sam said.

Jim looked at me. "Do you feel it's a gain?"

"Yes," I said. "But he still doesn't know me. He still thinks his food is poisoned. When I come to see him, he'd still rather hit me than sit next to me. It's like you catch a glimpse of the old Chase, but then it's gone again."

"He doesn't know you?"

"He thinks his real mother has been kidnapped by terrorists and is being held hostage somewhere and that's why she never comes to visit him," I said. I swallowed hard and told myself that I would not cry during this meeting. But it was hard to keep that sort of promise, especially when we had to walk through all of the facts of Chase's illness, and each one hit me anew, as if I had not watched him deteriorate but was confronting all of this for the first time.

"But you visit him?" Jim said. "Even though he doesn't know you?"

"Yes," I said. "Three or four times a week."

Jim nodded. He'd clipped a pad of paper inside a notebook and held the notebook open on his lap and he made a note. We watched him write. He looked up at us.

"And what's his diagnosis?" he said.

"He has autism and schizophrenia," said Dr. B. He said this as simply and dispassionately as if he were saying, I'll have the cheeseburger and fries.

I bit the inside of my mouth hard and bit it again but Jim nodded again and kept writing and then read another page of Chase's application. Then he looked at me with a perfectly level expression. "He has a history of violence? Property destruction? Self-injurious behavior?"

I paused. "He begged me to kill him," I said. "That was just before he came into the hospital. And then he threatened suicide with a knife."

"Was he holding the knife or talking about getting a knife?"

"Holding the knife," I said. "He was going to cut the pain out of his chest. And he tried to strangle himself with a microphone cord. And he made a plan to step out in front of a truck." I stopped. "I don't know," I said. "I'm not sure this represents a significant history." I shook my head.

When I look back on it now, I see the absolute absurdity of my statements. I can't imagine what I thought a significant history would have been. Perhaps if Chase had successfully committed suicide, I would have thought that counted.

Jim nodded and wrote something on his pad.

Chase moved past the window but I didn't see him pass by the door and appear on the other side. Sam cleared his throat. "I'm wondering," he said. "We all know Chase pretty well and we think he's pretty different from the kids we usually see. Do you have other boys like Chase on your unit?"

Chase peered around the door and his face alone appeared in the window. Then he pushed the door hard and stepped into the room. The door banged against the rubber doorstop in the wall and made a louder sound than I thought it should.

"Hi Chase," said Jim. "Would you like to join us?"

Chase walked into the center of the room and stood in front of Jim and Sandy and stared at them and then began to talk to the space beside him in a voice so low I couldn't be sure he was using words. He stood before us unsteady on his feet, like a particularly purposeful drunk, and waved his arms as if he moved without intention. Then he pointed at me.

"You're a drug dealer," he said.

"Chase," I said. "Come on."

"Chase," Jim said. "Do you want to sit down?"

Chase immediately fell into a blue vinyl chair and stared at Jim with dark suspicion.

Jim explained that he and Sandy had come to visit him and to learn more about him because they thought he might prefer living at Murdoch Center.

Sandy sat up a bit straighter in her chair and grinned at Chase. "Hi Chase," she said.

Jim looked at Chase. "What do you think?" he asked. "Do you think you'd like to get to know more about Murdoch Center?"

Chase jumped to his feet and nearly tipped over. He stood swaying over Jim and glared at him. "No," he yelled. "No Murdoch! No Murdoch! No! No! No!"

"Chase," said Sam. He stood up and moved closer to him. "Chase. Sit down."

"That's all right," said Jim. He looked at Chase. "Would you like to sit down?"

Chase didn't move.

"What do you like?" said Jim.

Chase raised his hand to his face and cupped his palm until his fingers curled next to his eyes and fired lasers, taking aim at the wall just above Jim's head. He muttered something and smiled to himself.

"He likes music," I said.

"Music," said Jim. "What music do you like, Chase?" His voice, which had been bland, became animated and excited, as if having an interest in music was an unusual and extremely interesting thing.

"Hey," said Chase. "Hey. I'm Zack de la Rocha." He patted his chest lightly once, twice, five times before dropping his hand to his side and tapping it on his thigh. He squinted at the ceiling vent and fired a laser at it with his eyes.

"Do you sing with a band?" asked Jim.

"Rage," said Chase. "That's my band, man." He bent a little from the waist and leaned in toward Jim and continued to smile his terrible smile.

"I know a lot of people who like music," said Jim. "What else do you like?"

Chase stared at Jim and licked his teeth.

"He likes comic books," I said. "Or he did."

"Comic books!" said Jim. "Who's your favorite comic book hero?"

Chase rolled his lips together and then opened his mouth wider but he didn't speak.

"He used to like Spider-Man," I said. "That was his favorite."

"Spider-Man," said Jim. "Wow. He's pretty cool."

Chase looked away from Jim. He started tapping faster and faster on his leg and we watched him.

"Do you get to play much music here?" Jim asked. "You know, at Murdoch Center people can have stereos in their rooms."

Chase closed his eyes and then opened them. He started tapping his other leg, and then drummed both hands against his stained black pants.

"Is there anything you'd like to know about Murdoch?" said Jim. "Do you have questions I can answer?"

Chase narrowed his eyes and looked at the ceiling and then abruptly stood up and in three long strides reached the door. He banged it open, stepped through it, and walked away. The door drifted to a stop and no one got up to close it. No one said anything.

Then Jim told us we could send the application if we wanted, but he could just about guarantee that PATH would turn it down. How did he know that? He and Sandy were on the review team and they would have to report what they'd seen here, and what they'd seen here made a PATH placement impossible. He could appreciate our need to find a place for Chase, clearly Chase was not going to be able to come home, obviously Chase had needs that were both dire and complex, but he was sorry, PATH was not the place to serve him.

"You understand," he said. "I have to think about the match with the unit. The boys on PATH have simple, classic, straightforward autism, if autism is ever straightforward. They are much younger than Chase. They don't have Chase's history and we wouldn't take them if they did. I'm sorry," he said.

I looked at him. "All right," I said tightly. "I understand. PATH won't take him. Okay. That's fine. Do you have any ideas? Any ideas at all? I hope you do, because we've looked all over the state of North Carolina and nobody wants him."

"Oh," said Jim pleasantly, "when I said Chase wasn't right for PATH I didn't mean Chase wasn't right for us. Chase is a BART guy."

"A BART guy?"

"Wouldn't you say?" Jim said and turned to Sandy. "Doesn't Chase look like a BART guy to you?"

"Much more so than PATH," she said. "He's a little bit younger than our BART guys but I think he'd fit right in." She smiled at me. "It's a good group," she said. "The boys all have a developmental disability and some other diagnosis, usually psychiatric, and BART takes them in when no one else will. They live together, and go to school, and have jobs, and have chores around the unit. They go on outings — didn't they just come back from a basketball game?"

Jim nodded. "I think so," he said. "It was that or the circus, I forget."

"They shop for food and make meals and some of them are part of our Special Olympics teams," she said. "The goal is to help them build the skills they need to live more independently."

"You can use the same application you wrote for PATH for the BART unit," Jim said. "We've got a review team meeting coming up in the next month or so and we can look at it then."

"Is there a bed?" I asked. "Do you have room? Could you be ready when Chase comes out of the hospital?"

Jim and Sandy looked at each other and then looked away. In that glance alone, I should have seen that trouble lay ahead. But all I could think was that maybe, at last, we'd found a place for Chase.

"What happens next?" I said.

"It's a process," Jim said. "We don't have any openings right now but we anticipate having one in the future. The review board is going to meet the first of May."

AFTER THEY STARTED the Clozaril I waited for change to come, as if it were possible that a change in him was certain. Clozaril was supposed to work magic on those who hadn't been cured by other drugs. Sam told me that an old friend of his was transformed by Clozaril and went from being someone who was practically living on the streets and completely incoherent to someone who could hold a job. The nurses told me they thought they could see some small improvements, day by day, but I didn't see that anything was different. Chase paced and tapped and fired lasers and fled when strangers came onto Five South. If he sat for longer periods of time in a classroom with other teenagers and stared silently at the wall instead of pacing and shouting, perhaps this was improvement. If he could write in a mysterious language, just sharp jagged shapes that sometimes looked like letters or backward letters or abstract symbols or Cyrillic or Greek but were something wholly Chase's own, perhaps this was improvement. Every Friday, a nurse came to him after lunch and had him sit in a chair in the dayroom so she could take his blood pressure, his temperature, and then his blood. He stared past her. I sat next to him and he talked to me about his mansion. One day, when the nurse was

finished, he told me to go look out the window and see for myself.
I followed him and he pointed to the red brick buildings of the
business school and explained that one of these was the mansion
where he would live one day.

"You know that's not true," I said softly.

"No," he said. "That one! The one over there! You see it? It's
right there!" He repeatedly stabbed his index finger against the
glass and then looked at me. "Right there," he said again. "It's
right there."

I looked out at the buildings. In the afternoon sunlight, they
were a dusty brick color, with neat white trim, shaped like the ho-
tels on a Monopoly board. The construction workers had diverted
some of the traffic from a site on Manning Drive, and I watched
cars snake past a big blinking yellow arrow. Chase stared impassively at the buildings. Then his mouth twisted a little. He glanced
at me and very quickly raised his fingers, squinted at me as if taking aim down the shaft of a rifle, and fired a laser at me.

SOMETIMES HE WAS ASLEEP when I came to see him and
lay on his side on his bed. He was thin and lay on top of his blankets and sunlight came in through the big windows. I stood in
the room and listened to a helicopter racketing overhead, getting
ready to land on the roof, and then the thundering thwacking
sound that meant it was just above us, the beating of the rotors
like something with its own life, and then the roar that meant it
had landed on the roof and then the sound of the engine dying
away in a dissolving whir. Chase slept on and I didn't try to wake
him. In the beginning, I would have. In the beginning, I would
have wanted us to have a visit. I would have wanted him to know I
was there. I didn't try to wake him anymore. I sat on the desk and
watched him sleep for a while, watched him breathe, watched him,

in that time, be without motion at last, and then I went over to
him and lay my palm on his forehead and felt his warm skin and
could see his thin chest rising and falling with each breath, could
feel the damp sweat of his skin. I stood like that and then I lifted
my hand away and I went out to the hallway where Sam usually
sat at the table in front of Chase's door. He explained about the
Thorazine, that they didn't use it the way it used to be used but
just to sedate someone who was having trouble getting himself
under control. And then the Clozaril had that as a side effect, too,
especially as the dose increased in the first weeks. Really, it was
hard to know what was making Chase sleep in the middle of the
day but it was something he needed, right? He looked at me when
he said this and nodded for emphasis. Then he told me that he
thought Chase was really tolerating the Clozaril well. He thought
he could see that things were getting a little better.

"It's hard for us to know," he said, "since we didn't know him
before." He stood up and looked in at Chase. Then he crossed his
arms over his chest and stood across from me.

"Do you think he's more like he was before?"

"No," I said.

He asked me to describe him and I shrugged. "He was verbal
and he made sense and he went to school and he had difficulties
with things but not like this," I said. "Nothing like this."

Sam nodded.

"He knew me," I said. "He knew his sister. He knew who he
was."

Sam nodded again.

"He always had trouble with things like getting dressed and
washing. He always had trouble being really clear about things.
But it was different then," I said. "It wasn't like it is now."

"So the psychosis just came suddenly, out of the blue?"

I studied the tops of my shoes. A few months ago, I would have said yes. But now I realized that Chase had been working up to this for his whole life.

"Chase's first psychotic symptoms came when he was five," I said quietly. "It's not like I really remember Chase without some sort of psychosis being there. But it was much more low level. Much milder than this." I wrapped my arms around my waist. "I'm being no help to you at all," I said. "I can't remember anything clearly enough for this to make sense."

Sam didn't reply but we stood like that for a time, both of us looking through the open door at Chase. He slept soundlessly and without motion and he'd folded his dirty hands into a position of prayer under his chin. He didn't shave yet and looked younger than fifteen. Sunlight fell in a pale block across his bed. After a while, I left.

EIGHTEEN

||||||||||||||||||||||||||||||||||||||||||||||||

One day, when we were still in awe of the mild North Carolina winters and Chase had just turned thirteen, I came home from work and Robertson met me at the door. He appeared suddenly, as if he'd been hovering in the hallway waiting to hear my key in the lock. Chase was upstairs, folding laundry, he told me. Then he asked me what would happen if Chase missed his seizure meds.

It was Robertson's first day on the job. He was going to be trained in seizure protocols the next week but this was during the time before state law changed and you could start your job without having fully completed training. This wouldn't have been such a big deal except for the fact that Chase would have a seizure if he missed his meds.

Robertson looked like Kurt Cobain in the months before he died, young and frail and downtrodden. He'd wrapped an old greenish cardigan around his thin shoulders and stood next to the sink, picking at the raggedy end of one sleeve. He was trying to look cool but he couldn't look cool.

"I didn't know what to do when I realized I forgot so I wanted to talk to you as soon as you got home," he said.

I glanced at the clock. It was five thirty. "Chase," I yelled. "Chase!"

We both waited. When Chase didn't appear, I turned to Robertson. "Go get him," I said.

I got a glass and filled it with apple juice, then went to the medication box, which had a counter, rows assigned to each day of the week, and below that, little doors that opened on tiny boxes for morning, afternoon, evening, and bedtime dosages. Chase and his worker filled these boxes on the first day of the week. This task was meant to increase Chase's independence, to help him understand the importance of the meds that he took, but it also had the additional purpose of teaching the worker the importance of the medication regime. I had shown the box to Robertson that very morning.

I opened the box for Monday and tapped the morning meds into the palm of my hand. As I did this, I made excuses for Robertson. It was his first day. He hadn't completed the training yet. He didn't think to call me at work. Behind these excuses I felt my own inadequacy: I had waited for the Autism Society to train him and hadn't trained him myself, I should have called home to see how things were going, I should have stayed home from work and observed.

Still, I told myself, it might be all right. All we had to do was get Chase's meds into him and hope that he still had enough in his bloodstream from his last dose yesterday to tide him over until these took effect. It had been twenty-two hours since his last antiseizure medication, ten since he missed his morning dose, but maybe it would be okay. Maybe he'd just go to bed and all would be well. When Chase followed Robertson into the kitchen, I gave him his juice and handed him the pills, one after the other.

"Next time, if you have a question, call me at work," I told Robertson. "No matter what kind of question. Large or small. It doesn't matter."

He nodded. He had a miserable, defeated look on his face. "I didn't know," he said. "I'm sorry."

I heard the crash while I was doing the dishes after dinner and right after that Robertson's panicky voice, shouting my name. I ran up the stairs and Robertson met me in the hallway, yelling, "He's in the bathroom. He fell, he fell, he fell."

Chase lay still on the cold bathroom floor. The shower curtain, half out of the tub, dripped water on the floor next to his head. The blue towel that had been wrapped around his waist had come undone. His eyes were closed. There was blood on his head, on the vinyl floor. The toilet seat had cracked and come off.

He was bleeding and still wet from the shower. I strangely found myself wishing that the CAP workers would do a better job of teaching him to towel off.

"Robertson," I yelled.

He was in the doorway already.

"Call 9-1-1," I said. "And then come back. Do you know the address here?"

He said he did. He said he could give basic directions. I turned back to Chase. I closed his towel. He wasn't seizing anymore but he'd clearly lost consciousness and fallen. He'd been brushing his teeth. His red toothbrush lay against the floor's shoe molding. I pulled another towel down from the towel bar to cover him. I hated seeing him on the cold floor. Robertson was back. He said the ambulance was on the way.

"Listen," I said. "Help me move him to his bed."

Chase stirred, eyelids fluttering. He still couldn't talk. He looked so cold, and his skin was wet and it wouldn't take much for the air blowing across his skin to cool him more. We were able to get him to his feet and then, with our hands under his armpits and our arms around his waist, move him the three or four steps to his bed. He was bleeding just above the ear or maybe it was his ear. I told Robertson to go downstairs and wait for the ambulance.

I looked up and saw Haley, who stood in the doorway in her pajamas, once again witness to some brutal thing that brought Chase
trouble.

"Mom?" she said. Her face was still and serious.

"It's okay," I said. "It's okay. It's okay. Don't worry, sweet pea.
It's okay."

She watched me intently. I used the towels to try and dry Chase
off. His eyes were open now but he was staring and still. I pulled a
blanket up over his damp skin.

"What's the matter with Chase?" Haley said.

I tucked the blanket around him and he watched me. His lips
looked bluish.

"Chase had a seizure," I said. "He got hurt. The ambulance is
on its way. But he's okay. He's okay." I paused. In my head, I'd
already called the neighbors to get Haley a place to stay. "Do you
think you can go over to Betsy's tonight, until I get home?" I said.
"I don't know how long I'll have to stay at the hospital. If you go
over to Betsy's, it'll be fun. It'll be like a sleepover."

She nodded, wide-eyed, unsmiling, frightened but willing to
do whatever I asked.

"Go get your jacket and your shoes," I said. "Get Giraffic."

She held her stuffed giraffe out in front of her. When Chase
first started having grand mal seizures, Haley would come to get
me and say, Chase is having a grandma. Now, whenever he seized,
she ran to her room and closed the door and got in bed with her
stuffed giraffe and pulled the covers over her head.

"Get your shoes," I said again. "And get your jacket." I looked at
her, small and thin, wavering in the doorway with her little solemn
face. "Don't worry," I said. "They're just going to take him to the
hospital and check him over. He's going to be okay. Don't worry,
sweet pea." She looked past me to Chase and I walked over to

her and picked her up and hugged her, and felt her arms and legs wrap around my body just the way they had when she was a toddler. The sound of sirens drew closer, and the neighborhood filled with whirling light. An ambulance pulled in the driveway and a fire truck had pulled up out front, along with a police car and the EMT car. It was a mild January night, still in the first hours of dark, when the neighborhood was awake. People began to open their doors and step outside to see what the commotion was. They walked from farther down the street and clustered in a little group under the streetlight in front of our house.

The paramedics came into the room with their gurney. One crossed to the bed and wrapped a blood pressure cuff around Chase's arm and then pumped the cuff until it was full of air. Robertson came into the room behind them, buttoning his ratty cardigan. "If it's okay with you, I'm going to go now," he said.

"What?" I said. I stared at Robertson as if he were an alien someone had inconsiderately dropped into my house. It didn't seem possible that he would leave now, when things had gone so terribly wrong, when this had happened on his watch.

"I'm going now," said Robertson. "If it's okay, I'm going." He didn't wait for my answer but turned and walked away from me through the hallway and I heard his steps on the stairs and then the sound of the front door as it opened and banged shut behind him.

A paramedic stood by my elbow and kept asking me what happened.

"He was brushing his teeth and he lost consciousness and fell," I said. "We think he had a seizure. He has a seizure disorder and he missed his meds this morning."

"And he'll seize when he doesn't get his meds," said the paramedic. He looked at me. "I'm just confirming," he said.

"Right," I said. "That's right."

"Where did this happen?"

"In there," I said. "In the bathroom."

"Did you move him?" asked the paramedic. His voice was sharp, curt, unsympathetic. He walked away from me and looked into the bathroom, where the toilet seat lay split on the floor and blood smeared over the tile. There wasn't nearly as much blood as I thought there had been but any blood was too much. Chase's blood.

"He was cold," I said. "He was bleeding and lying on the floor and I wanted to get him warm."

The paramedic looked at the toilet seat on the floor. "He hit that?"

I nodded. "It came off," I said stupidly.

"You shouldn't have moved him."

"I know," I said, pleading. "But he was bleeding."

Chase tried to sit up on the bed.

"No, no, buddy," said the paramedic, who was writing something on the sheet of paper on his clipboard. He opened his fingers and pushed gently with his palm flat on Chase's chest. "You just lie still, okay? I'm just getting your blood pressure. Can you tell me if anything hurts?"

"My neck," said Chase.

"Where?"

Chase raised his arm, his muscles loose and soft, and waved at the direction of his neck.

"Where?" said the paramedic. "Show me again." He knelt by the bed with his clipboard and stethoscope. He had a kind face and wore wrinkled blue pants and a rumpled blue jacket. I thought about the paramedic who had made a balloon animal with a face out of a latex glove during Chase's first ambulance ride. I thought about the paramedics who had lifted Chase out of the bathtub the year before, unconscious and wet and still seizing, blue lips, soft and still, and who lay him on his bed, with his blue blanket over him, and listened intently to his heart and heard it fluttering, beating rapidly, like a caged bird or a trapped mouse, frantic and pumping too hard, and made notes on the clipboard and then carried Chase over to UNC Memorial, and wouldn't take him to Duke Hospital, even though that was where my insurance said he had to go, saying he could die in the ambulance and they weren't allowed to risk that. They stabilized him at UNC and then transferred him to Duke, where a pediatric cardiologist diagnosed the too-rapid heartbeat of atrial tachycardia. The ER reports from both UNC and Duke say *status epilepticus* but no one said those words to me.

This latest paramedic was practically shouting. "Where does it hurt, buddy? Show me where it hurts." I noticed that as soon as someone realized that Chase had difficulty communicating, he raised his voice, as if Chase were deaf. The paramedic leaned over him and said, "Does it hurt here?" He lay his hand on the back of Chase's neck and Chase put his own fingers just above that, on the back of his neck halfway to the base of his skull.

"Okay," said the paramedic. "Lie still, there, buddy. Take it easy, now. Don't move." He called for a collar and a backboard. He held Chase's head steady while the other paramedic slipped a collar beneath it and then strapped the front of the collar in place. Chase's hands went to the collar like birds, loose and flapping but searching, as if to say, what's this? The first paramedic touched Chase's hands and said, "It's just a collar to keep your neck still. You can take it off when you get to the hospital." The gurney was already unfolded in the room and one of them braced it with one foot and used the other to drop the frame down until it was the same level as the bed. They slid the backboard under Chase and then carefully, tenderly, moved him from his bed to the gurney. Haley watched from the doorway and I said, "Go downstairs, quick now," and she ran off and I could hear her footsteps on the stairs, a little rabbity thumpa-thumpa-thumpa, and then they carried Chase out of his blue room with the wallpaper border of astronauts bouncing on the moon that Chase had picked out himself as soon as we bought our house and they made the difficult tight turn in the hallway and then carefully down the stairs and out the front door and then down the front steps, where they let the wheels of the gurney hit the sidewalk but all I heard was ringing metal, the sounds of metal against metal, things snapping into place. They checked the straps and tucked in the blankets and called out to Chase in cheerful voices. "You're going to get a ride in the ambulance! Hang on there, buddy! We'll get out of here in no time!"

And Chase lay on the gurney in the darkness, his eyes dark and watchful, his skin the bluish color of powdered milk, not moving.

"You can't ride with us," one of them said to me, "but you can follow behind. Just stay close."

"Are we going now?" I asked. Haley stood next to me, leaning her shoulder against my waist, watching the ambulance and the fire truck and the police car and the EMT vehicle.

"Soon as we call in, we'll be on our way."

Betsy stepped out of the deep shadows that separated her house from mine and asked if she could do anything. The firemen who'd been waiting in the driveway turned away from the house and jumped back in the truck. Doors slammed. Someone revved the engine.

"Can you take Haley?"

She nodded. "As long as we need to," she said.

"I don't have her sleeping bag."

"We've got extra," she said.

Someone called out, "Ma'am? Ma'am? We're about to get underway here."

Haley stood behind me, her face white and anxious, wearing her blue coat with the pink trim and her white rubber boots. She held back but also gave the impression of someone who was leaning forward, as if at the starting line of a footrace. I swung her up through the air and hugged her.

"You're going to hang out with Betsy and Laura," I said. "Isn't that cool? It's okay," I said, "it's okay. Chase had a seizure but he's going to be fine. You've seen him have seizures before and he's been okay, right? He's just got to go over to the hospital and get checked out. And I'll come get you as soon as we get home."

She shivered in my arms and then pulled away.

"Come on, Haley," Betsy said. "You can sleep in Laura's room. That'll be fun."

"Ma'am," the paramedic called again. "You following us?"

The ambulance pulled out first, then the white car painted with the words *Emergency Management Team,* then me. I turned to watch Haley walking up the steps to Betsy's front door and my stomach dropped as I thought of the things Haley had to bear.

That night, there was a basketball game. Cars on their way to the Dean Dome backed up along Manning Drive in front of the hospital and there was no getting close to the place, no special lane kept clear for ambulances. We sat in traffic, first the ambulance, then the EMT car, then me. The first two were able to inch forward and occasionally someone would let them squeeze along, because they were vehicles that looked like they were on official business, and had their spinners going, and every so often, the ambulance would let loose with a whirling bleat. No one saw my car as in any way connected to this caravan and I drove along,

sticking as close to the back of the EMT car as I could manage
and whispering to myself, "Okay, okay now, just let me through,
just let me get through." Once, I slapped my palms hard on the
steering wheel and yelped, "Hey, I'm with them!" In the stillness
of my car, my voice conveyed nothing but utter disbelief at being
blocked by the other cars, at the other drivers not being able to
know my predicament, my child in that ambulance, the bloody
freaking basketball game traffic in the way.

They parked the ambulance in the bay and I was able to find a
place out front. By the time I got back to the unit, they were wheel-
ing Chase along the hallway to a pediatric trauma room. They'd
slapped an oxygen mask on his face in the ambulance and as they
wheeled him under the bright greenish light, he began to vomit. The
team at his side cried out and hurried faster, and he vomited more.
He was in a neck brace and on a backboard so he vomited lying
flat on his back, with an oxygen mask strapped over his nose and
mouth. Someone reached down and pulled that back and then he
was in a room and two nurses were hooking up a suction machine
to clear his mouth and airway and another wiped his face and the
doctor came in and yelled about a CT scan of his head and the next
thing I knew, we were in radiology, and I was watching Chase as
the team gently moved him to a sliding table that would pass his
body through the big spinning donut that was the CT machine.
They invited me back to the control booth and as I watched, black
and white images of Chase's brain appeared, pools of light and
pockets of darkness, no really identifiable structures other than the
familiar shape of a brain in a skull, and below that the notched and
ringed latches of vertebrae locked together in a column, and then
the technician leaned forward and looked carefully, and punched
buttons, and the view changed, and she turned to me and she said,
"This is looking at the brain from above."

A little while later, the radiologist came in to read the pictures from the scan, now spread out like items on a menu on the screen in front of him. He took his time and leaned in and breathed deeply and looked again. He wore a long white coat; a pad of paper clipped together with a ballpoint pen stuck out of his hip pocket. He straightened and stood with his arms folded across his chest and leaned back a little bit on his heels and then bent from the waist and dropped his hands to the countertop in front of the screen and got in close for a very good look.

Finally he turned to me. "The good news is that his head is clear," he said. "I don't see any evidence of massive brain injury. We worry about that when someone comes in vomiting after a fall, after a loss of consciousness. The vomiting, whatever it is, is unrelated to the fall. It's from something different, maybe a virus he picked up at school."

He paused and looked back at the images. I sensed a "but."

"You see this?" he said and pointed to a black space surrounded by light that looked exactly like the black spaces surrounded by light above and below it. "Here," he said, "I'll get a better angle. Give me a lateral view," he said to the technician. She punched some keys and the image changed to the familiar image of the vertebrae that attach the skull to the neck.

"This is what concerns me," he said, and pointed to a faint shadow along the neck bones. "Frankly, I'm not sure what we're seeing here. I'm going to call neurosurgery for a consult. His head's clear but it looks like he may have sustained a neck injury. We wouldn't want him going home without having looked at that very carefully."

"Is that dangerous?" I asked. "What kind of neck injury?"

"It can be," said the radiologist. "You see where this is? Up high, at C3? That's of greater concern because of the location. Did he complain of pain in this area?"

I nodded blankly. I didn't yet know the language of neurosurgeons, the way each of the vertebrae in the spine is mapped and labeled, the way each has its own number and letter, starting with C1, for the first of the cervical vertebrae, descending first to T1 at the start of the thoracic vertebrae, and then to L1, for the beginning of the lumbar spine.

"I suspect there's an injury here," said the radiologist. He frowned at the shadow and pointed at something. "Hard to tell because of the swelling. Let's send you back out to the ER and have neurosurgery take a look."

Chase was back on the gurney by this time, with a foam collar cinched around his neck. We waited for neurosurgery in a glass-walled room in the pediatric ER. After a while, a boy came in with a broken arm. An exasperated woman who I assumed was his mother accompanied him. She wore gold capri pants and gold lamé mules and a dozen necklaces and yards of bracelets at her wrists and ankles; she jangled when she walked. The nurse pulled the curtain between us for privacy but there was no privacy at all. The broken-arm boy's mother was on her cell phone within minutes complaining in the same impatient tone, with the same infuriated words, to many different people, that she was stuck in the ER because her moronic son had been stupid enough to break his arm during his Little League game. She had other choice opinions of her child and no fear of sharing them. I sat next to Chase and after a few minutes reached over and held his hand. He'd stopped vomiting and lay still, languorous in the drowsy state I knew came over him after a seizure. I held his hand so he could feel me there, as if the things that had happened to him had happened to me as well, as if my presence could teach him patience in the face of these things that hit him like a bolt out of the blue, as if my presence could matter in any way at all. Mostly, I felt helpless and the white foam collar fastened around his neck made me swallow a sob.

The woman with the cell phone stuck her head around the curtain.

"What are you in for?" she barked.

"He fell," I said.

"Huh," she said. "These kids. This whole thing is a pain in my you-know-what." She studied Chase. "So what's wrong with him?" she said. "He looks pretty good to me."

"They think he hurt his neck," I said.

"His neck? My boy broke his arm! His arm! I don't know what I'm supposed to do about that, but I tell you what. I've had it up to here"—she violently slashed her hand through the air somewhere in the vicinity of her throat—"with his shenanigans. He does this stuff on purpose, you know. He's always trying to get my goat." She stared at her watch and then gave me a hard look, as if I might somehow also be responsible for the inconvenience of her evening. "Almost ten thirty," she snapped. "I can think of a million places I'd rather be. This is just insane!"

She flapped the curtain closed for emphasis, the way someone might slam a door. Then she was back. "Well," she said. "Good luck to you. I can see they're coming now. About friggin' time. Do they think we have all day?"

When the boy with the broken arm was fitted with his cast and gone, we waited for neurosurgery. Every so often, a nurse breezed into the room to check Chase's vitals, ask about vomiting, and tell us that neurosurgery had been paged but must have another patient somewhere else in the hospital. Around midnight, I told Chase to get some sleep but he was already quiet, his eyes closed. I turned the lights out in our room and sat in the dark while Chase slept. I leaned my head against the wall and tried to close my eyes.

I thought of Haley. I wondered how she was doing at Betsy's house. I wondered when we'd get out of there. I wondered if I should just let her sleep the rest of the night there or wake everybody up so I could bring her home. I wondered how much longer we'd have to wait. I wondered if I should go and try to find the doctor myself. I wondered if I was going to have to buy Chase his breakfast from the vending machines. I tried to remember how much money was in my wallet. I wondered if this was anything serious. I wondered how I would know.

Then the door banged open and the lights snapped on and I sat up bleary-eyed and Chase tried to sit up on his gurney but the short man in green scrubs and long white coat and green skullcap who stood in front of him said, "No, just lie still. I need to have a look at you." His voice was very soft, almost gentle and girlish. He turned to me and his glasses winked in the light and he said, "This is the boy who fell during a seizure?"

I nodded.

"Ricardo de Soto," he said. "I'm from neurosurgery. Can you tell me what happened?"

He nodded and wrote things down while I spoke. Finally he said, "I saw the CT scan. I agree with the radiologist. There's something there that needs to be more fully evaluated. I'm ordering X-rays. If there is a serious injury to the C-spine, it can be very dangerous for the person to go home without proper care. We need to see what an X-ray will tell us." He paused. "It's hard to be sure because of the swelling. He might have some spinal instability."

I kept nodding as if I understood what he was saying. I had not yet realized that Chase had a serious injury, that he was really injured at all.

"Let me do an exam before you go to X-ray." He turned to the gurney. "Chase," he said. "Can you wake up for me? Good boy! All right. Give me your hand. I'm going to have you sit up now."

Chase swayed sleepily on the edge of the gurney but followed the neurosurgeon's finger with his eyes and touched his nose with his own index finger and squeezed the neurosurgeon's hand and said "Ouch" in a convincing and irritated voice when the neurosurgeon began to prick his arms with a small pin and ask him if he could feel that or this or how about that?

Finally he asked Chase where it hurt and Chase tried to take off the foam collar to show him but the neurosurgeon said, "No, no, don't do that! Just show me without taking the collar off!"

Chase didn't move. I put my fingers on the top of the collar. "Does it hurt here?" I said. He shook his head no and his hand flew up and brushed the back of the collar, in the middle of his neck.

"All right," said Ricardo de Soto. "Let's get you down to X-ray."

At two, we were moved to the adult ER, where Chase lay on his gurney in the hallway because all the rooms were occupied by people who were just a little bit down on their luck. The woman in the room directly in front of us paced up and down in front of the glass window; she shook and moaned and occasionally cursed. A sheriff's deputy came around the corner and stopped at her door. He never looked our way but pulled out a fat pad of paper clipped with a ballpoint pen, paused as if he were bracing himself for a big leap from a high place, and then pushed the door open. The woman in the room began to wail as soon as she saw him and then she tried to run past him but he stood between her and the doorway and said her name over and over again: "Dorothy Weeks. Dorothy Weeks. Dorothy Weeks." Then he began to describe the amount of crack cocaine they'd pulled from her suitcase after the car was stopped. She stopped wailing and retreated to the corner farthest away from him and began to scream, "Mother fucker, *mother*fucker, *motherfucker*!"

Chase lay on his back and stared at the ceiling. I told him to get some sleep. He wanted to sit up. I asked a passing nurse if we could be moved, the motherfucker woman being who she was, but the nurse said that was impossible.

We went to X-ray. I followed the gurney and waited inside the room while Chase stood in front of a flat beige box and the technician slid the frame of film in behind him. Afterward, I could see the shadow that had everyone worried but I still didn't know how it was different from the shadow that lay above it or the others spread out below.

At four thirty, Ricardo de Soto came by and told us that Chase could go home, but only if he promised not to remove the neck brace and to return in the morning to get a different, better brace from the Brace Shop. He'd stapled directions to that department on our discharge sheet and pointed these out to me.

"What do you think is wrong?" I said.

"There's too much swelling to say conclusively but we believe he's got some spinal instability," he said. "We cannot rule it out tonight so he must wear the brace morning, noon, and night for the next week and then return for a second set of X-rays." He looked warmly at Chase. "Can you do that?" he asked. "Can you keep that brace on, no matter what? It's very important that you don't take it off."

"Cool," said Chase.

"Can you do it?" Ricardo de Soto said again. This time he put his hand on Chase's arm. "This is very serious. I need to know that you can do this."

"I can do it," said Chase.

"No taking it off at school," he said. "No taking it off because something feels itchy."

"Okay," said Chase.

He looked at me. "You understand?" he said. "The brace must not come off, not for any reason."

I nodded again and he seemed satisfied.

"I've written down the name of a pediatric neurosurgeon and we've made an appointment for Chase one week from today. Come thirty minutes early so he can go to X-ray."

When we left the ER the sun was starting to come up. Out in the parking lot, I scraped a thin sheen of ice off of our windshield while Chase shivered in the front seat and waited for the car to warm up. When I got in, he asked for U2 and I put the tape in before we turned west through town, traveling alone through the still and silent streets.

I should have supervised Robertson. I should have stayed home on his first day of work. When I learned that Chase had missed his meds, I should have made him lie in bed for the rest of night, where he would seize safely, no danger of falling. A million things came to me that I could have done differently. These were quickly replaced with a million thoughts of the ways I forever failed to keep Chase safe.

At dinnertime, we sat at the dining-room table and I brought plates of pasta and bowls of salad from the kitchen. I had to call Haley three times before she came in and sat in her chair across from Chase and picked up her glass of milk and began to drink, kicking one foot against the table.

"Stop that," I said and she stopped.

The brace held Chase's head and neck in place and he could not

bend his face to his plate. He tried to lift his fork to his mouth.
Food fell down his shirt and into his lap.

"Gross," Haley said. She was eight now, nearly nine. She moved
the flowers in the middle of the table a little bit so she would not
be able to see Chase.

"Let me get you a spoon," I said.

He didn't wait but dug his hand into the plate of pasta and
shoved it into his mouth. Curls of pasta fell from the plate and bits
of tomato dripped onto the floor.

"Chase," I said, my voice rising, the familiar tug of impatience
and sadness rising in me. "Wait a second, Chase." I said. "Just
wait. You're getting food all over the place."

I found a clean dish towel and wrapped it around his neck brace
and spread it out like a giant napkin so that it covered the front of
his shirt. "Here," I said. "Use your spoon. Just get closer," I said.
"It'll be all right."

He sat strangely straight and tried to maneuver the spoon from
his plate to his mouth. Food tipped onto the table and then the
floor.

Haley picked at the pasta on her plate and watched the tops of
her knees under the table. After a few minutes she looked at me
and said, "May I please be excused?"

"Haley," I said. "Your brother can't help it."

She kicked the table and picked up her fork and poked at her
food. She looked at me, her eyes grave, her face solemn, so serious that her expression seemed to exceed anything you ought to
see on a child's face. At night, I'd tuck her in and sit on the edge
of her bed and sing to her in the dark, the light from the hallway
cutting a clean trapezoid onto the floor, and hope that she could
hear in my singing all of the things I was sorry for: that she had
to live with Chase's troubles, that she had to live with me as I

took care of Chase's troubles, that she had lost her father, that she often got lost in the shuffle, that I had to work, that there wasn't enough of me to go around. I knew she played by herself most of the time and invented long stories for the people who lived in her dollhouse. I often found her in her room with the Sorry! board set up, each player a different stuffed animal save for Haley, who threw the dice for everyone and marched the little men around the board and congratulated her giraffe when he made a particularly good move.

CHASE LIFTED HIS SPOON and dropped pasta down into his collar. His face was impassive but I knew he was hungry and frustrated. And yet he just kept at it, trying to eat as best he could.

Haley looked at her plate. "My appetite isn't on this," she said.

"What's your appetite on?"

"Nothing." She put her fork down. "May I please be excused? Please?"

"All right," I said at last. "Go ahead. Just put your plate in the kitchen."

THE NEXT DAY, I made a point of taking Haley into the woods near our house so she could ride her bike. The bike had been Chase's bike, a dirt model that was supposed to grow with Chase until he was nearly six feet tall. When he was younger, he'd ridden everywhere on his Huffy, but he got this bike when we moved to North Carolina and he gradually lost interest in it, just as he lost interest in other things.

It was a good bike though, and I thought someone should get some use out of it. Haley got a lock for it that was her very own and sometimes rode it to school. This was around the same time she took up skateboarding and used to stand at the top of the hill in front of our house and step up on her skateboard and then fly down the hill in a straight, heart-stopping shot, bending her knees to steer around cars parked in the bike lane, the sound of wheels rolling on asphalt everywhere; she jumped off only when the skateboard had rolled to a sudden and silent stop. Then she scooted the board on one foot back to the top of the hill and did it again

She rode ahead of me out into the field and I followed behind. Just beyond the field, the trail dipped down into a natural culvert that was mostly dry but in spring could fill with water. Now it was glazed with crispy plates of silvery ice. Haley pushed off and put her feet on her pedals and rode down into the dip, her bike clattering faster and faster over the dirt and loose rocks and then flying up to the other side, where she dropped her feet back to the ground and stopped to look back at me, breathless, hair flying under her helmet.

It was a sunny mid-winter day awash in golden light. A soft breeze rustled through the dry yellow grass and as I passed into the field I glanced up into the pines and saw an owl standing still on a branch, so quiet I nearly missed him, and then so present, I couldn't imagine how he would not be visible to everyone who came by. A turkey vulture turned slowly on a coil of air over the field. High up and far away, he was just a slice of dark against the blue sky.

Haley turned where the trail made its way back under the trees, and yelled at me again and I jogged to catch up with her. The trail followed the hillside down to the creek; halfway there, some kids had built a big bike jump, mounding dirt into a huge pile and then tamping it down until it was smooth. You could see the tire marks that led up to the mound and the way the earth had become flat and bare on the other side of the jump from all of the times bikes and their riders had come down hard.

Haley pedaled down the path and pulled up next to the jump and studied it.

She looked back over her shoulder at me as I approached. "I'm going," she said.

"Are you sure?" I said. Then, not wanting to sound dubious or discouraging, I amended that. "I'll watch from here," I said. "That jump looks great!"

She wheeled the bike back up the trail. She threw one leg across the seat and put her hands up and tested her helmet and then pushed off hard with one foot and lifted the other to the pedal. She pedaled hard and fast down the path and leaned forward over the handlebars and bent down low, coming at the jump with as much velocity as she could muster. She rode up in a sharp curve and one bike wheel came up off the dirt but something caught the rear wheel and it did not follow. Instead, Haley left the bike, left the earth, and sailed out over the handlebars and somehow landed flat on her back on the packed earth below the jump.

"Haley!" I shrieked and started for her.

She raised herself on her elbows and pushed her helmet back out of her eyes. She looked at me and began to laugh. I leaned down next to her to see if she was okay and then sat in the dirt next to her and watched her laugh until tears rolled into her hair and she slapped the earth with the flat palms of her hands and then rolled up in a ball and clutched her stomach, laughing.

"Are you okay?" I said. "Haley? Does anything hurt?"

She shook her head, no, no, and wiped at the tears and straightened herself out. By now I was laughing, too, although I didn't know why, maybe just because it seemed like the only possible response. "You should have seen yourself go," I said and she howled anew.

After a few minutes, she grew still and lay flat on her back and sighed deeply, catching her breath, and looked up at the sky. I sat next to her in silence and listened to the wind move in the dry branches and to the distant sound of the creek moving its slow winter water past its banks. She turned her head to look at me and gave me a sly look. "Go again?" she said.

I could not say no.

A WEEK AFTER THE ACCIDENT, Chase and I went back to the hospital and donned our heavy lead vests so that Chase could have his neck examined. He sat patiently on the stool while the technician slid plates the size of small posters into a box behind his head and lifted his chin and told him not to move. Afterward, the pediatric neurosurgeon showed us the images, ghostly pale against a bluish background, the fine sharp white of bones, the chiaroscuro of luminous shadow, and explained that Chase had instability in his cervical spine. She explained the consequences of not treating this: quadriplegia at some point, when the spine slipped further out of place. The certainty of this outcome meant that Chase should have surgery. She reached behind her and picked up a tawny model of the human spine. It was shaped like an upside-down cobra and rattled a little as she moved it around, as she pointed to the parts of the spine injured in Chase's fall—up high at C3, meaning he was lucky to still be alive—and explained that she would come in from the back and stabilize the spine with titanium rods and allograft, the putty of bone mixed up from a cadaver donor.

"Can I see that?" Chase asked. When the neurosurgeon handed the model over, Chase held it in his lap and then touched the bones of the spine and made the spine move.

"Pretty cool," said the neurosurgeon. "Right?"

"Do you understand, Chase?" I said. "Do you know what we're talking about?"

He gently touched the bones at C3. "This is where you'll do it," he said.

"On you, though, Chase," I said. "Not on the model."

"I know," he said. "Right here." He patted the bones tenderly and looked up at us. "It's okay," he said. "I want to be able to walk."

WE CROSSED THE WALKWAY from the parking deck to the hospital before dawn so the building looked like a dark square against the darker sky, a square lit by blocks of white and yellow and greenish light. The air was thin and cold and smelled like rain. Chase took my hand as we passed from the covered breezeway out to the open drive and we made our way around the construction fences and orange pylons. Inside, the lobby was empty and we rode the escalator to the first floor, where I gave Chase's name to the man behind the counter. The room was dim and quiet. The palms in the corners were dusty. I tried to interest Chase in a magazine but he said no and sat with his bear on his lap and looked around. A family of three generations came in, the patient, his wife, and their four children, and his mother and his mother's sister, and they spread out in chairs across from the television set and the children immediately began to roll on the floor with one another, except for one small girl, who sat in her mother's lap and pushed her head back against her mother's sternum whenever the others came too close.

The man said something to the boys and they stopped wrestling and just then, a tall man in blue scrubs came through the door and we stood and followed him upstairs to the surgical suite. Chase was given a gown to wear and a paper hat and red socks with rubber chevrons on the bottom to keep him from falling if he chose to walk across the slick floor. The nurse came along and rubbed Emla cream on the back of Chase's hand and told us it would take effect in a little while; when it did, she'd be back to put the IV in. Chase sat in his vinyl recliner and stared straight ahead and I flipped through the TV channels to see if there might be something he'd be interested in and we settled on the news. When the anesthesiologist came along, I asked if I would be able to go back to the operating room with Chase and the man shook his head.

"We can let you walk down the hallway as far as the OR but we can't let you inside," he said. "How will that be?"

"Chase," I said, "I'll go with you to the door, okay?"

He nodded and blinked at me, his eyes big and dark. The nurse came with the IV and Chase asked her if she had a butterfly needle and she said, "Right here." She leaned over him and rubbed the back of his hand until a vein stood out and then slid the needle in place. He watched her and didn't flinch.

"That wasn't too bad, was it?" she said and he nodded. She hung bags of fluid on the metal stand and connected them to the tube running from the IV in the back of Chase's hand and said she'd be back in a few minutes. "You're just about ready to roll," she said. "I think they're just about ready for you now."

Then the OR team came to get him, and I stood and watched them slide him onto the gurney and then walked beside him down an unlit hallway to a bright, cold room. No one stopped me so I stepped inside and held his hand and kissed him. One of the nurses told me I needed to leave. I kissed him again and told him I would be right outside the whole time and he looked at me and he said, "Mom, Mom."

"It's okay," I said. "Don't be scared. You're brave and strong. I'm proud of you." He looked up at me, swaddled in his white blankets, the IV line already dripping something into his arm, the bag that swung in its crooked cradle, his eyes wide and scared, and yet already beginning to droop. One of the nurses looked at me and said, "We've started the medicine now."

"Chase," I said. "Don't worry. They will take good care of you. And I will be outside the whole time." And then the nurses gathered around Chase and slid him from the gurney onto the table and I kissed him again and made my way to the door. The surgeon was in the hallway outside the OR and she stopped me and asked me if I had any final questions and I shook my head. She squeezed my arm. "Don't worry, Mom," she said. "This is going to be okay."

But I found no comfort in her words and felt the fear of what was about to happen to Chase and told myself that this was something we had to do to save him, to protect him from a worse fate. I knew, or at least had had it explained to me, which is not the same as knowing, that he would be face down on the table in a contraption that would allow them to go at his spine from behind, and I knew that those careful medical words, posterior dissection, meant that the surgeon would take a blade and cut through Chase's skin and then his muscle, until she'd laid open his spine, and then his bones would be drilled and fitted out with screws and rods and she'd pack the disk area with allograft so that bone would lay over bone until his spine was fused and firm. Afterward, she warned me, Chase's head would swell to the size of a pumpkin and I must not be alarmed when I saw him, for the swelling would abate and his neck would heal.

I walked back to the family waiting room with the plastic bag full of Chase's clothes swinging at my side and found a chair. The surgical suite waiting area was fitted out with blond wood furniture, the upholstery some sort of contemporary print of interlocking geometric shapes in teal and eggplant, and with a big screen TV, where families could watch the *Today Show* while they waited for news of their patients. I sat down and held Chase's things in my lap. I could feel myself breathe, each breath something sharp that drilled down into the pit of my stomach, until each breath became a physical manifestation of wordless, bottomless fear.

THERE ARE TIME LINES for things like bone healing and bone fusing, and we knew the first surgery had failed when Chase's spine did not knit together on time. So the pediatric neurosurgeon decided to try again and Chase had a second surgery. This time, the neurosurgeon felt that Chase's chances of healing would be improved by the use of a halo. On the morning of the second operation, after Chase and I had once again come to the hospital in the predawn hours and he'd held my hand while the nurse started his IV, and after I shivered again, and after I thought how brave he was to go through this again, because this time he knew what it would be like, I sat in the waiting room outside of the surgical suite and strung lengths of fishing line with beads and small flat discs enameled with the yin-yang symbol because Chase had asked for decorations for his halo. The families around me wanted to know what I was doing and I held the strings up and they admired them just the way you'd admire a bit of knitting.

When I saw Chase in the recovery room after the first surgery, a catheter attached to a drain at the top of his spine filled with bright red blood and snaked over the bed rails. He was still hooked up to the heart monitor and some other machine that chimed every few minutes. He looked gray and still, as if the distance between him and the rest of us that was always implied had been lengthened and deepened by the surgery and there was no getting to him now. But when I saw Chase's swollen head suspended in his halo after the second surgery, my knees went out from under me and I stopped breathing. The nurses propped me up and told me that it looked worse than it was. After Chase got out of the hospital and was able to come home, he looked at the strings of beads and smiled to see the yin-yang, the thing he'd most particularly asked for, and stood very still while I tied the beads to the rods of the halo. When I was through, he lifted his left hand and very gently patted at the beads, which swung a little and made a rattling sound when he moved.

"Is that what you had in mind?" I said.

He patted the beads and they rattled again. "Yes," he said. "It's okay."

THE HALO'S STEEL RING encircles the skull but doesn't rest on it; instead, the halo is anchored to the head by four long sharp pins that pierce the skull on one end and screw into the steel ring on the other. The ring is connected to unmoving metal rods that are bolted to a rigid plastic frame inside an adjustable lamb's wool–lined vest. When the halo-wearer sleeps, his head is suspended in this device by the four spikes stabbed into his skull and does not rest on a pillow. Before he got the halo, Chase had been after to me to get something pierced; this went along with his desire to grow dreadlocks, wear black clothes, grow up to be a rock star. After he got the halo, he settled for my explanation that he'd already been pierced, that the halo was the mother of all piercings, that while other people just got their tongues or eyebrows pierced, Chase had gotten his skull pierced and how cool was that?

At first, Chase went outside in his halo but it was difficult to move around and it didn't take long for him to give up on that. The school told me to keep him home since they didn't want the liability of a child in a halo in their hallways, when throngs of middle-schoolers pushed and shoved their way from class to class. They sent a sleepy teacher to our house instead, who read the books assigned for language arts out loud while Chase dozed on the sofa next to her. Every day, when I came home from work, I sat him on a towel on the edge of his bed and spread another towel over his lap. With washrags and liquid soap and two plastic basins of warm water, I washed his hair, and then his limbs and torso and trunk and back. I showed him how to soap his skin with the rag, and then dip the rinse rag in the warm water in the second basin and wash the soap away. I handed him the soapy rag and told him to wash his face, neck, and private parts. Then I turned away. When he said he was through, I helped him stand, pinching the towel around his waist with one hand and drying him with a towel in the other.

A FEW WEEKS AFTER Chase got out of the hospital, the elementary school held its annual Wax Museum. The kids were supposed to impersonate wax figures of famous people and were given a list from which to choose: Johnny Appleseed. Martha Washington. Betsy Ross. Nelson Mandela. At the very bottom of the page, in small print, someone had noted that if the child wished to be a person whose name did not appear on the list, it was all right to approach the teacher and ask if the proposed individual fit the terms of the assignment. This meant the person had to be famous enough to be easily researched by a third grader. When Haley told me she wanted to be John Lennon, she pointed out that John Lennon must be as famous as Johnny Appleseed, who in her opinion was really more of a made-up story about a real person than a person who should be famous in his own right.

Haley's teacher didn't agree. "We think of these figures as historical in nature," she said stiffly.

"John Lennon's dead," I said. I rolled my eyes at Haley, who danced around in front of me in the kitchen while I held the phone to my ear and tried not to sound too much like either a former professor or a difficult parent. More than anything, I wanted Haley to have something she had picked for herself, something she believed in on her own.

"You misunderstand," the teacher said. "We think of these figures as people who contributed to history."

"Don't you think the Beatles made a major contribution to American culture?" I said.

Haley's teacher was silent. Finally she said, "That's more pop culture. That's not exactly the kind of history this assignment focuses on."

"Okay," I said. "How about this? What if Haley focuses on Lennon the humanitarian?" I imagined Haley describing the Toronto bed-in to the parents of her classmates and I grinned at her.

There was a long silence. "Well," said the teacher at last. "That would be suitable, I guess."

The night of the Wax Museum, Haley dressed in black pants and a black turtleneck and a midnight blue velvet blazer and a Greek fisherman's style cap. She carried an electric guitar we'd made by tracing a shape on cardboard. Just after supper, we got into the car and Chase carefully lowered himself into the front seat, unable to bend because of the halo, and I closed the door behind him. Haley got in back. When we got to the elementary school, the parking lot was full of other cars and we followed other families, each with a child dressed as a historical character, into the school. When we passed into the lobby, I asked Haley if she knew where to go. She nodded. "We're supposed to meet in my classroom," she said gravely and quietly.

"Okay," I said. "Have fun. We'll meet you afterward."

She nodded and slipped away from us into the press of people. As we began to walk through the hallways, children took up their places in long rows along the bright corridors, stooping to put paper buttons on the floor before them and then standing as still as they could. Parents stepped up and pressed the paper buttons with the toes of their shoes and the children sprang to life and began to tell the stories of their characters.

As we moved through the school, people cast glances at Chase and did not approach us. I walked with my hand on his elbow and when he was interested in a character, he turned his whole body to face the child and people stepped back and looked at him and looked away and looked back again. Their fascination was the fascination of the morbidly compelled. You could tell that they did not find joy in Chase standing before them, saved from a lifetime of paralysis, but instead saw him as a freak in a strange cage, who perhaps had something contagious, who compelled them to study him even as they recoiled in shock. We moved and they fell back and away but still they watched him openly, with undisguised curiosity. People have this way about them and it's not to be spoken of contemptuously, because it's begotten out of an uneasiness that is truly not their fault. If long ago there were freak shows, now they have been replaced with allegedly educational programs on the Discovery Health channel about medical mysteries and strangely formed babies and men with giant tumors. We have all looked at that which is curious to us, as if it is impossible to look away.

But my generosity was tenuous that night, just as it was when people came up to Chase in the grocery store and asked him questions about this thing that could in no way be construed as their business. As we walked the halls, I wanted to tell everyone who stared at Chase that I understood why they looked but this was just a boy here to see his sister—no show folks, turn away.

We found Haley's friends, the girls who came to our house for her birthday parties and her sleepovers, and I stepped on their paper buttons and admired their performances. The PTA had set up tables of refreshments outside of the gym and I asked Chase if he wanted a cold drink or a cookie but he said no. He stood by himself and flinched when the mothers and fathers gaped at him.

"Let's go see your sister, okay?" I said, and took Chase by the elbow and steered him out and away from the crowds.

Haley was halfway down the corridor that led to the lunchroom, standing still as a statue in front of a row of black windows, her cardboard guitar on its paper strap slung over her shoulder. A man in a pale pink shirt walked up to her and said, "John Lennon! How cool!" He stepped on her button and she began her speech, carefully written and memorized, in a voice so low that the man had to lean in and listen until his smile became fixed and he shook his head a little. When she was through, he thanked her, and she nodded without smiling and resumed her pose.

AT NIGHT, I LAY in the dark in my room and thought of Zip and wondered what he would think of these things that had befallen his son. And some nights, I thought of our days as a family, when we walked through northern woods at Christmastime and picked the tree and Zip cut it down while Chase and Haley ran among the rows of trees whose dark branches stood crisp and green against the snow. In my dreams, I heard their laughter across all of time.

ON THE DAY OF Haley's ninth birthday party, twenty minutes before eight little girls were supposed to come for cake and games and a sleepover, Chase's halo dropped four screws on the kitchen floor. When I called the hospital, the neurosurgeon told me to bring Chase in. As I hung up, the first girl arrived, bearing her birthday present and a furry sleeping bag shaped like a bear.

I put Chase in the chair in the kitchen by the front window and told him not to move and then called every CAP worker I knew until I found Andrew. More birthday guests arrived. Their parents glanced curiously at Chase and then chatted with me about pick-up times in the morning. When Chase and I left, Haley put her arms around me and I felt a little shiver run through her, as if all she ever expected was for me to disappear with Chase and keep disappearing.

Chase's dim X-rays demonstrated that the grafts had failed again. At eleven o'clock that night, I sat in a conference room on the sixth floor of the hospital and listened while the neurosurgeon told me the thing to do would be to have the pediatric neurosurgeon take Chase back into the OR. I said, as politely as I could muster, that I would not give permission for that.

The neurosurgeon shot me a funny sharp look. "Chase needs surgery," he said. "He can't stay like this."

"I agree," I said. "Still, I think with two failures behind us, Chase has earned the right to be treated by the best spine person you have. Not the person who did this to him."

The neurosurgeon studied the top of the table. After a minute or two of this, he sighed and said, "I believe you're right. Chase has earned the E-ticket ride next time."

"Thank you," I said.

The head of the spine center did not usually take pediatric cases but he saw Chase and agreed that at age thirteen, and at more than six feet tall, he was the size of many adults. Dr. T could consult with pediatric folks if the need arose. He was the kind of surgeon who corrected other people's mistakes and spine patients came to him from around the country. On the day we went to see him, we ran into the pediatric neurosurgeon in the hall. She said she understood my decision and of course I was entitled to see any doctor

I wished, and she'd heard I'd been to Duke for a consult, and she wanted to be clear that I could certainly take Chase there, if that was my wish, but still, she said, she hoped I would give her another chance and Chase's failure to heal was not her fault. "I would like the opportunity," she said, "to do the next surgery." Her voice was choked with tears and anger and I just shook my head.

"I'm sorry," I said.

THE THIRD SURGERY was successful in the fusion but destabilized the spine just below the new bone. The head of the spine center showed me the X-rays and said, "This looks like it's just going to keep marching down Chase's spine. We need to think about doing another surgery, where we come in from the front and the back both and stabilize his entire C-spine." And so, in June, as school let out, that's what he did. The surgeon lifted all of the existing hardware out and began again, this time working from C3 to C7. The surgery took more than twelve hours and afterward Chase ended up in pediatric intensive care.

In the months after that, when Chase wore his neck brace, and then took it off, and then got sick and heard voices and waited for the nailers, and then went into the psych ward at the hospital and seemed to get worse, we entered a time where the ordinary things that other people did seemed like stories I'd heard about when I was a girl. In this time, we were forced to find hope when hope seemed beyond reach, beyond expectation.

NINETEEN

I rested my arms on the rails and watched Haley lead Lightning into the center of the ring. He was a brown misshapen horse with a head that was too big for his body, and a body that was too short for his legs, and a wiry black mane and a brushy black tail. He reminded me of everything that was misshapen in Haley's life, as if this disabled horse, whom she loved and feared, could stand in for her disabled brother, whom she also loved and feared.

It was spring. Chase was on Five South and Haley was eleven. Out at the barn, the air still smelled of cold; the pond next to the big ring was skinned with gray ice, and the horses in the dirt lot below the barn blew clouds of smoke with each breath and walked delicately over the frozen mud. Haley finished tightening the girth and then looked around for the mounting block.

She took the reins and settled in her seat, her limbs long and graceful, her seat easy, as if she'd been made to sit a horse, and began to walk Lightning in a big slow circle close to the fence. He tried to walk with his head down but she perked him up and then moved him into a slow trot, posting gently, trying not to come down too hard in the saddle. He shook his head and she sat a little taller. She'd ridden him three or four times in lessons and the woman who owned the barn said she needed someone to work with him and Haley could have extra saddle time if she could come out one or two afternoons a week and just ride him in the little ring. On those days, I got home from work early and each time she was waiting for me, ready to go, wearing her jodphurs and her first pair of riding boots, her black gloves already snug on her hands, her helmet resting on her lap. She said her homework was done and her room was clean and could we please get going?

She moved him through his paces, walk, trot, walk, trot, and forced him into the corners where he preferred not to go while I stood on the side and watched for things that might spook him, a blowing plastic trash bag coming on the breeze across the field, a bird that might suddenly fly up and out of the long grass, anything at all. But the ring was still and no birds flew and the grass rustled but nothing came across the pasture, not even leaves. I breathed and watched her ride and felt myself settle a little. She had a crop and when he didn't do what she asked of him, she put it to him and got his attention and he did as he was told. But he didn't move easily from walk to trot, and he didn't move easily back to walk again, and he fought her at the corners, and he fought her when she changed directions, and he fought her when she asked him to halt. His eyes rolled and popped a little whenever she gave him directions, and he blew and flattened his ears. So she held him and finally he stood still; she sat back hard with a grim look on her face. After a time, she leaned forward and said something to him and he pricked his ears forward and she patted him on the neck and then gently tapped him with her heels and he set off at a walk.

Over the black trees beyond the pond, a lone hawk sailed on a long open span of air and I watched it rise and lower on outstretched wings and then rise and lower again, not flying by intention but being taken by the wind in ever-widening circles until it was gone into the horizon.

Haley took Lightning to a trot and when he was trotting well

and she had him in the far corner, she put her leg to him and
asked him for a canter. This was a gait that was new to her and
one that she and Lightning were trying to learn together. When
she squeezed him, he turned his body halfway sideways as if to
look back at her and then straightened himself out and flung himself forward just as he put his head down and arched his back. She
sat hard and hauled on the reins and her body slipped to one side
and she stuck and stayed on and then he stopped and breathed
plumes of smoke and I saw the bluish white of his eye and his flat
ears. Then Haley put her heel to him and hit him with the crop
and said, "Canter." I watched with my stomach dropping while
Lightning put his head down and bucked again and Haley lost
her balance. She lost her stirrups and grabbed his mane and he
could feel her dislodged and in that felt proud of himself, for he
stopped again. She sat for a longer time this time and then found
her stirrups and shortened her reins and pressed him forward into
a walk. When he had come down the long side of the ring, she
asked him to trot. He shuffled along and tossed his head and she
kept him at an even pace until she got to the far corner and then
she called for a canter again and whipped him with the crop. I
stopped breathing. He took three steps in canter and then threw
his head down and flung it up again and bucked in four short
hops. She held him and held him and did not come off, but when
he finally stopped and stood blowing under the afternoon sky,
she swung her leg over and jumped down. She ran her stirrups
up and took him by the bridle and then yelled to me to open the
gate. She passed me and I could see that she'd been crying and
her mouth was set in a line as straight as a hyphen and she didn't
look at me as she led him through the gate. "I hate Lightning,"
she said fiercely.

"I'm sure you do," I said, even though I knew she couldn't hear me.

But she never quit riding, not even the difficult horses. It was as if her struggle to control them stood in for something bigger that Haley had yet to master, a road she felt herself to be on, and often alone. In the beginning, it was all she could do to get on. As time passed, her voice grew clear and strong when she gave commands and she rode hard over high jumps, and the horses turned to her hand and felt her on their backs as someone who knew she was in charge.

ONE MONDAY EVENING I wheeled the trash barrel out to the curb. I walked back over the grass to pick up the blue plastic recycling tub and put it down in the gutter next to the trash barrel and then stood at the top of the driveway and looked back at the garden I'd planted with Chase and Haley, the cherry tree and the redbud and the candy lilies Chase had picked out, and Haley's iris and the dry brown bones of the butterfly bush that in summer sent purple blooms like fat tubers out at the end of its branches, and the roses that in winter were still green but green as if green could hibernate and turn with the seasons into sleep. The front windows behind the garden were warm yellow squares and the front door stood open where I'd left it, with only the glass of the storm door between the view of our front hallway and the sofa in the living room beyond and me. Anyone who passed by and looked inside would see what I saw, the back of a chair, a lamp, a picture on the far wall. That passerby would see something that looked entirely quiet, entirely serene, as if nothing about us were different, as if nothing in this family had been disrupted to the core. I walked down the driveway and leaned against the hood of my old blue car and turned my face up to the stars. There was no moon that night and the stars were bright and filled me with the idea of hope. I watched them for a while, and watched the spaciousness of the

sky and the distance between light and here, and then a plane
came along, high above me, and made its way below the galaxies,
its lights blinking softly as if to signal that it was of this world and
no other, just as I seemed to be, and I breathed and breathed and
said to no one at all, or no one to whom I had ever spoken before,
"Help him. Please. Help him."

IN THE FIRST WEEK of June, Dr. B called me at work and
told me that he'd had the last conversation he was able to have
with the representative of my insurance company and they had
decided that Chase no longer required acute care and should be
discharged from the hospital to another care facility immediately.
Today. Tomorrow morning at the latest. Dr. B had argued that
no such facility had been identified but he explained that he really didn't have a leg to stand on, for Five South was not in the
business of providing long-term care and he knew the insurance
company would not go for it. Not surprisingly, they hadn't, just
as they had not gone for the description of Chase's symptoms or
his need for medical management or the fact that he still thought
he was a rock-and-roll singer who had himself long since abandoned his band to go do political work of an unspecified nature in
the jungles of Central America. Dr. B had explained that we still
didn't know if the Clozaril was going to have any beneficial effect
but he'd been forced to agree that there was nothing left to try,
that Chase was on the drug of last resort, and if it didn't work, it
remained the case that he'd need long-term care somewhere else.
The insurance company representative was unmoved by the argument that long-term care for someone acutely psychotic did not
seem to exist and Dr. B wasn't able to make the argument that his
unit should provide it in the absence of other possibilities. He'd
tried to make the case that Chase continued to be unstable and

in need of crisis-level care, but the insurance company made an alternate determination. Chase, in their view, still needed care, but not care at the acute level.

"What do I do?" I asked Dr. B.

"You have the right to appeal this decision," he said. "But you should be aware that the meter is running while you wait for the results of the appeal, and if the appeal is unsuccessful, you'll be financially responsible for every single day Chase remains in the hospital until that decision is reached. They have a procedure they follow," he said, "and I don't think they'll hear the appeal for forty-five days."

"I want to file an appeal," I said. Then I said, "How can this be? What do they expect us to do?"

"He'll have to move to John Umstead Hospital," said Dr. B. "That's a state hospital. They'll have to take him."

I waited but he didn't say anything more. I felt the words *John Umstead* reverberate through me. No one had mentioned the possibility of the big state hospital in Butner before. No one had prepared me for the fact that this could happen to Chase.

"How can they do this?"

Dr. B cleared his throat. "Because they can," he said. "This is how the system works. All you can do is appeal."

"How will we move him?" I asked at last. "Do you expect me to drive him?" I turned the phone cord between my fingers and looked out of my office window across the green lawn of the university. A car screeched its brakes on the road. People walked up and down in front of stores as if this were an ordinary day.

Finally Dr. B said, "Usually, the patient will be transported by the sheriff's office. He'll be handcuffed and they'll take him down and out through the ambulance bay."

"No," I said. "We can't do that."

"They're trained to deal with people who might need to be restrained," said Dr. B.

"Chase is not a criminal," I said.

"It's the usual way," Dr. B said.

"But Chase is terrified of death squads and executioners. He thinks he's in a concentration camp and government agents are out to get him," I said.

Dr. B was silent for a time. Then he said, "We might be able to get an ambulance to take him. You'll have to pay for it. Your insurance company probably won't see it as medically necessary."

"That will be better," I said.

"You should get a letter by certified mail today or tomorrow. It will tell you that Chase's care has been decertified and that the insurance company will no longer pay. They'll give you the exact time you will become the responsible party. Chase needs to be moved by that time. It will probably be tomorrow. We'll start the transport paperwork here today."

"How are we going to prepare him?"

"I don't know that we can prepare him."

"Do you want to tell him or should I?" I said.

"We'll tell him," he said. "One of the nurses will start talking about it with him this afternoon."

I nodded and then realized he couldn't see me. "Okay," I said. "I'll be there."

I CALLED JIM at Murdoch Center and explained that Chase was about to be moved to John Umstead. I said that he needed a bed right away. Jim said Chase hadn't yet been approved for admission. Even if he had been accepted, they had no way of securing a bed for him. There were twelve beds on the unit and someone who needed to be in one filled each of those beds right now.

"Isn't there something that could be turned into a bed?" I said. "How about that observation room at the front of the unit? It has a bed and a dresser."

Jim sighed. "That's a therapeutically necessary room," he said. "We use that in the event that someone is suicidal or needs twenty-four-hour observation. It makes it possible for us to keep from sending people back to the hospital. We don't use it a lot," he said, "but we need to have it available at all times."

"Let's say Chase is approved," I said. "Where does he fall on your waiting list?"

"Our waiting list?" said Jim. "Well," he said. "Right now, today, Chase is pretty much it. When there's a bed, he'll be first in line for it."

"What should I do?" I said.

Jim waited. I listened to him wait.

At last he said I should call the man who oversees all the hospitals and care facilities for the state division of health and human services. He named him and told me he worked in Raleigh and then said, "You understand? He's not only responsible for the developmental-disability sites but also runs the mental-health facilities and the substance-abuse facilities and the system of group homes and area mental-health units. If anyone knows of a facility that can take Chase, he'd be the one."

He rustled something on the other end of the line. "Here's his number," he said.

I couldn't get through but left a message explaining Chase's situation. The woman who answered the phone listened and wrote things down and asked questions so I knew she was trying to get the story straight. When I hung up, I called Linda, who had gone with me to see the PATH program in the winter; I asked her if she had any new ideas about where we could take Chase. She said she'd been working on nothing else ever since she got word that Chase was to be released from the hospital but that nothing new had emerged. "I just don't know what to tell you," she said. Then she said it again.

"Who else can I call?"

She considered this for a minute. "Unless you call Raleigh, I don't know what else to tell you to do."

"I already did that," I said.

"What?" she said. "You called the head of the division?"

"This afternoon," I said.

"That was mighty bold."

I blinked. "Was that wrong?" I said. "I don't know what else to do. Not unless you know how to help me."

"No no," she said. "Don't get me wrong. That was a good thing to do. But boy. I don't know too many parents who would just pick up the phone and call that man."

"It's his job, isn't it?" I said.

Linda laughed. "Well," she said, "yes. I guess it is his job."

SEVERAL DAYS EARLIER, I'd gotten a call from the guidance counselor at the middle school. She told me that she and Haley's teachers had met; they'd looked at her progress over the course of the year and decided that she was in real danger of failing sixth grade. We needed to meet. So that afternoon I went to Haley's school. I was the first one to the conference room and I sat on the far side of the table and waited for Haley's teachers to arrive. The bell rang and the hallway outside the guidance office filled with kids who bumped along and talked and jostled and walked away. I drummed my fingers on the table and then sat back and stopped drumming. There were drawings pinned to the bulletin boards of children with smiling faces, blue paper with red

Magic Marker, or green paper with black ink. The hallway grew louder and then stilled and then there were no children anywhere except for a girl who sat on a chair with her earth science book on her lap.

Haley's math teacher was the first to arrive, and then her guidance counselor from the elementary school, who'd come over to explain to the middle school what she'd seen in Haley in the past. The exceptional children's coordinator came next, and Haley's current guidance counselor, and then her language arts teacher and her science teacher.

"We're here to talk about Haley's academic progress," said the current guidance counselor. "I think we all agree that Haley isn't achieving to potential. Or do we need to discuss that?"

The math teacher shook his head. "I think that's accurate," he said. "I see a smart girl who isn't doing well, mostly because she doesn't turn her homework in or doesn't keep track of assignments or doesn't seem to be paying attention in class. Is that what the rest of you see?"

The language arts teacher and the science teacher nodded.

"It's hard to understand," the science teacher said. "She'll be going along fine and then all of a sudden, she'll stop doing her work."

"Haley does her work," I said. "I see her homework."

"Do you check it every night?"

I shook my head. "I used to do that but when it was always done, I decided I didn't need to check it as often."

"Maybe you need to start checking it again," the language arts teacher said.

"I can see that it's done," I said.

"It's not getting turned in," said the math teacher. "She might be doing it. We just never see it."

"Is there some strategy we can use to help her remember to turn it in?" I said hopefully. "Something that happens the same way in each of her classes that we can agree on today?"

The math teacher looked uncomfortable. "I don't know what that would be."

"I don't know. Some sort of system? A reminder? A note on the board that she looks for?"

The language arts teacher frowned. "I can't do that," she said.

The math teacher shook his head. "The problem is," he said, "if we did that for Haley, we'd have to do it for all of the kids in the classroom. And we've got twenty-six kids and just can't do something special for everyone."

"If you put a note on the board, where everyone could see it, then maybe everyone would benefit from it. It wouldn't have to be something special for Haley. It could be something for all of the kids."

"That's just not going to happen," said the math teacher.

"But what have you done to help her be more successful in your classes?"

The language arts teacher looked down at a piece of paper in front of her and began to read items that sounded like they'd come from a college textbook on how to teach. "We look for ways to increase her ownership of her own education," she read. "We seat her in close proximity to the teacher's desk. We seek to bolster her self-esteem."

"How?"

The teacher looked uncomfortable.

"I just wondered if you could give me a specific example," I said.

No one spoke.

Haley's elementary school guidance counselor looked carefully at the wall behind the teachers' heads. "This isn't the first time Haley's had academic difficulties," she said. "When she was in elementary school, she had difficulty paying attention and staying on task and getting some of the bigger projects done that she needed to get done. Do you remember?" she said and looked at me. "We all thought that it was because of her brother and once you got things with her brother sorted out, things would be easier for her. But it doesn't sound like that's happened. I wonder if maybe we might have missed something."

The middle school guidance counselor looked at me. "Did Haley's brother go here?"

"Chase," I said. "Do you know him?"

The guidance counselor blanched and recovered. "Of course I knew him," she said. "We all knew him. How's he doing? He had that terrible injury and he didn't really come back to school after that, did he?"

"He came back for a few weeks in the fall but then he was admitted to the hospital and he's still there," I said.

"He's still there? Is it the neck injury still?"

"No," I said. "He had a psychotic break and he isn't really getting better."

The room was still. The chairs outside in the hallway were empty now and the secretary pushed back from her desk and stood up and walked over to a revolving rack with slots behind plastic windows for pamphlets and began to sort fresh copies into the different slots.

"It's safe to say that Haley's been under a lot of stress for the last few years," the elementary school guidance counselor said. "She's really a great kid and she's had to cope with an awful lot. There was a divorce and a move and her brother's disabilities, which have been significant and ongoing. It sounds like we might be better off getting her tested now, just to make sure nothing fell through the cracks. These things you see in class might be stress related. But what if they're not?"

"We can test her or you can test her," said the middle school guidance counselor. "If we test her, you'll have to wait until fall, since there won't be any way to get this on the school psychologist's schedule between now and the first week in June. If you test her, maybe you can get it done over the summer and we can come back for a meeting in the fall and work on developing a concrete plan, if that's what we need to do."

"And in the meantime?" I said.

"You should check her homework and we will sign her planner to make sure she's got her assignments written down. But it's going to be up to you to make sure that the work gets turned in. Otherwise, she's going to fail sixth grade."

AFTER DINNER, HALEY picked up the dishes from the table and I stood at the sink and rinsed them before putting them in the dishwasher. She stood at the end of the counter and watched me and then crossed behind me to the old green wicker chair and sat down and crossed her arms over her waist.

"Can we play cards when you're done?" she said.

I nodded. "What do you want to play?"

"Rummy."

"Oh, god," I said. "You'll have to teach me again."

"It's easy."

"I know. I just can't remember how it goes."

"I'll show you."

"Did you do your homework?"

"Yes."

"Are you sure?"

"I did it," she said and looked away from me.

"What was it?"

"Math and language arts."

"But what did you have to do?"

"I had to read for my reading journal and then do a worksheet."

"Can I see?"

Her face closed. "Fine," she said. She pushed one foot out in front of her and frowned at her arms. "Can I ask you something?"

I nodded.

She studied the floor and picked at a piece of loose wicker under the chair arm.

"Don't do that," I said.

"What?"

"You'll break the chair."

"It's already broken."

"I know," I said. "But more. You'll break it more."

She stopped snapping the loose wicker and shifted in her seat and the chair creaked. I wiped the pan I'd cooked the chicken in and then folded the dish towel over the edge of the sink. The refrigerator hummed behind me.

"How come you stayed home from work with Chase when he came home from the hospital but you didn't stay home with me when I was sick?"

The winter before, Haley had been home with something that looked like the flu and later looked like mono and finally had no name. It took her six weeks to feel better.

"Because I couldn't," I said. "I wanted to but I couldn't."

"Why not?"

"I only get so many days off from work and I'd used them all up when you got sick," I said.

"That's stupid."

"But it's the way it works," I said. "If I took more days than that off, they wouldn't have paid me."

She looked away from me.

"I did the best I could," I said. "I went to work late and I came home at lunchtime every day. I know it wasn't enough but it was all I could do. And I'm sorry that that was all I could do. I wish things were different. You have no idea how much I wish things were different. But they aren't. I have to go to work and earn a living and I can't be everywhere everyone needs me to be at once. But I am sorry. I wish I could have been with you every day. Do you understand?"

She shrugged.

"Haley," I said. "I love you and I never want anything bad to happen to you."

"I liked it better when Chase was here."

"I know," I said. "Me, too."

When the man from Raleigh called, it was nearly ten and Haley had gone to bed. I was sitting in the half dark of the living room telling myself that I could read a book if I just paid a little more attention to it. The house was still and cool. I had the windows open, for it was early June and the nights could still be mild and pleasant. The telephone sliced through the quiet.

He introduced himself in a huge voice and asked me if I was the parent of the boy who was about to be released from Memorial. When I said I was, he asked how I expected him to help me. I asked him if there wasn't something his office could do to find a place for Chase to go.

"Already done," he yelled into the phone. "He's going to John Umstead Hospital tomorrow. I arranged for the transfer myself."

"Chase has developmental disabilities," I said. "I don't believe that John Umstead Hospital can or should provide long-term care for him."

"This is what we do," he said loudly.

"I might be wrong about this," I said, "but haven't there been lawsuits about housing people with developmental disabilities in state psychiatric hospitals? Isn't it against the law?"

"In these circumstances, it's understood that we will provide the best possible care for your son while we continue to work to identify an appropriate placement for him," he yelled. "What does your area mental-health unit say about this?"

"They've been working on this since Chase first went into the hospital. They haven't been able to identify an appropriate placement," I said.

"Have you even been to any facilities?" he shouted.

"There are only two places in the entire state where the operators were willing to consider Chase. I visited one and she rejected the application as soon as she got it, telling me that Chase is too complex and too much in need of services for her to be able to take him. The other unit told me they would reject Chase if he applied. They suggested that we make an application to the BART unit and we did that, but the BART unit has no beds."

"What office do you work with?"

"Orange-Person-Chatham," I replied.

"And they haven't been able to do better than this? It's up to them to find a place for him."

"They can't find what doesn't exist," I said. "I feel confident that they've given it every effort. I'm turning to you because we've come up empty, Chase still needs care, and he's about to be released from Memorial without a place to go."

"He's going to Umstead," the man shouted. "I said that already."

"Umstead is not an appropriate placement for him," I said. "You know that as well as I do."

"It's intended for the short-term," he said.

"I don't see how it will be short-term if the state doesn't have facilities to offer him."

He sighed. "Chase is an outlier," he said. "You can't expect the system to work easily or well for an outlier case."

"I'm very concerned about his placement at John Umstead Hospital because the hospital doesn't treat children with developmental disabilities," I said.

"You say the BART people would take him if they had a bed?"

"That's what I understand."

"How about this, then?" he said. "Let's get your son over to Umstead and then have the BART people consult on his care over there. Come over, put treatment plans in place, whatever will be most helpful. If they're on the ground, day one, is that going to do it for you?"

"Do you have any other suggestions?"

"Look," he yelled, "look. Of course we're going to keep searching for a place for him that would be better long-term. And a bed is supposed to come available at BART at some point in the next year. In the meantime, let's get him settled at Umstead and then get the Murdoch people over there and go from there."

When we hung up, I stood in the kitchen and rubbed my eyes with my fists. Behind my lids, I saw stars and universes and whole galaxies explode.

THE NEXT DAY, the staff got together and decided to throw Chase a going-away party with pizza and cake. One of the residents took Polaroids of all of the nurses and therapists and glued the pictures to sheets of construction paper. Each person wrote something to Chase on his or her page and the resident bound the pages together with yarn from the arts-and-crafts supply box. When I got there, the nurses were sitting at the table in the dayroom where everyone ate lunch and Chase paced in front of the nurses' station. He had cake on his shirt. The chief nurse pulled a slice of pizza out of the wax paper–lined box and tried to hand it to me; when I said no, she put the slice down and cut a slab of cake and put it on a paper plate ringed with pictures of flowers and balloons. I shook my head.

"Well," she said, "sit down anyway."

The nurses told stories about Chase just as if he could understand them; one told me how he'd nicknamed Chase "Manhattan" because Chase always talked about moving to New York City and having a penthouse apartment in the sky. This nurse was called Big Butchie and had grown up in upstate New York several hours from the town where we had lived when Chase was young; we both commented on the snow and the cold. He'd given Chase a small stuffed mouse to keep in his pocket and had named the mouse Little Butchie for him. "Just in case he gets scared," he told me. "You understand."

"The thing about Chase," Sam said, "is that he's so cool. He's like the arbiter of cool. Like he pays attention to cool and nothing else. Was he always like that?"

I nodded. "Always," I said.

Chase walked past the table in the dayroom and turned away from us into his room. He stood at the window with his back to us. Dr. B handed me a clipboard with a form clamped on it and pointed to the lines where I would have to sign. He tore off the bottom copy and handed it to me.

Sam had pulled Chase's clothes out of his storage closet and packed them in plastic bags with drawstring tops that had the hospital name stamped on the side, and the words *Patient Belongings*. These were lined up in a neat row behind the nurses' station.

"I don't know when the ambulance is scheduled," said Dr. B. "This afternoon, I think."

Sam looked at his watch. "We just called them and they're supposed to be on their way."

"How will this work?" I said.

"When they get here, we'll take him out through the ambulance bay. We have enough staff to escort him downstairs," said Sam. "And we gave him some Thorazine and some Ativan, to help him stay calm."

He explained that I should take Chase's things down to my car and then bring the car around to the ambulance bay and meet us there. He called for a cart and said he'd go with me and wait by the hospital front door with Chase's bags while I brought the car around. After that, I needed to go directly to the ambulance bay so I could follow the ambulance up to Butner.

Someone said something and Dr. B looked at me and said, "Are you ready?" Then he said, "That was the ambulance driver. He says they're about fifteen to twenty minutes out."

The orderly with the cart buzzed at the front door and the nurse buzzed him in. She was eating a slice of cake behind the nurses' station. I thanked Dr. B and he smiled and said, "I wish we could have done more. It's been a difficult case. I wish we'd had a better outcome."

We shook hands and I looked over his shoulder at Chase, who stood with his back to us and stared out the window.

"Does he know he's going?"

"Yes," said Dr. B. "We had the party for him and he seemed to understand."

Sam had loaded the cart with Chase's bags and was waiting by the front door. "Are you ready?" he asked.

Downstairs, I got the car and paid the parking attendant and drove up to Neurosciences and Sam helped me load the bags into the trunk. "I think I got everything," he said. "You can call and tell me if anything's missing."

I looked at the clothes and jacket and papers and art projects done by other people with Chase's scrawl on them and the big pillow from his bed and the extra blankets and finally found his bear and reached in and pulled it out.

"You know where the ambulances come in," said Sam. "Right?" He looked at me.

"Around the back."

"You just drive over there and we'll bring him down."

I nodded.

"Good luck with everything," said Sam.

"Okay," I said. "Thank you."

I waited in the car after I parked. Two ambulances stood in the bay. The one farthest away was empty and being readied to leave and two paramedics tossed things in the back and one stepped up on the bumper and looked at something inside and then dropped to the pavement and pulled the doors shut. The ambulance closer to me had both of its rear doors open and the driver stood by the passenger-side door and spoke to someone on his cell phone. When he was finished, he snapped the phone shut and put it in his shirt pocket. I got out of my car and walked over to the ambulance and stood there with my arms folded across my chest and waited. The air smelled of exhaust. When the breeze came up, you could smell the hot grease from the Wendy's inside the hospital. I watched the paramedics in the ambulance step down from the back of the vehicle and watch the hospital doors with great attention. One of them turned to me and said, "Are you the mother?"

I nodded.

"It'll take us about forty-five minutes to get there," she said.

One of the nurses from Five South walked up to me from behind and called my name. She was carrying a case of chocolate Boost. "We thought we should send this with him," she said. "It's paid for and we don't need it for anyone else." She followed me to my car, where I took the Boost from her and slid the case onto the backseat.

"Well," she said, "good luck to you."

"Did you see Chase?" I asked. "How is he doing?"

She looked past me and worked at a smile. "Don't worry," she said. "They're bringing him down. They had to get a few extra people to help but I think it's going fine now."

I walked up and down in front of the hospital doors and then went to stand by the doors where gurneys are pushed through in an emergency. I could see the back hall of the emergency room, its pale walls, its yellow light. Behind me, the ambulance driver answered the staticky sound of his dispatcher and then hopped out of the ambulance cab and leaned against the door.

Someone was screaming and then they were through the doors, six of them surrounding Chase with their hands on his arms and shoulders and waist, and Chase was thrashing and turning and screaming the same thing over and over again. "I didn't do anything wrong, I didn't do anything wrong, I didn't do anything wrong." He flailed blindly at the men who surrounded him, throwing his fists and kicking out and the men stepped neatly backward to avoid his blows and at the same time kept their hands on him and called to one another to look out, look out. And someone called his name and I saw that these were not just men but that Sam was among them and Big Butchie and the young resident who always called Chase "Dude" and two of the male nurses from Five South and then a man I didn't know at all but who wore a hospital security uniform. Six of them in all and in the middle

Chase turning and pummeling the air and screaming finally, "No! No! No! No!"

I turned away when they tried to wrestle him into the ambulance, turned and leaned over and sobbed, and the young resident came over while the others banged and clattered and yelled and said things like, Hold him, easy now, steady, and then Sam said that he'd ride up with him and he got in the ambulance first, and after that Chase screamed and screamed without words and I bent and wept and the doctor put his arm around me and said, "It's okay, it's not that bad, I've seen worse, it's okay." I looked at him, at his flat white face and his frightened eyes and yet I allowed myself to be comforted, although there was no comfort in that moment and there is none in the remembering.

I FOLLOWED THE AMBULANCE up I-85 through Durham and then north across Falls Lake, and then down through the center of Butner, where there was a firehouse and a public safety office, a store that sold hunting gear, a bank, two gas stations—one out of business—and a public park where rusty iron picnic grills studded the weedy lawn. Sometimes I could see Sam in the ambulance's rear window. I could not see Chase. When we got to John Umstead Hospital, we turned onto a service road that ran up to a set of double doors at the rear of a newer building marked Admissions. Beyond it were the residents' units, red brick buildings that looked like barracks. I parked behind and tried to follow Chase inside but a nurse stopped me at the door and said, "You need to park your car out front and we'll call you when we're ready."

I asked to see him. I explained that he was very frightened. I held his bear in front of me. "I need to give him this," I said.

The nurse looked doubtful. "Just for a minute, then," she said. I followed her inside.

Chase shuffled around a small hallway, his face white and haunted. I walked up to him. "I've got your bear," I said. "Here's Brown Bear."

He took it and stared at me and then began to chew on the bear's nose.

The nurse came up to me and told me I needed to wait outside until they decided whether or not they would admit Chase.

"It's a transfer," I said. "That's already been decided."

She looked at her clipboard. "I have no record of that," she said, "so our doctor is going to have to take a look at him."

"I spoke to Raleigh yesterday," I said. "They assured me that Chase would be taken here and we'd get people from Murdoch Center over here right away."

The nurse looked skeptical. "Our doctor needs to decide," she repeated. "There's a family waiting area out front that you can use after you park your car. Be sure to park in the visitor spaces in the lot across the street."

Chase chewed on his bear and stared at me.

"It's okay," I said. "It's all right. You'll be okay."

His hair was still long and it fell in deep bangs over his eyes. His orange shirt was stained with cake. He was wearing his dirty black parachute pants. He stared at me and chewed on his stuffed bear and didn't say anything at all.

I waited in the family waiting room. A woman behind a glass window pointed me to the chairs. I was alone at first but after a while a man came in and sat down in a chair near mine and stared at the wall in front of him. A brown wooden door at the rear of the waiting room opened and two women appeared, a young one and an older one; the young one moved slowly as if in a trance and the older one was telling her that her father had just gone to get the car and he would pick them up out front. The woman behind the glass called to them and waved. "Have a good break, Niki," she yelled. "See you tomorrow." When they were gone, I waited near the man who stared at the wall and tried to look at the ragged magazine in my lap. *Field and Stream.* 1997. I stood up and walked over to the magazine rack and examined the contents and then picked out a *Good Housekeeping* from 2001 and brought it back to my seat. It was a holiday issue and there were many articles explaining crafts the whole family could make or cookies by the dozen that you and your kids could bake together. There were photos of children smiling next to grinning parents. There was a long article about how to obtain a Christmas miracle and I tried to read that. The first paragraph was confusing so I tried again.

"She's going to do better this time," the man near me said and I looked up.

"She's been out for almost a year but we were planning our wedding and it must have got to be a little too stressful for her so she's back for a tune-up," he said. He looked at me this time so I knew he was talking to me.

I nodded, once, and turned back to my magazine.

"It's nothing shameful," he said. "You got someone here?"

I nodded again.

"It's all of us in this boat together, trying to take care of these people we love. Mine's is okay most of the time. Mine's just needs a little help now and then." He spoke evenly, as if this were not a big deal. "She's got to look after the house and maybe that's too much for her. I don't know. I might could do some more for her."

He waited for me to tell my story. Finally he said, "Is it your husband?"

"No," I said. I studied the magazine in my lap.

"Is it your mother?"

I stood up and crossed the room and sat in a chair where I could see the front door. No cars passed on the road out front. The man who'd been looking at the wall stood up and went outside and smoked a cigarette, leaning his weight on the foot he propped on a planter full of red geraniums. The woman behind the glass window answered the phone. I paged through my magazine. When I got to the last page, I closed it and left it lying in my lap for a moment and then flipped open to the first page and started again.

When I looked up, the man was gone. I looked around the empty room and tried to hear any sound that might be coming from the room I couldn't see, where Chase was waiting with the doctor. I stood up and walked over to the front door and stepped outside and looked at the sky. The clouds were the color of dust. It was late afternoon by now and the breeze that blew through the ambulance bay had died down. I watched a red pickup truck make its way along the road between the hospital and the water treatment plant. It turned in behind the plant and disappeared from view. I pulled the door and walked back into the waiting room and sat down again. I stood up and tried to find another magazine. I looked for a clock but couldn't find one. Then the wooden door at the rear of the room opened and women began to pass through the waiting room on their way to the front door, calling goodnight to the receptionist as they passed, so I knew it must be just about five o'clock. The receptionist came through a door in the wall next to her glassed-in booth and looked at me and said that someone would be with me soon and I should just continue to wait.

"These doors stay open until nine o'clock tonight," she said. "You'll see security come by from time to time to check on things."

After she left, I listened to the telephone answering machine answer the phone but then the calls stopped coming. I tried to read the *Good Housekeeping* again but that was too difficult so I began to thumb through *Field and Stream* and look at pictures of fishing lures and guns. I walked up and down and looked for other magazines and finally settled on a *Reader's Digest,* where I could read little anecdotes of things that were supposed to be funny.

When the doctor came through the brown wooden door at the rear of the waiting room, his wristwatch said six-twenty. He approached me gravely and softly and I stood up to meet him. He shook my hand and introduced himself and said, "We're going to keep your boy."

I nodded.

"Can you tell me—" he said. "How long has he been like this?"

"He's been like this for the last seven-and-a-half months," I said. "He was at UNC Memorial and he was transferred here today when my insurance company didn't think he needed acute care anymore."

"I see," he said.

"His records were supposed to come in with him," I said.

"So they tried various things at Memorial?" he said.

I nodded.

"And nothing worked?" He glanced at his clipboard. "I've got the list here."

I nodded.

"How about the Clozaril?"

"The Clozaril seemed to have some small benefit," I said.

He nodded gravely and looked at his papers and then looked at me.

"We're admitting him to our adolescent acute-care unit," he said. "That's where he'll go tonight. In the morning, the team will meet and decide how best to care for him."

"Can I see him?"

The doctor shook his head. "Not tonight. It'll be best for him if he just goes over and gets settled in. You'll want to come back tomorrow and meet with the social worker. We've already set up an appointment for you. You can see him after that."

"He can't care for himself."

The doctor nodded. "That's why it's a good thing we can take care of him here."

When we were through, he shook my hand and wished me luck and smiled very gently and told me not to worry too much. Outside, the air was still and cool. My car was among the last three or four in the parking lot. I got in and sat behind the wheel and looked at the buildings and looked at the tall chain-link fence around the playground in front of the children's unit and looked at the many windows without light or movement. There was a sign instructing visitors to lock all of their personal belongings in the trunks of their cars and not to bring anything inside and this sign was repeated throughout the parking lot. I looked at the broken gravel at the edge of the crumbling asphalt lot and the old concrete steps leading up to the old glass doors with big metal handles, and at the scrubby bushes that lined the foundation around the front doors of the different buildings and the flat, plain, mown grass, cut to within an inch of its life, and at the long, low field that lay between the hospital and the water treatment plant. Then I turned the car south and headed for home.

TWENTY

||||||||||||||||||||||||||||||||||||

The next day I drove the same highway back to Butner and parked in the same desolate parking lot. I buzzed the doorbell by the front door and then signed in at the front desk, where an assistant sat behind a large sliding-glass window. Outside, a swarm of ladybugs seethed along the brick face of the building. "You can go sit in the waiting area," the assistant said and handed me a tag that said *Visitor.* She looked down at my name. "You need to write the time, too," she said. "Right here."

I wrote the time and then looked blankly around. A hallway bisected the foyer and signs pointed to the Whitaker School to my left. To my right, the hallway disappeared into dimness. Right in front of me, a heavy wooden door with a small window; next to that, a sign: THIS DOOR MUST BE LOCKED AT ALL TIMES. Everywhere I looked, I saw linoleum floors that had been polished to a gleam and old walls with an old paint job.

The assistant glanced back at me. "Just go down that hallway and you'll see some chairs. That's the waiting area."

The hallway was lined with shabby wooden doors, each with a nameplate, each one closed up tight. Staff offices. The space felt airless and dank and there was no sound of any sort. In the waiting area, the chairs were old and battered, with bald patches in the upholstery and greasy spots where heads had lain against the cushions. I heard a door close and the click of footsteps but no one appeared. Then the assistant walked past me on squeaky rubber-soled shoes and smiled and knocked on a door across from me. When no one answered, she returned to the foyer. I sat in the chair with my hands resting on the arms and looked around. The last time I'd been in a state psychiatric institution was in 1975, when I worked at Fountain House and went to visit the boy named Robert, who sat nearly naked in his room, his board-stiff legs drawn up before him.

The very fact of this boy had not occurred to me for almost thirty years. I remembered his catatonia and the unforced cheerfulness of the nurse who stuck our meager bouquet of daisies into a vase and the memory of that vase stopped me, for surely that could not have happened, surely no one could have permitted a glass vase in a room with a boy who had stopped eating, who stared at the wall, whose gown did not have ties or snaps. A vase in the hands of that boy was a weapon or a doorway, depending on your perspective, but either way, it offered a conclusion that surely could not, should not, be borne by the boy or by his parents. For a few minutes, I sat in the chair in the hallway and stared down at the covers of old copies of *Martha Stewart Living* magazine — "Have a Perfect Easter!" "Sixteen New Things to Do with Squash!" — and worried about that boy, who so many years ago may have been in danger, and may have seized an opportunity. I felt my heart race with fear for him and for his family, and even though I knew that decades had passed, that whatever was going to happen had happened long ago, and to another family, to another boy, I thought of that boy's mother and what she must have endured, back in the days when psychiatrists glibly blamed mothers, as if psychiatric illness was a failure of maternal virtue, when nurses may have left glass vases in a patient's room, as if safety was something that fell only within parameters that included snaps and ties.

I heard a door open and close loudly and a brown-haired woman in her fifties appeared in the hallway and said, "You must be Chase's mom?" When I nodded, she strode over to me with her hand outstretched and introduced herself as May, Chase's social worker, and told me we'd go upstairs to fill out the forms and I could see Chase after that.

Behind the heavy wooden door with the sign that said it must be locked at all times, we walked down a long hallway lit by long rows of windows on each side. Because Umstead had been a military facility in the beginning, when they converted it to a hospital they built long halls to connect the buildings and now there were miles of corridors.

"You have to have a staff person with you at all times," May said. "Each door is locked and only a staff person will have keys." She looked at me. "I know it seems shocking," she said. "But it's really in everyone's best interest."

I followed her up the stairs and then down another hallway, past empty areas furnished with the same kinds of chairs I'd seen downstairs. We passed a large room and I could hear shouts inside and the sound of a ball bouncing.

"That's the gym," she said. "We have recreation time there, with staff supervision."

She pointed out the visitors' room and explained that I would see Chase there. I would not be permitted to go onto the unit or to see his room. We turned down another hallway and then stopped at a battered wooden door. Inside, a worn wooden desk and desk chair stood under a single window. An old computer hummed to life when she touched the mouse. But she let the screen go dark again and opened a file on her desk.

"Please," she said. "Sit down here." She gestured at the only other chair in the room, a straight ladder-back chair with a tired cushion tied to its seat. "I'll need you to answer some questions," she said, "and this will take a while. We try to be as thorough as possible here and begin at the very beginning." She reached for her pen. "By the way," she said. "I believe I heard that Chase will be moved today. He's on the adolescent unit but we know that that isn't safe for him. I believe he's going to be moved to the boys' unit, where we keep the ten- to twelve-year-olds. There aren't many kids on that unit now and he will be safe because he is so much bigger than they are."

"He's not safe?" I said. I felt my stomach sink.

"You know, the children we have here often have criminal histories," she said. "This is really the end of the line for them. Often, they've come here in lieu of a jail sentence. They are very street smart, very savvy. Chase is not a member of that population so we believe there is some risk in keeping him with those boys and girls. There are more than twenty-five of them on that unit now and that's too many for him to come into contact with. We saw it last night. We decided he needed to be moved and I believe that's what they're doing now."

"And he'll be safe?"

She looked at me. "The boys on his new unit are younger and smaller. We don't think they'll mess with Chase because he's so much bigger. Plus, they aren't quite as incorrigible as the kids on the adolescent unit. And there are only three of them. This should be a more secure environment for him."

I shook my head. "If he's not safe, he shouldn't be here," I said. "When will the folks from Murdoch be here?"

May said she didn't know what I meant.

"I spoke to Raleigh the night before Chase was transferred here," I said. "They said that Murdoch folks would consult with your staff, create a treatment plan for Chase while we wait on the bed over there."

"I don't know anything about that," said May, "and I've never heard of anything like that happening before. It sounds highly irregular."

"You've had no contact with Raleigh about this?"

"This is the first I've heard of it."

I looked away from her and then looked at her again. "You should know that I want him out of here," I said. "I never wanted him to come here in the first place. I'm appealing the insurance company's decision and I want him transferred back to Memorial."

"Give us a chance," said May. "We do pretty well here."

"I'd like to see where he lives," I said. "I'd like to know how well he's being cared for."

May frowned.

"Look," I said. "These are throwaway kids. You just said so yourself. The end of the line. Criminals. Chase is not a throwaway kid. He's very much loved by his family. No one understands his illness. It's a terrible illness. He hasn't responded to treatment. No one knows what to do. But he is not like the other kids here and we are not like the other families and I will visit him and I will see that his needs are met."

May watched me as I spoke. Her face softened a bit and she turned her pen in her fingers. "I'll see what I can do," she said. "Once he's moved and settled in, maybe you can make a brief visit to his room."

We began before the beginning, with the pregnancy and how much weight I'd gained, and what Chase's father and I had done to make our livings, and only after May was satisfied with those answers did we move to the birth and Chase's early years. She wrote steadily in spaces provided by the forms and I watched her write, her black ballpoint moving slowly across the page.

"All right," she said. "Let's talk about family history." She finished what she was writing and turned the page over and didn't look up while she asked me about my grandmothers and grandfathers, my mother and father, my sisters, the multiple histories of repeating illness that might run through my family, something that might account for Chase.

Then she asked me about Zip and I told her all I knew. She wrote and wrote and wrote as I spoke and I felt the unsteadiness of everything I said. After that, I felt the aching familiarity of everything I said, as if there were things that marked Zip and Chase as father and son, even more than the facts of their eye color or the shape of their heads.

"Did Chase's father abuse Chase?" May asked. She watched me as she spoke.

I thought of Zip's hands on Chase's neck, his hard thumps on Chase's back, that snowy morning in the Midwest. "In my opinion," I said. "Yes."

"And how often does he see Chase now?"

"Not at all," I said. "Hasn't for years."

She paged through her forms until she found the space she was looking for and carefully wrote a few lines. She stopped and lifted the point of the pen from the page and looked out the window.

"So we have breast cancer and high blood pressure and diabetes," she said, "but no one has neurological problems?"

I shook my head.

She turned the pages back until she found the family history space and wrote something next to a small box that she also checked.

Outside, the sun brightened suddenly, as if it had come out from behind a cloud, and then darkened again. Down the hall, a phone rang and rang and rang and then went still.

"Anything else?" said May.

I shook my head. "I can't think of anything," I said.

She wrote for a while, then turned her form over and continued writing. When she stopped, she paged past two more forms and pinched several pages between her thumb and her forefinger. "These are financial forms," she said, and passed them to me. "They explain that you are responsible for paying for Chase if his Medicaid plan doesn't pay. Sign at the bottom. There. And there." She pointed to another line. "Date it."

When I had signed everything I needed to sign she turned to a thick stack of papers stapled together. She handed these to me. "This is our handbook," she said. "It explains something about us and gives you all the rules about the unit."

SHE LED ME BACK down the long hallway and we turned the corner and walked past the gym. She stopped in front of a wooden door with a window high above the doorknob.

"You can see Chase now," she said, and pulled out her keys and unlocked the door. "Just go inside and wait. Someone will bring him around." She held the door with her foot while she spoke to me and watched me walk inside. "This door will lock behind you," she said.

The room was furnished with a brown vinyl sofa, a brown vinyl chair, a wire-frame chair with a black plastic seat, a wobbly table, a wastebasket, and a telephone on top of a dog-eared directory. Two windows looked out over the parking lot at the rear of the children's unit, where cars lined up on the broken asphalt. Old green paint on the walls. Old brown linoleum floors. I sat on one of the chairs and then stood up and walked over and looked out the window. The windows were made of thick glass and the glass encased wire mesh. There was a noise in the hallway and a single file line of adolescent boys bumped and jostled by the window. I watched them but none tried to look my way.

I sat down again and waited. It was a big place that you would expect to find full of sounds but it was mostly quiet. I could hear the sound of the air-conditioning system as it put out lukewarm air. I rolled the tips of my fingers on the arms of my chair and then stopped. When I crossed or recrossed my legs, the vinyl on the chair squawked. I sat down and then stood up and walked around again and then sat down and was sitting when someone came to the door with a set of rattling keys and I heard the bolt slide back in the lock. Chase followed the nurse into the room. He wore blue hospital pajamas. The nurse sat on the wire-frame chair and flipped open a file and looked at her watch and then made a note on the page in front of her.

"Chase," I said softly. "Hey Chase."

He didn't look at me but paced up and down in front of me. He was talking under his breath, grimacing and sighing and pointing to unseen things. The blue pajamas sagged around his waist and his hands were dirty. He walked around the room as if he were the only one in it.

"Would you like to sit down? Chase?"

He stalked the room in front of me. The room wasn't large so he could only take five steps before he had to turn and then take five steps back to the opposite wall. He tapped his chest and then his thigh as he paced, and then fired lasers. He didn't look at me or at the nurse. He paced and paused to strike a strange pose and then paced again. Then he crossed to where I was sitting and tried to kick me. I ducked away and stood up. The nurse jumped to her feet and opened the door that led back to the ward.

"Visit's over," she said.

Chase stalked through the door. The nurse looked back over

her shoulder at me. "I'll see that he's in his room and then come and let you out," she said.

"Can I walk with him to his room?"

"Against the rules," the nurse said. The door closed behind her.

WHEN I GOT HOME, I took off my good clothes and put on a pair of old paint-splattered shorts and a paint-splattered T-shirt. I lay newspaper on the floor in the hallway and taped off the baseboards and the door frames with blue painter's tape. I backed the screws out of the switch plates with an old screwdriver.

I pried open a bucket of paint with a church key and then stirred it until the color was true. I carried the bucket into the hallway and set it on top of some doubled layers of newspaper and took a brush and began to cut in around the doorway and the taped-off moldings. The hallway was the last room in the house due for a new coat of paint. After I'd painted Chase's room, I'd decided that my room needed painting, too, and then the living room, the dining room, Haley's room, the bathrooms. I'd decided we needed to get rid of the old carpet and Haley and I had spent one weekend pulling it up and prying hundreds of carpet staples out of the old subfloor. Haley used the crowbar to jack up the carpet strips along the baseboards and I knelt on the floor with a rubber-handled screwdriver and pulled the tacks. We swept up all of the dirt and Haley came along behind me and drew pictures all over the floor and wrote messages for the men who would come on Monday to lay the new wood floor, encouraging things like, *Keep up the good work!* Or, *Good job! You're almost there!* They got a big kick out of that. I borrowed a friend's truck and we cut the carpet into sections as we pulled it up and then rolled the sections and together hoisted them into the back of the pickup and drove out to the landfill. We lost part of our first load on an empty country highway and had to go back, laughing and moving fast, to pull our old living room carpet off the dark turning road.

I had apparently decided that everything about our house needed to be changed, as if by making a new house I could start us over again, as if I could build health for Chase out of paint cans and new floors. I worked the brush around the door frame and thought about Chase adrift at Umstead, nothing in place, no one talking to one another, until I couldn't stand it anymore. I dropped the brush into the kitchen sink and closed the can of paint and turned the faucet on so water ran over the brush and used the handle of the screwdriver to tap the lid back onto the can. I washed my hands and turned the water off and left the brush to drain and wiped my hands on the tail of my shirt and walked over to my desk, where I'd written some phone numbers on a pad of paper. Squinting, I dialed the last number on the page and got Umstead's medical director on the first try and asked him about the consultation with the Murdoch folks. He explained that he'd just now gotten off the phone with Raleigh and they would get the thing set up. He expected it would take some time, these things normally do, but within a week or two, they should have things in place.

"What are you doing about finding a place for your son?" he asked.

The million-dollar question.

I gave him the short history.

"You know that we aren't equipped to care for children with developmental disabilities," he said. "This is not a desirable place-ment for Chase. We would want a strict time line so we'd know that he was going to be moved along quickly."

"I think you might want to say that to the people in Raleigh," I said.

"My idea was that you would," he said. "It will carry more weight coming from a parent."

"I don't think I have that kind of weight," I said. "But I'll try."

"And I'll send them an e-mail this afternoon detailing our concerns," the medical director said. "I'll tell them in no uncertain terms that an appropriate placement for Chase must be identified. It's in everyone's best interests to have him moved as quickly as possible."

WHEN I SPOKE TO the man in Raleigh the next morning, he told me that he had said all he was going to say in our first conversation and he was going to have me speak to a customer-service representative for the division. From now on, I must direct all of my calls to him. He was the only one who would be able to help me, for he was an advocate for the customers of the system and would know the process I needed to follow.

The line went to Muzak and then someone picked up the phone and said, "Leonard Button." He had a youthful, eager voice but he let me know that he'd been doing this work for twenty-five years and had two grown children and a PhD in anthropology. He said he'd been fully briefed on Chase's situation the day before and was in possession of the e-mail from Umstead's medical director and he felt he knew the whole picture well. He asked me about the area mental-health unit. He wanted to know what they'd done to locate a placement.

"It's really up to them," he said. "They're the ones who need to step up to the plate. What's your local unit again?"

"Orange-Person-Chatham," I said.

"It's surprising. They're one of our best. I'd think if anyone would be able to help, they would."

"I don't think they can help because the kind of facility that Chase needs doesn't seem to exist."

"Come now," he said. "Tell me the places you've sent in applications."

I listed them. "Most places won't take an application from us," I said. "Once they hear about Chase."

"They just need to get a little bit creative," he said. "They just need to put their heads together some more."

I told him about the joint meetings between the developmental-disability and mental-health staff; I described the trip to Jacksonville and the director of that facility's flat rejection of Chase, the way she'd flipped through the application and immediately said no; I explained that PATH had turned us down and that BART had no bed for him.

"I think it's the state's responsibility to provide a bed for him at the facility that's been identified as the only facility in the state for him," I said.

Leonard deflected that opinion. "I think you'd better call up your local worker and give her what for," he said. "I think that's the place for you to start."

"You'll forgive me for saying so," I said, "but I don't see that as the most productive way to resolve this. The area unit has done all that it can do. That's why I called your boss in the first place. It seems to me, if he can't solve it, and you can't solve it, that the next place for me to call is not the people who work for you."

"Now, now," Leonard said in an unctuous voice. "Now, now. What we've got to do is give this thing a little time. Lawyers aren't usually the best way to resolve things."

"I'm not talking about an attorney," I snapped. "But I would like to know how much more time you'd like me to give this. Chase was in Memorial for seven-and-a-half months. During that time, no placement appeared. He should not be at Umstead and yet he's there. The hospital medical director doesn't want him there. I don't want him there. The state doesn't want him there, because it's illegal to house him there. How long do you want me to wait for a placement given these conditions?"

"I think you should call me whenever you have concerns," Leonard said. "I think that's the best thing for now. Call up your area unit and see what they can do for you and then call me if you don't think you're getting anywhere."

YOU MIGHT THINK that the man who told me these things would have a hard time looking at himself in the mirror. I hope he does. But he is not the problem. Our profound unwillingness to care for those among us who cannot care for themselves: that's the problem. Our entrenched blindness about illnesses of the brain: that's the problem. The fact that we share these beliefs and assumptions in untested and misinformed ways, that before Chase I shared them, that you share them today if you have never come up against this illness in someone you love: that's the problem.

THE PLANE TILTED just a little to the left as we came in over Manhattan and Haley looked out the window at the great shapes of buildings below her and the open green rectangle of Central Park and the wide gray avenues of midtown. Everything was bathed in a yellow light so the city looked almost golden. I watched over her shoulder and yet she stayed transfixed by the view. Finally she turned to me and said, "What is this place?"

"That's New York City," I said.

"That's New York City?" she repeated.

"That's right. That's where I used to live."

She looked from the view to me and back to the view again as if she had discovered a piece of information that challenged something essential. All through the spring, Haley and I had kept

on. I had taken her to Washington DC. In June, we borrowed
a friend's house on Nantucket. It did not seem possible that we
could get away, but it also did not seem good for Haley to continue
to live in her brother's shadow. We were held hostage to it as surely
as if someone held a gun to our heads, in part because I believed
that at any moment Chase would come back to us and I wanted
to be there when that happened. But as weeks became months, I
thought it might be okay to plan a trip in the early summer, just
for a week. I'd take Haley on her first plane ride. We would fly to
Manhattan and then get on one of the little props that flew out to
Nantucket and look at the ocean and watch as the coastline of the
island came shimmering into view.

At LaGuardia we had to run for the plane but they held it for
us at the gate while the other passengers coughed and fidgeted and
read their newspapers impatiently in their seats. When we were
airborne out over the Atlantic, Haley stared down the aisle and
out the cockpit window into the vast luminous blue of the sea and
air. I pointed to the tiny white wakes behind boats and the ruffled
waves that meant sandbars but Haley just shook me off and stared
straight ahead. The noise from the props was deafening so she had
to wait until we were unloaded onto the Nantucket tarmac to tell
me how much she hated flying.

We stayed in the last house down a sandy road where dunes rose
on either side and wild roses crawled over the split-rail fences that
fronted all of the gray-shingled houses. We arrived at sunset and
unloaded our things and then in the new dark found our way to
a corner market with creaking wooden floors and old glass cases
filled with meat and fish where we bought bread and cheese and
tea and eggs and toilet paper and milk and juice and wine.

"Dinner and breakfast," I said. "We'll find a supermarket
tomorrow."

We could hear the ocean shushing into the beach as we loaded our paper sacks onto the backseat of the car I'd rented. Haley buckled up and her chin drooped onto her chest as I made our way through the soft sea air. She was already asleep by the time we got back to the house and I wished I could carry her inside, as if she were a much younger child, as if I could turn back the years for her and recover everything that had been lost.

In the morning, we ate breakfast with our plates on our laps, sitting in the living room where we could look out over a greenish pond. Herons stood delicate sentinel in the cattails and marsh grass. Gray clouds lay over the horizon but for the most part the sky was blue. Haley drank apple juice and slowly ate her toast. When she was through, I washed the dishes and we put on our swimsuits and our sweatshirts and loaded a plastic tote with towels and a blanket and sunblock and a couple of plastic pails and then we set off down the road to the beach. Here the ocean seemed a dark blue and the combers stood out stark and white. The sand was as rocky as I remembered it and Haley kept her flip-flops on while she walked down to the foam and let the sea rush up over her feet.

She screamed and jumped back. "It's cold," she shrieked. "It's cold! It's cold!"

I came up beside her and let the water wash up to my ankles. I guessed the temperature to be below sixty. Haley danced on the sand and shivered. "That's the northern Atlantic," I said and stepped back from the waves. "Not quite like home, is it?"

"N-o-o-o-o-o," she chattered.

"Put your sweatshirt back on. It's only June. It might be too cold to go in. But we can go beach-combing."

We gathered up our pails and I reminded Haley to put sunblock on her face and her legs and the tops of her ears and feet.

We made our way along the beach with our heads bowed, as if our walk was some extended meditation or prayer. Haley ran ahead and came back to me and ran ahead again. I couldn't stop thinking of Chase, of how much he would love this, the plane ride and the beach, that view of New York City. And then I wondered if these were things that Chase would ever know. And then I shook my head hard as if I could cast those thoughts upon the water and reminded myself that this was a vacation, this was about giving Haley a normal girlhood. And yet I felt again how small our family had shrunk and how the two of us stood alone.

I watched the sand, looking for something special to hand to my daughter. The surf here was rough and most shells were crushed before they were cast up on the beach. There were the long shells of razor clams, pretty much intact, and the creamy yellow scallop shells I remembered from my childhood, and the occasional tiny jingle shell lying on the dark sand as luminous and pearly as inlay in a lacquered box. I picked my way through seaweed festooned with little waxy golden balls, like Christmas ornaments, and past rubbery fronds of brown kelp. There must have been a storm recently for so much plant life to find its way to shore. I looked down the beach and here came Haley, running toward me, calling out to me.

"Look at this, Mom!" she yelled. "Look what I found!" She splashed through the backwash no longer worried about the cold and opened her cupped palm, where she held a tiny cache of perfectly smooth, perfectly oval, flat black rocks. It was as if they'd been polished by the sea and then given over to her, flawless and whole. And I suddenly recalled that Haley used to pick up rocks wherever she went and the door pocket in our car next to her seat was always full of tiny pieces of quartz or acorn caps or interesting sticks or tiny pebbles that Haley remembered for the places she'd

found them. She'd point to a pale granite chip and say, "I found
this on Grandfather Mountain that time we went with Chase."
When she said things like this, I got the feeling that behind every
one of Haley's tiny objects stood a whole story, as complicated and
dense as memory.

"Let's look for more," she said, and pushed her wet hand through
her blowing hair, which was beginning to work loose from its elastic. We spent the morning working our way down the beach and
found black stones and gray stones and white stones, these last
heavy as lumpy eggs. When we got back to the house and I made
lunch, Haley washed the stones with water from the garden hose
and lay them out in the sun on the front steps to dry.

EVERY DAY I WATCHED the answering machine for messages, for I worried that something would go wrong while we were
out of town and John Umstead Hospital would not know where
to find me. Chase was new there, and they were new to him, and
I didn't know how things worked yet. But I'd left our number
with May, who said that was all I needed to do, and turned away
for seven days. When the light flashed on the third day, and my
heart stopped and I sucked in my breath, it wasn't the hospital
at all. Instead, my friend Vickie's old friend Bryce, who lived on
Nantucket all year round, wanted to take us out on his boat. The
next day, we met him at the dock, with his wife and their baby son
Ignatius and we loaded coolers of beer and sandwiches and ice for
the fish we'd catch into the boat's cabin and we strapped life vests
on and Bryce explained that, when we were on his boat, he was
completely in charge, and Haley nodded solemnly and took her
seat at his direction. He winked at me and then piloted us up the
channel and out past the lighthouse at Long Wharf and turned
north along the coast until we felt the chunk-chunk-chunk of a

different sort of wave as we pounded around Great Point, where the harbor ended and the open sea began. When we were opposite Brant Lighthouse, Bryce throttled down and let the boat begin to drift. He baited a hook and then handed a pole to Haley and showed her how to flick her wrist and send the line whizzing out over the water and then patiently wait for something to strike.

Which happened almost immediately. "Oh," she yelped. "Oh! Oh! What's that?" And her pole bent and she took two involuntary steps forward but Bryce was right there and he held her and showed her how to begin to crank the reel and bring the fish in.

"Look at you," he said. "You're a natural!"

She struggled with the crank and looked over at me and I said, "You can do this, Haley-Bird." So she leaned back against Bryce and he put one arm around her waist and eased her into the chair and then strapped her into the white leather harness and stood the pole in the pole stand and stepped away and said, "Attagirl!" And Haley leaned back and cranked and cranked and cranked until pretty soon there was a thrashing dark thing alongside the side of the boat and Bryce reached down with a big net and scooped the fish into the boat and water flew from it in a silver sheen and Haley looked at it, this flopping flippered thing, and Bryce said, "You got yourself a big blue! Good job!" He knelt down and pulled the hook from the fish's mouth and then tossed the fish onto the ice.

We fished all afternoon. At the end of the day, after we came back into the dock, I took pictures of Bryce and Haley and the fish. Then I took a picture of Bryce holding his baby upside down by the ankles, as if Ignatius were a fish Bryce had been lucky enough to catch out on the big dark sea. And again I thought, Chase would have loved this. And again I tried to put that thought away.

• • •

AT NIGHT WE SLEPT as if we had not slept for months. We ate lunch in town at a place that overlooked the harbor and we took a tour of the oldest house on the island. We went to the whaling museum and stood slack-jawed under the hanging skeleton of a baleen whale and Haley intently studied the pictures of men in boats, men fated to be lost at sea, as if she knew that this, above all else, was what a man could expect. We window-shopped through Nantucket's cobbled streets and Haley took pictures of things that interested her: doorways, and street benches, and the shadow from a sign cast across the road. She bought a stuffed horse in one of the shops and I took her into a drugstore with an old-fashioned soda fountain so she could eat a toasted-cheese sandwich and drink a chocolate milk shake at the long marble counter. At night we walked along the beach and listened to the boom and rush-shush of the waves and looked up at the stars and pretended that we never had to go home.

AFTER WE GOT BACK, I drove up on Saturdays to see Chase. I would park in the visitors' lot behind the building and climb the three concrete steps to an area that looked like a small loading dock, where a black urn filled with wilting red geraniums had been used by many people as an ashtray. A box hung on the brick face of the building next to the door and in the box was a telephone. I would dial a number and wait a long time while the phone rang and rang until someone answered and told me to wait right there, someone would be down to get me. I would stand on the loading dock and wait. It was always hot. Across the parking lot was a shed crowded with heavy equipment and the air smelled of diesel exhaust and earth.

In the beginning, I would bring him a soda and a candy bar and stand the soda next to the candy bar like offerings on the wobbly table in the visitors' room. The keys would rattle and I'd hear the bolt slide back on the door between the visitors' room and the unseen world that Chase now occupied and then the nurse would encourage him to come into the room and he'd take two steps into the room and look at the table for the soda and the candy bar. He was wearing street clothes now. The hospital had wanted him to wear pajamas even though no one else did, because it helped the staff to remember that he was the one on fall precautions and seizure precautions, but I objected to this and said the pajamas made it clear that Chase was different than everyone else and singled him out as vulnerable to the tough kids and he already had enough trouble with that.

The nurse would settle into the chair by the door and Chase would drink the soda if I opened it for him. He'd stay as long as it took for him to finish his drink. I began to bring him hamburgers and French fries and thick milk shakes that took a long time to eat.

One day, he sat at the wobbly table with his hamburger wrapper spread flat on the table top and his box of fries lying flat on a yellow paper napkin that I'd unfolded and treated as a plate. His hands shook when he tried to bring the hamburger to his mouth and the slice of tomato slid onto his shirt and hung there while he ate and then fell to his lap. I reached for the pile of napkins and reached for his lap but he kicked at me and the nurse said, "Chase," and I stepped back.

"Who is this?" the nurse said. "Is this your mother?"

Chase said, "My mother's clothes. My mother's glasses. Not my mother."

"This is your mother," the nurse said. "Who else would come to see you every Saturday?"

"Chase," I said. "Chase. I'm your mom."

He wiped his hands on his pants and stood up and began to walk up and down, up and down, in front of me. "Making movies now," he said, and looked at me with a weird smile on his face. "Out there." He said something else I couldn't understand. Then he said, "Giant insects. It's going to be good."

"Do you know where you are?" I asked.

He looked at me. "Prison," he said. "This is a jail for juvenile delinquents."

"I can understand why you feel like it's a prison," I said. "But it's a hospital."

"Murderers. Here. I have to resurrect everyone."

"They're trying to help you," I said. "You had to move because the insurance company wouldn't pay for you anymore at Memorial. Do you understand? It wasn't my idea to bring you here. I didn't have any choice."

He stared at me as if he'd never seen me before. Then he crossed the room in two strides and kicked me as hard as he could. I twisted away and jumped up and the nurse jumped up and she put her palm on the small of Chase's back and steered him away, back onto the ward.

I THOUGHT ABOUT ZIP and I thought about Zip and I thought about Zip. Everyone had thought that they knew him. I had thought that I knew him. And I felt certain that he was not a liar, that he had believed in the plain truth of everything he'd said. But the things he'd told me didn't really hold up: he'd said he could fix any car engine he saw, but couldn't fix my car; he'd said he was an expert marksman, but I never saw him handle a weapon; he'd said he quit school because his parents stopped paying, but his mother told me that she had spent her days at a factory for a big department store, bagging dresses and coats she'd never be able to afford, and all so she could pay that loan, month after month, until Zip was through.

At night, when I couldn't sleep, I sat and sorted through old family pictures and felt that, instead of excavating a mysterious past, I was being turned inside out by things I didn't know. I had photos of family ancestors on Zip's mother's side, big-bosomed women in fancy dresses with high necklines ruffled in lace, big men with large, light eyes wearing dark suits and small hats. But Zip's father's side remained more or less a blank. The only time I ever saw Joseph was in the picture from his wedding, where he stood next to Mary and cut into his wedding cake; he wore his uniform because he was just back from the war.

I studied these pictures as if I could find traces of Chase, traces of Zip, behind the carefully composed faces, the beautiful clothes, Mary's family's obvious prosperity, Joseph's family obscured by mystery. I thought that no one should imagine having a child until they've seen the story told by the family photo album. One night I called Zip's cousin and asked her if anyone in the family was known to be a little strange, a little different, a little eccentric, a little odd.

She laughed when she heard my questions. "Do you mean was anyone crazy?" she said.

"That's a hard thing to ask," I said. "Just out of the blue."

"Let me think," she said. I listened to silence and then she said, "The only one I can think of was an uncle who really kept to himself. I always thought it was a cultural thing, something left over from the old ways, but it could have been something else. Nobody ever saw him except once or twice a year when there'd be some kind of get-together. And when he came to those, he kept to himself, as if he expected you to come up to him. I always thought he was trying to hold court so I avoided him. I remember him being mostly alone and he died alone in his house and no one found him for a week or more. That was a sad thing."

She paused.

"The family's big on grudges," she said at last. "Little things set them off and they keep it up for generations. Two of the sisters lived in this town; they lived half a mile apart and they didn't speak to each other for their entire adult lives. More than sixty years. I heard someone say the whole thing started because one wouldn't do a favor for the other. It was something simple, too, like mailing a letter because she was going that way anyway. They were a mysterious bunch because of things like that. I don't think anyone ever came out and said any of them was crazy, though. But who knows? Times were different then. No one talked about such things. The families tried to keep this hidden because having someone who was crazy in your house, well, that was a shameful thing."

I BEGAN TO THINK I could only believe things I could corroborate. I didn't trust myself as a witness. It seemed to me that I had bought into Zip's view so deeply that my own vision made me blind. Now, when I looked back, my entire life with Zip was nothing I'd thought it was. It was not just an unsettled feeling that came upon me when I realized this, but instead I felt unmoored, unbound, undone. I had been married for a long time to a man I thought I knew better than I knew anyone else in the world but who, it turned out, I had not known at all.

It's a common place for divorced people to say that the person they once loved turned into a stranger before them. I suppose that may be true; when we fall out of love, the familiar grows extraordinary and then strange, as if all the equations we've been working from suddenly add up to a different set of numbers. But this is not what I'm describing. The more I looked for credible witness to the things that Zip assured me were true, the more the man vanished. The very fact of him disappeared like smoke.

Remembering a favorite story of his, I decided to try to find out if a drummer who pointed a .38 at a woman who was dating a keyboardist had missed and hit Zip. It seemed to me that this was the sort of story that would have had a public life; surely it could not have happened without a written mention somewhere. So I looked through online records of his hometown newspaper and, when those didn't yield anything, I contacted the county library and told them I was trying to find out anything I could about a shooting among members of a rock-and-roll band, maybe in their hometown, maybe just somewhere nearby. The librarian who responded was very sorry but she couldn't find anything in the newspapers in their holdings for ten years on either side of those dates. She suggested I try the historical society. Before I did that, I picked up the phone and called Zip's mother and asked her to tell me whatever she knew about the time Zip was shot.

There was a long silence.

"Zip was never shot," said Mary. "Not that I know of."

"Never shot in the groin at a band meeting by the drummer of his band?" I said. "Never spent six months in the hospital learning to walk again?"

"He went in when he was in junior high school for a couple of days for his adenoids," she said, "but he was fine." She was silent for a moment. "I don't know what he told you," she said, "but he was never in the hospital for six months."

I hung up and crossed the kitchen to the window and stood and looked out at the street. The neighbor's yellow dog padded by, followed a minute later by our neighbor, who glanced at my garden, saw me, and waved. I waved back. When she was gone, I watched the breeze work through the leaves in the crepe myrtle. Everything was strange.

DAYS AT UMSTEAD PASSED, one like another, until Chase had been there for months. There was no hope of school. At the treatment team meetings, they told me it wasn't safe for Chase to leave the unit with the boys under twelve to mix with the other teens in the classroom. I pointed out that Chase was entitled to an education. The psychiatrist leaned back in his chair and then leaned forward and fixed me with a steady look and pointed out that Umstead was no place for Chase. He wanted to know what I was doing to find an appropriate placement for him.

Every day, two orderlies walked Chase down from his room in the children's unit and out to a waiting hospital van. Some days he went quietly. Other days, he fell to the ground and thrashed or he tried to bolt and run, perhaps down the long broken asphalt road that led from the hospital back into the center of town. The orderlies got him into the van. They sat one on each side of him while the van traveled three blocks to Murdoch Center. At Murdoch, he went to the BART unit and, with the help of the teacher, played a few computer games in one of the classrooms. Then he had lunch. After lunch, again flanked by the orderlies, he returned to Umstead and spent his afternoons drowsing on the sofa in the dayroom. Someone checked on him every fifteen minutes and each time noted that he was asleep.

May asked me to bring some items from home that might interest him and I packed a plastic box with plastic figures of Batman and Spider-Man and one Thursday drove with them up to the hospital and met her in the waiting area downstairs near the front door. She made an inventory of the things in the box and then told me if I didn't tell anyone, she'd take me back along the long hallway on the unit to see Chase's room. We entered through the blank locked door of the visitors' room and found ourselves on a long green hallway with rooms opening off of it, each the size of a large cell, perhaps eight feet by ten feet. Each held a metal bedstead with a thin mattress made up with sheets, a flat pillow, a single blanket. There was a large bathroom with toilets without stalls, showers without curtains. Nothing could be done that wasn't under surveillance at all times. Chase's room was down on the right. He stood in the room and swung his arms, his back to the door. When he heard us he turned and left the room. His room held his bed and his clothes piled on two shelves that were built into a recess in the wall; a third shelf held a toothbrush, a bar of soap, and a comb.

May held the plastic box with the action figures inside.

The nurse brought Chase back.

"Chase," she said. "See what your mother has brought you?"

He didn't look at the box or at us but crossed to the window and stood with his back to us.

May put the box on the shelf next to his pants. "The staff will work with him with these," she said. "Some play therapy," she said doubtfully.

They increased his Clozaril and increased it again and he began to drift through his days in a wordless state where he said nothing comprehensible and seemed not to comprehend anyone around him. When I saw him in the visitors' room, he nodded off like a heroin addict and spittle ran from his mouth and the nurse with him began to carry a rag so that she could wipe up his drool. His shirts were wet with it. His gait was increasingly unsteady. His hands shook. At first the acute-care-unit psychiatrist cared for him but after a month or six weeks he was switched to a psychiatrist who specialized in more long-term cases. I wondered if this meant hopeless. We met in a room off one of the waiting rooms and Dr. A told me he was working hard to make sense of Chase's case and he hoped to find some answers soon.

These were the warm days of late summer, when the air seemed dusty and yellow and leaves hung exhausted in the trees. The room was brown and yellow like the air outside and the light of the sky and paint peeled from the wall next to the door where an old leak had once stained the wall a deep ocher.

"Have you had any luck in finding him a placement?" he asked.

I shook my head. "He was accepted at BART but they don't have a bed," I said.

"Do they have any idea when they might have a bed?"

"They won't say. Maybe sometime within the next year."

"It would be better for him if he were in a place where people could really meet his needs," Dr. A said. "We can't do that here. All we can do is what we would do for someone without a developmental disability but that is not in Chase's best interest."

"I know," I said. I explained that the people from Orange-Person-Chatham were still looking for a placement. I explained that I had written to the man who supervised the man who oversaw all of the hospitals and facilities in the system and when he didn't reply, I'd called his office and asked to set up an appointment with him. The woman who answered told me she was not going to do that. When I hung up, I contacted the Governor's Advocacy Council for Persons with Disabilities and explained Chase's situation to them. It took weeks for me to hear from them, but finally they wrote and said that Chase's case was far too difficult for them to take on so they would take a pass on it. I wrote again and told them they should be ashamed of themselves for refusing to help Chase because they thought it might be too hard. The program assistant saw my letter and approached one of the attorneys, who agreed, grudgingly, to look into things for Chase. She had his case for three weeks but did nothing before she left to take another job. After that, no one did anything while they searched for a new attorney and it had been many weeks with no help on the case. I'd called Carolina Legal Assistance for Exceptional Children and they asked me if I wanted to sue. When I said I wanted to find a solution that did not involve a lawsuit because I was worried that a lawsuit would guarantee nothing but a long stay for Chase at Umstead, the attorney advised me to call back when I was serious about a suit. I wrote to the secretary of the Department of Health and Human Services but she ignored me. I called Leonard Button twice a week and asked for his assistance. He played mind-numbing games. I called Linda at Orange-Person-Chatham and could hear the catch in her voice when she heard from me, her discomfort with the fact that she had nothing new to tell me. Someone in her office heard from Leonard Button by e-mail; he wrote to tell them that, at the moment, I did not seem litigious, and so all was well. I explained to Dr. A that I would become litigious when I was certain that I'd exhausted all possibilities, but that I knew a lawsuit would take years to resolve and when I saw Chase languishing at Umstead, I knew we did not have years. We had to find a way to solve the problem now.

Afternoon sunlight fell on the wall behind him and he blinked a little. Chase's new social worker, Patrick, had joined us halfway through the meeting. Now he stood and crossed the room and adjusted the blinds so that he and Dr. A could sit without the sun falling across their faces and into their eyes.

Dr. A had a new theory about Chase. He thought the normal EEG gotten upon admission to Memorial was very provocative, given Chase's history of abnormal EEGs. "Sometimes," he said, "when a person's epilepsy is treated so thoroughly that he no longer seizes, and his EEG appears normal, the consequence is a huge upswing in psychotic symptoms. They call that situation forced normalization," he said, "because the control of the epilepsy has resulted in an EEG that is forced by medication to appear normal. But the downside is the severe psychosis."

He spoke softly, in a gentle voice, and watched me carefully for my reaction.

"So if we let Chase seize, his psychosis will resolve?" I said.

Dr. A smiled and nodded. "That's the theory, anyway."

"I don't think I'm comfortable with that," I said.

Dr. A blanched. "No," he said. "I'm not suggesting we let Chase have a seizure. What I'd like to do is look into this a bit more, maybe get Chase seen by his neurologist, consult on this as a possibility, make sure we've pursued every angle on this case."

After the meeting, Patrick waited in the hallway for me.

"Do you have a minute?" he said.

I nodded.

We watched Dr. A walk back through the hospital, turn a corner, unlock a door, and disappear from view.

"Let's just go back inside," said Patrick, and gestured back at the visitors' room. I sat down and he sat across from me in a worn rocking chair. He was a slight man with longish hair and Chase had become convinced that he was his father and would not speak to him. Patrick told me that he'd been reading reports of my visits with Chase and he noted that I experienced a great deal of aggression from Chase during these meetings.

"The thing is," he said, "you can't argue with psychosis. Think of the worst zealot you've ever met and how impossible it is to have a conversation with him because his beliefs are so entrenched. Chase is a thousand times worse than that. Your impulse is to have a conversation with him about family matters, but he's operating in a world of beliefs that no longer acknowledges family matters. When you talk to him about these things, he just gets more hostile, more agitated. You're just succeeding in getting him worked up. And then you have a visit that is not acceptable to you, either."

He leaned forward. "I'm going to ask you to accept that Chase doesn't know who you are. This is hard," he said. "But this is the way it is and this is the way it's likely to be for a long time to come. If you can find a way to just sit with him and let him set the tone of the visit and just agree with the things he says, maybe he will come to like seeing you. You may never be anything more than the lady who brings him a sandwich once a week, but at least you can have a relationship with him as the lady who brings him the sandwich. You can have that relationship with him for the next thirty or forty years." He paused and reached behind the sofa and found a box of tissues and handed it to me so I could wipe my eyes.

"I know plenty of parents who have been where you are," he said. "They've watched mental illness take their children. But the thing about Chase that's different is that you and he have lost the primary relationship, the one between parent and child. The other parents I've known, their kids still recognized them. This is harder because of that. And it's harder than death because it's so unresolved." He shook his head. "This is a very severe case," he said, "and it's hard to accept. But you need to accept it. Chase is going to need twenty-four-hour, one-to-one institutional care for the rest of his life and it's probable that he will never know who you are again."

I sobbed once and wiped my eyes and looked away and then looked at him again. "I'd like to visit him," I said and Patrick nodded.

"I'll take you up," he said. "I think they're expecting you. But I want you to remember what I said."

THE INSURANCE APPEAL had long since come back, indicating that Chase was still in need of acute care and, therefore, the case was dismissed, so I could have moved him back to Memorial. But I remembered the day he was brought to the ambulance and his anguished cries and his struggle to break free, and I decided that the only thing to do was to minimize the number of moves he had to make to the one where he moved from Umstead to BART.

ONE SUNDAY EVENING I turned my car away from town and drove along a road that passed a house shaped like the spaceship in *When Worlds Collide* and a cemetery that stood alone on the top of a knoll and a Southern plantation – style house with a red tin roof and a new layer of gravel on the drive circling in front of the big front porch. I left the trees and deep woods behind and crossed the county line and looked to my left, at the big boxy apartments in the complex where Chase and Haley and I had lived when we first came to North Carolina. Then I turned right and followed a much smaller road down a hill and through a stand of hardwoods and over a bridge. Two deer stepped out of the long grass at the side of the road and stopped and stared at me. I turned at the iron gates and passed by the community garden and an open space filled with iron fencing and fireplace tools and metal parts of things now incomprehensible and found a parking spot on an embankment.

The evening had turned cool and the sun was almost down behind the black trees, the sky just a glowing band of deep yellow, the dense blue of early night on the rise, and someone had already lit the fire in the round fireplace in the center of the gazebo and pulled the sliding-glass doors shut to keep the heat in and lit the candles below the stained-glass window that had been forged in the shape of the yin-yang sign. A man sat on a cushion on the floor with a harmonium before him and touched the keys and squeezed the bellows and a woman winched a round iron ring stuck with candles back to the ceiling now that the candles were lit and looped the pulley rope around a bracket and tied it off. Others arrived. A tall man with a gray beard brought a tabla and a mandolin. A woman walked down the path from the parking area playing a cedar flute. A man carried his guitar down the path and a woman walked three feet behind him and carried a bag of rhythm instruments. I sat on a meditation bench to the right of the man with the harmonium and waited with my legs crossed beneath me and my eyes closed and then the practice notes of the harmonium gave way to a chant about Krishna and the man who leaned over the instrument began to sing. I opened my eyes and watched the yellow fire curl and roll over the dark logs in the fireplace and listened to the song and listened to the voices of the others, who sang immediately and without hesitation. Another man began to beat a tom-tom, and another man finished unpacking his *djembes* and he, too, began to play. When the Krishna chant was through, the man at the harmonium let the bellows go and the air rushed out of the instrument and he picked up a rattle and began to sing about Wakan-Tanka and the others followed and a woman jumped to her feet and sang loudly and shook a rain stick with her right hand and turned her left palm upward and turned her face upward and beseeched the ceiling.

The sky outside turned black and the iron lampposts standing in the woods turned off, one by one, and darkness closed in around us. I sang when the others sang and I paused when the others paused and I looked past the fire and out the big glass windows and into the black woods where no light shone. Then I stood up unsteadily and crossed the stone floor of the gazebo and reached into a cardboard box full of ground cedar and scooped up a handful

and stood before the fire, the ground cedar scattering around me
but still some held in my hand, enough for a hope, a wish, a prayer,
and I held my hand to my heart and then held my fist over the
fire and opened my fingers and the ground cedar sprang up as red
and orange sparks and I asked for help and I asked for an answer
and I didn't know to whom or what or even if to anything at all
I directed this supplication but I knew I should have done more,
handled things differently, made some sort of Faustian bargain,
if such a thing could have been made, but I had not. Instead, I
must have done everything wrong that one could do, or else we
would never be here, and so I stood in a wooden gazebo while old
hippies and true believers sang around me and asked someone or
something to take our lives and make them right. Then I closed
my fingers and sang some more and afterward walked up the path
under the waving dark trees and drove home.

I MET WITH THE director of Murdoch Center and with
members of the Orange-Person-Chatham area unit who were responsible for finding Chase a place for long-term care. The director's
office was a wood-paneled place in the center's administration building. When I parked my car out front, Linda was just stepping out
of her black Honda. Inside, a group of people from Murdoch were
waiting—an outreach coordinator, the center's associate director, a
client advocate. After a few minutes, Linda's boss from OPC arrived,
with a woman who worked on the mental-health side of things for
the unit. We sat in chairs that made an approximate circle and I explained that I'd asked for this meeting because I thought we might
be able to find a solution if we worked together. I explained that
Chase was not doing well at Umstead and Umstead didn't want him
there. I explained that Umstead was unable to provide the services
he needed. I explained that I was not getting any real help from

Leonard Button's office. I explained everything carefully and was careful to keep my voice even and measured. I told them I sought their collaboration, that as a team we might be able to do more than I had been able to do as a parent alone.

Everyone nodded. Linda talked about the many meetings OPC had had about Chase and their many efforts to find a place for him. She talked about coordinating all of the materials for the applications, first at the place in Jacksonville, then at the PATH unit, and how Chase had been rejected by the place in Jacksonville and then reviewed by the admissions committee for PATH and was also rejected, but then was reviewed for BART and was accepted.

The director of Murdoch talked about that admission being essential to anything we might do but, at the same time, he wasn't sure what it was we could do, realistically speaking. What we needed was the one thing he couldn't offer us, and that was a bed. He knew we were in a difficult spot. It was not a desirable situation. But he could not come up with a bed when a bed was not to be had. He asked me what sort of contact I'd had with Raleigh beyond Leonard Button's office and I explained that I'd called the man who oversaw all of the hospitals and group homes and that had gotten Chase the consultations with Murdoch that were now in place. Otherwise my contact with him had not resulted in movement on a placement, so I'd written to his boss and, when he'd failed to respond, I'd written to the secretary of the division. She had also failed to respond. Right now, I was left with conversations with Leonard that were less than helpful, but I was trying to come up with more people to talk with and had contacted my state representative and my congressman. The congressman had said he could not do anything because this was not a federal matter; the state representative was looking into the situation from her office.

When I was finished, no one looked at me. Murdoch's director thumbed the papers in his lap and studied his shoes. Finally he turned toward me and said, "I think you might need a miracle. I'm sorry to put it that way, but it might be that this is what it's going to take."

IN SEPTEMBER, THE HOSPITAL sent Chase to see his neurologist so he could further explore Dr. A's theory of forced normalization. His neurologist met us in an exam room at the famous hospital where he taught and reeled backward when he saw Chase, for he had not seen him since the summer before Chase went into Memorial. "How long has he been like this?" he asked, and I explained. He nodded and shook his head and made murmuring sounds and looked aggrieved. Then he turned to Chase and said, "How are you, young man?"

Chase rolled his lips together but didn't speak. He patted his chest and then patted his thigh.

"It's sound communication," he said at last and twisted his face at us.

"Let's sit down here on the table so I can get a look at you," Dr. S said and Chase sat on the exam table.

Dr. S examined Chase and then told me he had a note from a doctor at Umstead who was interested in his opinion on forced normalization. He said, "In my opinion, there is no such thing as forced normalization, or if there is, it's a fleeting, short-term thing that can't possibly explain the condition we find Chase in now."

Chase sat on the table and squinted at the lights and then turned to the ceiling vent and moved his lips.

"There's no chance that this could be behind the psychosis, then?"

"No chance?" Dr. S said. "No chance? There's always a chance of anything. But the point is that, in Chase's case, that chance is so unlikely as to be practically nonexistent. Forced normalization, or so the theory goes, explores the relationship between epilepsy and psychosis and suggests that the more aggressively you treat the epilepsy, the more severe the psychotic symptoms become, and if you let the epilepsy alone some, the psychotic symptoms will abate. It's never been proven and is highly controversial. I don't think it applies here at all. This is something else."

"What?" I said.

"Oh, that I couldn't tell you," he said. "That's not something I'd be able to hazard a guess on."

Chase said something and Dr. S and I both looked at him and I said, "Chase?"

Chase began muttering and then he said something about the executioner and the nailers. He patted his thigh.

"It's okay," I said. "We'll be done soon."

We waited but Chase didn't say anything else. Dr. S shook his head and came across the room and clutched my hand in his. "We'll get him back for you," he said urgently. "Don't worry. We're going to get him back."

But he didn't say how.

At the hospital, Dr. A ordered an increase in Chase's Clozaril. Then he ordered a swallowing study to make sure that the reason Chase was losing weight had nothing to do with his ability to eat. One morning Chase surprised everyone by saying in a loud, clear, strong voice, "I'm ready to be discharged to Murdoch now." He said it twice. When nothing happened, he sat on a sofa in the dayroom and slipped into his fog. Two days later, he arrived sobbing at breakfast convinced his mother had been killed. Right after that, he began to tell the psychiatrist that Little Chase lived

inside him and caused him to do bad things and that was why he'd
been sent to jail.

I RARELY WENT INTO Chase's room at home, for each
item in it reminded me of Chase before he got sick. After I'd carefully boxed up all of his belongings and stacked the boxes in his
closet with the labels facing hopefully outward so I could easily
put my hands on anything Chase might ask for, as if he might ever
ask for anything again, the room still seemed to be his, and was
therefore in its emptiness too big a reminder of what the emptiness had replaced. I couldn't look at photographs, either, or at the
videotapes we'd made when Chase and Haley were young. I wept
at unpredictable times and could not stop myself. People asked
about Chase but then, when I could not tell them that he was getting better, in acts of kindness that cut through me like a bitter
sweetness, stopped asking. I met new people who had never known
Chase and did not know that I had two children and thought that
when I said, "My family" I meant just my daughter and myself. I
grew silent about the facts of my life, for I could not imagine saying, *You don't understand, we were once a family of four and then
some strange illness came among us and first took their father and
then, in the most horrible way, took my son, and Haley and I have
tried to figure out how it is that we are a family still, with half of us
lost to some kind of darkness so truly impenetrable by light, so truly
unknown, so utterly mysterious—for what else could be the definition
of darkness but the absolute absence of light and knowledge?—that it
doesn't even have a name.*

I wanted to be like the mother in the film *Lorenzo's Oil* and find
a cure that doctors had overlooked. I scoured the Internet for syndromes, relatively common things at first, and then for more rare
and unknown disorders, things locked into Chase's mitochondria

or his metabolism or his dopamine receptors. I looked for genetic conditions and I tried to match his symptoms to the symptoms of other children in other families. I read about complicated seizure disorders and illnesses of copper deficiency and untreated PKU. I looked into syndromes so rare that fewer than fifty people were known to have the illness, and of those fifty, thirty-eight were from Norway. I believed the diagnosis of schizophrenia and then I didn't. I believed the diagnosis of autism and then I didn't. I believed the diagnosis of schizophrenia and autism in one person, a condition that was said to be nonexistent, unknown, impossible, and then I didn't. I called the psychiatrist who'd treated Chase while we still lived in the Midwest and explained what had become of Chase and asked him if he had any thoughts about his early diagnosis. He told me he remembered Chase well, for it wasn't every day that you saw a child like Chase, and he was very sorry to hear of the current state of things, and yes, he'd used the atypical autism diagnosis but secretly had worried that what Chase really had was that rarest of all mental-health catastrophes, true childhood schizophrenia. He'd avoided that diagnosis because there were other ways to explain Chase's symptoms and he preferred those to the childhood schizophrenia label because the prognosis was so grim, so dire.

"And now?" I asked and listened to the psychiatrist breathe slowly on the other end of the phone and wasn't surprised when he told me that now, of course, now, given everything I described, now it was impossible to resist and he thought that childhood schizophrenia probably was the thing that Chase had had from the very beginning, even taking into account the seizure issue that might also have had some behavioral manifestations.

AND ALL THE WHILE, Chase staggered around Umstead with drool hanging in drippy strings from his lower lip, a towel laid open and flat across his chest when he dozed in the dayroom chair. He slept and slept and slept and slept. After our visits, I walked back through the long halls of the hospital and thought it was entirely possible that Chase would die there.

THE STATE REPRESENTATIVE called me several times. She commiserated and told me she was doing all that she could, but that turned out to be little more than telling me that she was a grandmother herself so she understood how painful this situation must be for me.

"I'm a taxpayer," I said. "Chase is a citizen of this state. The state is required to provide appropriate care for people like Chase. That's not just my opinion," I said. "That's the law. The state psychiatric hospital is not an appropriate place for Chase. They want him out of there as much as I do. They aren't trying to keep him. If I could bring him home, I would. But I can't. It's just not possible. And it's certainly not in anyone's best interests."

"And there's no movement on the bed at BART?" she said.

"No," I said. "Not yet."

She was silent. "Community-based care," she began.

"Is a great idea, in theory," I interrupted. "But what happens when they won't take people like my son? Where is he supposed to go? So far, my only experience of community-based care is that it seems to be a strategy to deny services to the people with the greatest and most complex needs."

"I think . . . "

"You can't blame the providers," I raged. "Financially, it's not in their best interest to take someone like Chase. They can't make a profit with a case like him. You have to look at it from their perspective. He's going to be a financial black hole for them. Of course they don't want him."

She sighed. "I'll call Raleigh in the morning," she said. "I'll set up a meeting and let you know what comes of that."

WHEN I WENT TO work, my boss asked me if I'd found a place for Chase. When I shook my head, he said, "Have you talked to our friend across campus?" I shook my head again. I didn't know how to explain how presumptuous I felt, asking that man for help. I knew that everyone said he was the most powerful man in the state, that three governors were indebted to him, that John Edwards had had to get his okay before he got into politics. I'd heard those stories. I knew they were true. But I could not imagine that he would take an interest in me or in Chase. So I told my boss I hadn't approached him because I wouldn't know what to say to him and had no idea if he could help, even if I asked. My boss's eyes widened a little when I said this and then he smiled gently. "You ought to give it a try," he said. "You might be surprised, if you just ask."

ONE SATURDAY, CHASE COULDN'T hold his head up and could barely speak. The nurse tried to make him comfortable in the visitors' room but he slid on the sofa and seemed barely conscious, his face pale and fragile and slack, spittle hanging from his chin. A technician dabbed at his face with a plain white towel.

"It's the medicine," the nurse said. "It can have this sort of side effect."

She flipped through the pages of Chase's chart. "It's right here," she said at a last. "Dr. A ordered an increase in Clozaril and they started that on Wednesday. The side effects can be worse right after the dosage is increased."

Drool threaded from Chase's lips and we watched the technician wipe his chin. I waited for a while but Chase never grew more alert. Instead, he stared at the wall behind me. Every so often, his lips twitched, as if he was trying to form a word but had lost whatever it is that is in us that allows us to speak.

PATRICK WANTED TO KNOW if I'd made any progress on Chase's placement. I sighed. I sat in my office at work and turned my chair toward the window while we spoke. I explained that the people in Raleigh thought that Chase was an outlier and therefore seemed to be treating his case as if it was not really their problem.

"Stick to your guns," he said. "I saw a family have to take a boy home this week who should never have gone home. He was so disabled that he had to be housed on a unit all by himself, with twenty-four-hour nursing care and staff support. The mother couldn't find a placement for him. She'd sit at the table and weep. We pressured her. I'm sorry to say it but it's true. We pushed her because we wanted to discharge him. We didn't want him here. He was severely developmentally disabled and he really didn't belong here. So we pushed and she caved. Maybe she didn't know that she didn't have to release him, that we couldn't discharge him without her consent."

"I can't bring Chase home," I said. My voice rose. "How would I do that? I can't care for him. I don't have twenty-four-hour nursing staff here."

"I know," he said. "I'm telling you this so you don't even try."

After we hung up, I looked out the window in my office. College students walked along Franklin Street with their backpacks and baseball caps, and soft brown leaves sailed one by one down from the oaks on McCorkle Place. It was a bright sunny day toward the middle of October. I watched the students for a while and then I swiveled my chair around so I could face my computer.

I scrolled through my files until I found the letter I'd sent to the man who supervised the man who oversaw all of the hospitals and facilities for people like Chase in the state. I printed a copy and lifted the fresh copy out of the printer and read it again and then read it again. Then I stood up and left my office and walked across campus to a small white house. Would-be kings had stood in this spot with less desperation than I felt. When I went inside, the lobby was cool and dim and silent. I knocked on the assistant's door and explained why I was there and held the letter in front of me and turned it in my hands as I spoke and she asked me to leave it and said he'd be out for a few days but if I came at the end of the week, she thought he could see me then.

TWENTY-ONE

IIIIIIIIIIIIIIIIIIIIIIIIIIIIIIIIIIIIIIIIIIIIIIIIIIIIIIII

"It's a very good letter," he said. "Very well written. Very thought-ful. Gives one the whole picture." He'd invited me to come in and sit down and I sat in a chair across from him. His curly white hair was carefully combed and he wore a pristine navy blue suit with a crisp white shirt. He had my letter on the desk in front of him. There were plants in the window behind him and a large framed photograph on his desk of his wife and his four boys when the boys were still young. The boys were dressed in pale summer jackets and ties and lined up according to height, each smiling, all of their hair blowing a little as if the picture had been taken on a breezy day.

"This man over at the Department of Health and Human Services," he said. "He won't answer you?"

"No," I said. "I called and asked to set up a meeting with him and his assistant said she would not do that."

"Do you know if he's from this state?"

"Michigan," I said.

"Well, that's why," he said. His face darkened. "He doesn't un-derstand that this is not the way we do things here. We take care of our own in this state." He leaned back a little in his chair and looked at me. "Now," he said. "How can I be of help?"

"I've done everything I can," I said. "I've talked to everyone who will talk to me and I've had meetings with anyone who will have a meeting with me and I've done everything the state has asked me to do, but I haven't been able to budge anyone in Raleigh. I just want to get Chase the help he needs and a lawsuit takes too much time and doesn't seem like the best way to get everyone to work together to find a solution. But I feel like I've hit a brick wall." I stopped and took a breath. "I wondered if you had some advice for me," I said. "I thought you could suggest some strategy I haven't tried."

"Well," he said. His voice was kind, immediate, clear. He smiled encouragingly at me. "Would you like me to make a call?"

I felt the air rush out of me. "Yes, yes," I babbled, "if that wouldn't take up too much of your time."

He waved that off. "Today's Friday," he said. "I believe the secretary of Health and Human Services is in Mexico on vacation but I have her number and I'll give her a call there. Let's see what we can find out by early next week."

On Monday, he called and told me that it took a day or so but the secretary had returned his call on Sunday and they'd had a talk about Chase.

"She's going to get with her people when she gets back this week," he said. "I'll keep you posted."

I could barely speak so I nodded and said, "Thank you."

"Oh, don't thank me," he said. "I haven't done anything."

A week passed. I made no phone calls. I visited Chase. I played cards with Haley in the evening after dinner. We got her Halloween costume ready. She was going to be a goddess of fire and had a long red dress, shot with gold, and a flame headdress. I remembered the year that Melissa had made costumes for Chase and Haley, when Chase was a swamp monster in a huge papier-mâché mask, and Haley was a centaur, with a long Mylar tail. Her hooves were painted yogurt cups. Chase loved Halloween. When we lived in the Midwest, we made a graveyard every year with cardboard tombstones his father cut out of empty cartons and carefully lettered with elaborate inscriptions. A ghost hung from our lightpost and we carved jack-o'-lanterns and one year I carved tiny faces into turnips that we hung in the apple tree, each turnip filled with a votive candle, each face a spark of light.

On Tuesday, the phone on my desk rang. The person on the other end identified herself as the social worker at Murdoch who worked with incoming clients. "I understand Chase will be joining us this week, maybe tomorrow, maybe the next day," she said. "I need you to answer a few questions and you'll have to sign some forms."

"What?" I said. "You mean because of Chase's day visits?"

"Oh, no," said the social worker. "He's at Umstead Hospital? And he'll be moving here? At least that's what I was told."

"What do you mean?"

She paused and then spoke slowly. "It's my understanding that a bed has come available for Chase and he'll be moving to the BART unit within the next day or two. Do you think you can be available for a treatment team meeting on Thursday? I think that's the day this will happen. I just don't think we can be ready by tomorrow so it's probably best to plan on Thursday."

"Yes," I said. I took a deep breath. "What time?"

"Well, you'll need to go to the hospital and sign his discharge papers first and pick up his belongings. He'll come over here from there. I guess we'll have the meeting around two. Is that okay?"

"Two will be fine," I said. "Two is perfect."

"All right then," she said. "I'm just making a note that you and I have spoken and you think two will work for you. You can call me and change that if the timetable doesn't work with the Umstead staff. In the meantime, do you have a fax number? I'm going to fax some documents that you'll need to sign and date. You can bring them with you to the meeting on Thursday. You'll be signing releases for medical information. We try to gather as complete a picture of the client's medical history as we can. We want to have all of those records in one place, on-site. So, let's start at the beginning. Can you tell me where he was born and who his pediatrician was when he came home from the hospital?"

I began. I listed his hospital and then all of the pediatricians and developmentalists and neurologists and neurosurgeons and psychiatrists and psychologists and occupational therapists and speech therapists and geneticists and pediatric cardiologists Chase had ever seen, a long line of names that spooled out from my memory in uncertain starts and stops, each name leading to another name, each place to a memory, those failed MRIs, the undiagnosed seizure disorder, the trips to the ER by ambulance with light cutting through the night, the school meetings and long evaluations and uncertain conclusions, and the gradual but unmistakable changes, the deterioration, the mysterious encephalopathy described by another doctor, unnameable, unquantifiable, unmistakable, uncurable, and running alongside all of that the years and years where I told myself that if I just tried harder and found the right doctor and the right treatment and the right medication and the right situation that I could help Chase improve, even when he was at all times slowly losing ground, so that each time something went wrong I told myself that we just needed to get Chase back and we could and this would be the time. I flipped through my Rolodex and wiped my eyes and gave her addresses and names and she said she'd send me release forms for each of these and I said, "Yes, that's fine, all right."

When she hung up, I put my face in my hands. Outside, a group of school children screamed and ate their lunch on the lawn.

I walked across campus to thank him but his assistant said he was going to be visiting lawmakers in Raleigh that day. On Wednesday I ran into him on the brick path that ran alongside Old East. "I understand everything's been set right," he said. "Is that true?"

I took both of his hands in mine. "Thank you," I said. "Thank you. Thank you."

He smiled and squeezed my hands. "I just did what was right," he said. "This is not the way we treat people in this state. It's very hard on the families and I understand that. I'm just glad to hear that all is well. We'll get your boy back. We're going to turn his light back on. You keep me posted," he said. "I want to hear how he does."

Linda called. "How did you do it?" she said. When I started to explain she interrupted me and said, "You're not supposed to know this, but it was the governor himself who called Murdoch. He called on Tuesday and he said that Chase would be living there as of Wednesday or he'd know why. That's what we heard. And then they opened that bed that they needed to open."

"It's really amazing," I said. I paused. "I am worried about one thing," I said. "I hate that this might be at the expense of another family. I don't want Chase to get services by someone else losing his."

"No," Linda said firmly. "From what I've heard, the other family is happy with how things worked out. From what I've heard, this helped them, too."

On Thursday I drove to Umstead and parked on the crumbly asphalt in the visitors' lot across from the children's unit and locked my purse in the trunk of my car. At the top of the steps, I put my finger on the buzzer and someone buzzed and I opened the door. I signed the visitors' log and told the woman behind the sliding-glass window that I was there to see Patrick.

Chase had gone to BART in the morning, just as he usually did, and when he was gone, the nurses packed his belongings into plastic grocery bags and while I waited for Patrick, an orderly brought the bags down and set them on the floor. There weren't many. When Patrick came along, he had one of the hospital teachers with him, who asked me to help her falsify Chase's education plan. He'd never gone to school at Umstead so they had never completed the document but he could not go to another state facility with paperwork that was incomplete; the hospital would get in trouble. All I had to do was sign. We were sitting at a picnic table out in front of the hospital and I thought about all the services Chase had not gotten at Umstead but reminded myself that it didn't matter.

"Just show me where," I said.

When all the forms were signed, Patrick helped me put the bags with Chase's belongings into the trunk. Then he stood on the dusty lawn in front of the hospital and watched me while I drove away and I waved as I turned out of the lot and headed toward town. It was less than a mile to Murdoch Center, but it lay at the end of a long road with many turnings and a landscape far different than any I had ever imagined.

HALEY TOOK AN OLD halter from its place on a nail and walked out from the barn along the dirt path to the lower pasture. A white horse grazed under an oak tree. When she was close, she stepped softly in the long, green grass and came up to the horse on his near side and with one gesture dropped the lead rope around his neck and the horse lifted his head and looked at her but didn't try to move away. She pulled the halter up over the horse's head and then clipped the lead rope to the ring under the horse's throat and walked the horse back through the pasture.

She put the white horse in cross ties in the schooling barn and brushed him with a currycomb. She leaned into his shoulder and lifted his foreleg and examined his hoof and used a pick to clean out the mud. She cleaned each hoof in turn and then positioned a dark green saddle blanket across his back. She hoisted the saddle on top of that and rubbed the horse's belly before she reached under and took the loose end of the girth and brought it up and cinched it on the near side. The horse swished his tail and gave her the stink eye but she talked to him and he settled and she patted his neck and rubbed his nose. She lifted the bridle from a hook on the wall and hung it over one arm and put the reins over the horse's head, unhooked the cross ties, and unfastened the halter and let it drop to the barn floor. She lifted the bridle until the bit came up to the horse's mouth and she pressed and he took the bit and she pulled his ears through the crown and then the rest of the bridle slipped into place and she fastened the throatlatch.

The instructor stood in the center of the ring and squinted at the riders from beneath the visor of her baseball cap and called for a trot. Haley moved Willy easily from a walk and posted easily and casually, waiting, and waiting, and then here it was, the word, *Canter*. At that, she kicked with her outside leg and drove with her seat and rocketed past me without a look, the sound of her horse's hooves thundering in the dust, her hair blowing out behind her. Just like that, she circled and circled and circled the ring. Willy blew and snorted and Haley kept her leg on him in the corners and his tail flew out behind him like a banner, and beyond the ring, two horses thundered up the pasture, turning and nipping, and turning again. The instructor's dog raced out from the barn, chasing the swallows that flew up and out from the dim rafters, and the girls in the ring kept cantering until the instructor called for a walk. She had them line up in the middle of the ring as she described the jump course to them. Haley sat her horse and watched while Helen rode the course and watched again as Elsie rode.

When it was her turn, she turned Willy to the rail and picked up a trot and drove him to the first jump and Willy cleared it easily and she cantered him to the next jump, which was really three jumps in a row, where Willy took one stride in between each of the three and Haley lifted her seat and kept her hands up his neck. She turned him back to a fence made of lattice and when he was over that, to the cross rails, and then to a jump painted with blue and green stripes, and a pink fence with plastic flowers hanging from the sides in buckets, and then crossed the ring and came around and took a red fence, and then came in a straight line to the last jump, a blue fence over bales of hay. When she was finished with the course, she rode back to her place in line, and Willy stood swishing his long, beautiful tail and Haley turned and said something to Elsie, who laughed and shook her head. Haley leaned forward and patted Willy's neck and he turned his head to look out at the pasture, where the other horses stood, and then she sat back in her saddle but dropped her stirrups and let her legs hang. She always wore a T-shirt with her riding pants and on this day wore a bright blue T-shirt with the Superman insignia on front. I sat on a bench beside the ring and she looked over at me and grinned.

When her lesson was over and she'd ridden with the other girls under the turning trees and along the back pasture into the woods and up the road to cool the horses off, I walked down to the barn and watched Haley lift the saddle from Willy's back.

"How big was that last fence?" I said.

She bent down and picked up a cross tie and clipped it to Willy's halter. "Two feet," she said.

"I thought it looked big."

"I know what I'm doing, Mom," she said.

"I know. But I'm still allowed to be nervous, aren't I?"

"You don't have to be," she said. "It's fine."

"I know. But two feet's a pretty big fence."

She looked at me and smiled. "Mom," she said. "It's okay. I like it. I'm not scared."

Willy snorted and Haley found the blue plastic bin filled with horse treats and came back to him with a hand full of grain. He lipped it from her open palm and shifted his weight. She leaned over him with her brush and worked, moving the brush in steady overlapping circles over his back and shoulders while he snuffled and stood, one hoof lifted delicately, as if he was poised to walk.

After she put Willy in his stall, we drove back into town. The road ran out before us and as we came around a curve I slowed and then swerved to avoid a pack of orange- and yellow- and red-suited bicyclists who bunched along the shoulder of the road. Dozens of turkey vultures circled in a big spiral overhead and Haley watched them.

"So can we go to Franklin Street or not?" she said. "I need some more hair dye." She acted like this was no big deal but I remembered what it was like to want something that would seem to make things right when nothing else would do, in the days when everything looked like it was in my control. I thought of Haley on horseback, her hands far up Willy's neck as she came up to the first big jump, how much it seemed that she had mastered, and yet, because of Chase, how far she would always still have to go. If she wanted to dye her hair blue and ride her horse to the stars, I would let her, if these were the things she needed to know that she could manage the world into which she'd been born.

"I guess so," I said. "After lunch."

She pushed buttons on the CD player until a song she liked came on and rode beside me, looking out the window. Farmland dipped away from the road, brown cows standing in short shade under low trees.

AT FIRST, CHASE HAD class in the morning while the BART staff reduced his medication. His Clozaril levels were near toxic when he was admitted and he sat in the dayroom with the TV on, his head lolling on his chest, spit hanging from his chin, a towel spread flat on his chest. He'd grown and grown and was now almost six feet seven, but weighed 165 pounds. They taught him the token system and taught him that he would have chores to do just like everyone else, and the first one would be to empty the dishwasher before his group had dinner, and they assigned him to class, where he nodded off over his Jumbo Workbook and dozed with his fingertips resting on the computer keyboard. He spoke to no one but everyone spoke to him. Even before he began to talk again, the staff got him to give everyone high fives when they passed, as if touch was a connection that would tell him he was at home among friends. Halloween was his first day on the unit and he went to a dance and nodded off in a chair while everyone else moved to the "Monster Mash." I brought a big sheet cake on his birthday in November and a pan of his favorite mashed potatoes but he didn't eat them. At Thanksgiving, he walked and patted and walked and patted and when they finally got him to sit down for dinner, he ate a slice of turkey and a roll.

I drove up to see him on a Saturday morning just before Christmas. He was in the dayroom on a blue sofa. Someone had put a blue and green plaid throw around his shoulders to keep him warm and spread a white towel over his chest and when I came in, his chin was dropped to the towel and his eyes were closed.

"Chase," I said. "Hey buddy." I sat down next to him on the sofa and put my hand on his arm and said his name again. He flinched awake at my touch and struggled to open his eyes.

"Sit up," I said, and he leaned forward and struggled to get himself upright, raising his thin body from his waist like a hinge opening. He looked at me and his eyes rolled and he blinked and his head lolled and he jerked it upright and opened his eyes wider and tried to say something.

"It's okay," I said, with my hand on his arm. "It's okay. It's hard to wake up, isn't it?"

He nodded. His mouth worked and his eyes filled with tears and his mouth twisted and worked and worked and he wept and I found some paper towels on the counter across the room and came over and tried to wipe his face. He kicked at me and I stepped back. He turned to me and his eyes were half shut and he tried to open them and sounds began to come out of his mouth and I leaned in and told him I couldn't understand, he would have to use words, and he leaned his head back and with his eyes closed and his face turned up to the ceiling he cried, "This is basically a home. I don't want to be here. I just want to come home."

When he spoke, his words were like wails and he kept saying this over and over again. "I want to come home. I want to come home." And as he spoke he wept, and as he wept he tried to keep his head up, and he stared angrily at me when he could keep his eyes open and he fell to one side of the sofa and pushed himself up with the palm of his hand.

"This is the right place for you right now," I said. "Chase. Listen to me. You've been very sick and you need some help getting yourself back together. That's what they're going to do here. It's a good place for you. It's not a home. It's a school. You've got a roommate and classes and you'll make friends here and pretty soon you'll like it."

"No," he said. "I want to come home. I'm not sick." His mouth twisted as he said this and he slipped down on the sofa and didn't bother trying to push himself back up. Spittle ran from his mouth and I asked him if it was okay to wipe his chin and he looked away and didn't reply so I wiped his chin and he let me.

"Not sick like you're going to throw up," I said. "Sick in another way. Sometimes your brain doesn't work the way it's supposed to and then you get sick from that."

He didn't answer but patted his thigh and patted his thigh and patted his thigh. I couldn't tell if he'd heard me.

"Do you remember when you were at John Umstead Hospital?" I said.

"Umstead's not a hospital," he said.

"Yes it is."

"It's a jail," he said. "They have an electric chair in the basement. Torture chambers. They killed children there. I saw them do it." He raised his head and looked at me and then jerked upright.

"It's a hospital," I said. "I can understand why it would feel like a jail." I stopped. He'd begun crying again and was saying over and over again, "I want to come home, I want to come home, I want to come home." His eyes were closed and tears ran out through his eyelashes and his head was tipped back so the back of the sofa supported it. I tried to wipe his face but he hit out and I leaned back. I sat next to him and tried to soothe him and tried to comfort him but nothing I did mattered at all. After a while, he stood up and left the room and walked down the hall to his room, where he closed the door firmly behind him. I walked out to my car, where I sat with my forehead pressed against the steering wheel while tears dripped into my lap.

I told myself that Chase was like someone who'd been in a coma and was beginning to wake up and wouldn't understand why he was at BART, or what had happened to him. That Saturday,

I'd come to see him in the morning because the staff had told me he had his most lucid moments in the morning, an hour or two after he'd taken his Clozaril—that he'd be sleepy but he would also know who he was. They'd begun to taper one of his drugs, an anticonvulsant that sometimes induced psychosis, and they told me they thought Chase was brighter and clearer every day. They said positive things, encouraging things, and kept telling me not to lose hope. The social worker told me that all of the boys on the BART unit were in bad shape when they came in, and the ones coming in from a hospital were often in the worst shape of all, but within a year, they were all transformed by the program and this would happen to Chase, too. She told me not to give up hope. She told me to keep trying. She thought there was even a chance that Chase might recognize me one day. But she didn't tell me that when he was lucid, he'd be angry. She didn't tell me what to say to him when he told me that he wanted to come home. His room waited for him, with its neatly labeled boxes containing his model of the solar system, his electric train, his books about weather and castles, his tornado tube, his music collection. The stuffed dog I made for him for Christmas the year he turned one sat on his bed, next to the red wool felt dinosaur I sewed for him on his second birthday. But he could not come home.

As I pressed my forehead to the steering wheel and didn't bother to wipe my tears, I thought of a day when Chase was fourteen and I found him hitting his sister. By the time I got to them, she was crying and I stepped between them and took his arms by the wrists and told him he had to stop or he would not be able to live with us anymore, that I would be forced to send him away, and he pulled his wrists away from my grip and dropped his arms to his sides and then turned and stalked up the stairs. I regretted it as soon as I said it, for I had no intention of sending Chase away, not then, not ever, but after all the TEACCH methods failed and he still hit his sister, terrific whumps on her back that shuddered through her whole body, I said that I would send him away if I had to, and now I wondered if he thought of this, too, and couldn't forgive me for making my threat come true. I wanted to take it back and I wanted to explain that no one knew that he would spend a year in the hospital while the doctors argued about what was wrong and then about ways to try and fix it, while he seemed to grow worse with everything they tried. I wanted him to understand that I hadn't meant it; that even though I threatened it when he was fourteen, I hadn't sent him away.

There was a time, not long after Chase went into the hospital, when I looked around our silent and empty house and I thought, Haley and I are like the survivors of a shipwreck. It's as if we are afloat in a big deep sea on a small raft and we are paddling and we believe we will make it to shore, but we can't escape the fact that Chase drowned, and Zip was lost, and we are down to two now. In my mind's eye, I see her watching me from across the raft, looking to me to tell her what we should do. And she should: I'm the mom, I'm supposed to be able to take care of things. So I pick up my paddle and I hand her hers and I tell her we are fine and we will make it to shore. And then I look for the horizon and I push off and tell her that she can rest when she needs to but that I will keep stroking until we wade up through the surf to a sandy beach, until we are safe.

Behind us, the ocean closes over our loss. And there are only memories then of the boat that went down and the people we loved. There is no single thing that explains what happened to them. There is only silence, moving water, the past.

A CAR PASSED AND I lifted my head and reached into my purse for a tissue and wiped my eyes and blew my nose. I felt hollow inside, but hollow with a kind of empty pain that would not

quit, like someone had amputated my heart and all I could feel was
the pain of the place where my heart used to be.

WEEKS PASSED, THEN MONTHS. I drove up every Saturday to see Chase and we met in the dayroom, or in the conference
room, where he could sit at a table and eat his hamburger and
French fries while I watched him, or in the classroom across from
the kitchen. One day, as he came down the hall toward me, an
aide at his side, he turned to the aide and said, "I have no idea who
that woman is or why she's here." Another time he looked up from
his fries and studied me and finally smiled and said, "You're Aunt
Annie, right?" And I shook my head and said, "No, Chase, I'm
your mom." His face darkened then and he rose and walked away
from me and I cleaned up the remnants of his meal after the door
closed behind him.

The BART unit was a locked unit and I'd come up for a visit
and stand outside the door and knock until someone heard me.
Sometimes, I could see Chase as he paced up and down the hallway behind the door; if he saw me when I knocked, he would not
come toward me but instead would disappear behind the manager's station. A few minutes later, an aide would walk toward the
door with his keys out and welcome me inside and tell Chase that
it was his mother, here to visit with him, and Chase would shake
his head but reach for the soda I held out to him.

On Mother's Day, he made a card for his mother and the staff
encouraged him to give it to me. Reluctantly, he retreated to his
room and then brought the card to me. It was a single sheet of
paper, laminated, bearing his photo, taken by a staff member with
a digital camera while he stood between two desks, his back to a
concrete block wall, his face expressionless. *Happy Mother's Day!* it
read. *Love, Chase.* He walked over to me with the card and he held
it out to me and then he pulled it back and looked at the aide.

"It's for my mother," he said.

"This is your mother," said the aide.

He hesitated.

"It's okay," I said. "You can keep it if you want."

"Give your mother the card, Chase," said the aide. "You made it for her."

He looked at the card and then at me and then very uneasily handed the card to me and I thanked him but he seemed worried that he'd done the wrong thing and then the visit was over.

AFTER DINNER I DID the dishes and Haley turned the lights on in the living room and sat on the sofa under their yellow glow and looked through the open doorway to the kitchen. She watched me load the dishwasher before she turned to the drawer in the end table and pulled out a deck of cards. She slipped the cards out of their box and into her palm and fanned the cards and selected the two jokers and set them to one side. She put her feet on the coffee table and leaned back against the sofa and watched me. She dropped her feet to the floor and put the stack of cards on the table in front of her and split the deck in two and shuffled the cards and then shuffled them again. At summer camp she had learned how to make the shuffled cards arc and fly together and she did that now, and did it again.

"Are you ready?" she said.

"Almost. What do you want to play?"

"I don't know."

"Rummy? Poker? Crazy eights?"

"I don't know."

"We don't have any chips for poker. We could use pennies."

"I know."

"Is your homework done?"

"Mom."

"I need to check it before we play."

"Mom."

"I'm serious," I said. "Your teachers asked me to do this. I have to do this. If you turn your homework in, I don't have to do this. It's really up to you."

She slapped the cards down on the table and stood up. "Fine," she said. She crossed the room and I heard her feet on the stairs and then I heard her bedroom door slam. I squeezed the sponge under water at the kitchen faucet and wiped the counters. I rinsed the last plate and put it in the dishwasher and then put dish detergent into the dishwasher and closed the dishwasher and pressed start. I heard Nirvana, and the familiar thump of the bass line through the floor. I folded the dish towel and lay it over the counter and then leaned against the counter and waited. After a time, I turned out the lights in the kitchen and stood at the bottom of the stairs and looked up and saw Haley's door outlined in light.

On Saturday morning, Haley dropped two blueberry waffles into the toaster and leaned against the counter and looked at me.

"Can we go to the CD place today?"

"I don't think so," I said. "I have to go see your brother."

She looked at the toaster.

"Why don't you come with me to see Chase?"

Her eyes widened and she shook her head and took a step back from me. "No, thank you," she said.

"It won't take long," I said. "And we could stop at the CD place on the way home."

The waffles popped up and she leaned over the toaster and examined them carefully and then pushed the lever down.

"Why don't you ever want to go see your brother?" I said.

She looked away from me. "I just don't want to."

"But why not?"

She shook her head and lifted the lever on the toaster and popped the waffles up and put them on a plate. "I just don't want to," she said.

"What are you going to do today?"

"I have horseback riding."

"After that."

She lifted one shoulder and dropped it.

"Play guitar?"

She shrugged again. "Probably."

"Could you clean up your room?"

"I like my room the way it is."

"He's better," I said. "You haven't seen him in a while. He's doing better."

"Does he know who you are?"

I shook my head.

"Then he's not really better," she said.

"He's better than he was," I said. "Every time I see him, he seems a little bit better."

She looked away and then back at her plate and then picked up her waffle and took a bite. "I don't want to have an autistic child," she said.

I nodded. "That's reasonable," I said. "I didn't want to have an autistic child, either."

She studied her waffles and narrowed her eyes and gave me a puzzled look that felt accusatory at the same time, as if she believed that I had had a choice in the matter and had chosen this for Chase and for us, or as if I had secret information that she needed and was refusing to give to her.

I explained that there was no predicting that something would go wrong with Chase and that even now the doctors were confused about what that thing was. "I can't promise you that you won't have a child with a disability," I said, "but I think the odds are strongly in your favor that you will not."

She looked at me again, not with a hard look but with a face so bland and quiet that I knew whatever she was asking had a great deal of importance to her.

"What about my dad?" she said. "Isn't he sick?" She kept her voice casual, even. She looked at her plate but at the last minute raised her eyes and looked at me. When I didn't answer right away, she took a bite from her waffle and acted like she had all of the time in the world.

I sighed. "No one knows," I said. "I think so, but no one really knows."

She looked skeptical.

"Dr. LJ says that if there is a genetic issue, it will show up earlier and more severely in each subsequent generation," I explained. "All we know is that Chase is really sick. It might be genetic and it might be on the male line. But it might not be. Since no one really knows, no one can say anything definite."

"So I won't have an autistic child when I grow up," she said.

"Oh, Haley," I said. "Probably not. No one knows for sure so I can't make you any promises. But probably not."

Haley kept a picture of her father in her bedroom, a photo of Zip pulling Haley on a sled across our backyard while it was snowing, next to a snowman that we'd made in the afternoon, when all the schools in town closed early. She told me she didn't really recognize him in the photo. Sometimes, she remembered the way her father picked her up and flew her through the air like a bird, flew her through the kitchen and the dining room, the living room and up the stairs, to her bedroom and her bed, as if she herself was flying on her own wings. Over time, as he never showed up or called to talk with her or sent her a birthday card or Christmas present, I could see her father disappearing from her memory, not abruptly, but slowly, like a long slow drip, where each drop that fell was never to be recovered and took a long time in the letting go. She began to test her memory of him. Every once in a while she'd say something like, "My dad liked the *Titanic,* right?" And I'd recall Zip's obsessive interest in the subject, the way he collected books about the sinking and then read them over and over and over again. He kept those books on a shelf next to his collection of toy soldiers, little iron figures dressed in the coats and puttees of the First World War, each in a pose that a soldier from that era might assume: here were the artillery men, and the foot soldiers, the messengers on bicycle, the riflemen lying prone, and the radio operator and the cooks.

When I told Haley that her father was very interested in the First and Second World Wars, she nodded as if this was confirmation that she'd had a father and could count on the fact that she would remember him.

She wanted to know about his rock-and-roll band so I pulled out the old posters and tapes and she took them to her room, where silence followed for a time. After a while, I heard Zip's voice and the siren clamor of Mickey's guitar as he imitated the whine of bombs falling from the belly of a plane. When I went into her room after that, I saw that she'd propped the poster up where she could see it from her bed. She wrote the name of his band, the Strangers, in repeating lines like a list over the knees of her jeans.

She took up guitar and I could hear her trying to learn Nirvana songs in her room when her homework was finished. She had a black and white Telecaster knockoff that I'd gotten her for Christmas the year she turned twelve, with an amp and a webbed nylon strap. She began to save up for distortion pedals; later, when she was thirteen, we would be making weekly trips to the local music

store, where she could try out better guitars or test different pedals
and feel herself admired by the young men who staffed the store
for the fact that she was learning to play. She wanted to form a
band and waited for one of her friends to get a drum kit so they
could get started. She worked at the guitar and felt that this was
something all her own. I smiled when she said this and thought
that she had either gotten the guitar-playing DNA from her father
or else had taken up the guitar as a way to supply his presence.

Now she finished her waffles and put her plate in the sink.

"Why don't you come with me today?" I tried again. "He's a
little bit better. You can see for yourself."

She raised and lowered that same shoulder, that same eloquent
shrug, the lifting of loss and the inability to fully embrace hope,
and she lifted and lowered it again. "Okay," she said. "I'll go."

EIGHT MONTHS HAD PASSED since Chase came to Murdoch. The weather had turned warm and we had begun to take
walks when I visited and, when we walked, the visits assumed a
predictable shape. We walked after Chase's meal and we always
walked the same inner loop of driveway that circled behind the
Murdoch Center cottages, and Chase always walked along the
inner gutter, where concrete made a path different than the asphalt. An aide came with us, for Chase did not yet have campus
independence. We walked without speaking. Afterward, Chase
walked with me to my car and, when his aide directed him to,
waved when I left.

We kept reducing his medication; he no longer drooled or slept
for half a day. He spent more time in the classroom and he learned
the token system and he moved up to unit independence. He had
a speech and communication therapist and a recreational therapist
and an occupational therapist and a psychologist and a nutrition-

ist. He had pet therapy with a dog named Tucker. I brought him a photo album filled with pictures of his family and his therapists worked with him and worked with him. No one debated his diagnosis anymore and eventually I stopped asking what was wrong. I began to understand that in searching for a name I was hanging onto the idea that there was yet a treatment out there, yet a cure that we might find, and in fact neither of those things was true or possible. I stopped seeing Chase as a child I just had to get back on track and saw him as he was, tall and painfully thin and unable to care for himself, unable to communicate, beset with the unseen, the unknown, the unnamable, but arrived into himself completely, as if all of this had been hardwired, preordained from the start. Dr. LJ tried different words when the treatment team met every quarter to review Chase's progress—Lennox-Gastaut syndrome, movement disorder, psychosis NOS—but finally said that if he was going to be completely accurate, the only thing that he could call what plagued Chase was "Chase NOS"—Chase Not Otherwise Specified. "He's a population of one," he said.

When we walked, I talked with Chase about his childhood. I talked about his trains and our big drafty old house in the Midwest, and the way we had played red light–green light when he was a little boy riding his bike in upstate New York. I talked about the trips to the playground where he had loved the slide and about the days we spent swimming in the lake or about that time we got so sunburned and about the day that his cat came to live with us. I talked about the year the Christmas tree fell over and the year he had a windup train on top of his birthday cake and the time we went camping with our friend Donna. We would scuff along the driveway and step to the side when one of Murdoch's white laundry trucks came by. The driver would slow and wave to us through the open door. When we would pass other cottages, their patients would often be sitting outside in the shade and we would wave to them as we walked by. Former residents, long gone into their regular lives out in the world, still came back to visit with the oldest members of the staff. Murdoch had become a place where there were twice as many staff as patients, but under the reform movement, it might be forced to downsize, and services would be lost. I worried about BART closing, because beyond BART, there was no place in the world for Chase.

But today with Haley was a hot summer day and the pale sky was big and empty, limitless and infinite, and the three of us set out from the BART cottage and crossed the lawn behind the cottage and turned up onto the circle. Haley walked beside her brother and looked up at him and then looked away and then walked without looking at him at all and then looked at him again. Chase looked at her and looked at me and he said, "Not Haley." And I said, "No, that's Haley, it is." He looked again and said, "Shorter. Different glasses." I stopped and stood with my son and my daughter under the open, endless sky, under the bright sun and the cloudless infinity, and put my hand on his arm. "Chase," I said, "this is your sister. Some time has passed and she's gotten taller and she got new glasses. But this is your sister." He looked at her with interest and Haley said, "Hi Chase." He looked at her and his lips began to twist a little and then he looked closer and said, "Are you in tenth grade?" She smiled and said, "No, I'm going into seventh."

"You go to McDougle?" he asked.

Haley nodded.

"Cool," he said.

I touched his arm again. "So this is Haley," I said, "and I'm your mother." But his face went blank and his lips were moving and his hand patted his thigh and he turned to the space beside him and said something and laughed and then he turned away and started walking again and Haley and I walked along behind him, following the gray trough of concrete that circled the ring of cottages, and passed the Munchroom and the gym and the outdoor pool, and none of us spoke.

When we had gone twice around, Haley and I followed Chase beyond the cottages to an open lawn, where short, dry grass crunched crisply under our feet. He walked and walked until he was in the middle and then he opened his arms and spread them wide and began to turn circles under the sky, a long shadow falling from him toward the road and then spinning away as he turned.

Haley watched him and then I came up to him and he turned toward me and smiled and stopped turning and took my hand. "Hey Mom," he said. "Mom. I've never been in this field before."

It took a year but there came a time when Chase always knew me.
I drove up to Murdoch on the weekends and he saw me when I
came through the door and he smiled. "What's up, Mom?" he
said, and came toward me with his hand raised, ready for a high
five. After a while, when I came to visit, he leaned over me and
gingerly folded his spindly arms around me in a delicate hug, as if
his body were a bony cage.

When Chase had known me quite consistently for quite some
time, the treatment team decided it might be therapeutic for him
to go off campus for visits. I'd pick him up and then we'd stop for
burgers and drive down to a little lake in town, where we could
picnic under the trees and watch people fishing from the docks.
The lake was man-made and a small waterfall ran along one side,
where the blue lake rolled over a cement dam into a broad brown
creek. On our shore, where we sat with our burgers and fries, there
were hardwoods right up to the water's edge, their roots tangled in
bare dirt, and a rocky lawn.

Chase didn't say much to me on these trips but when I wanted
to remind him that we were together, I'd lift my hand, palm out
and he'd lift his and touch his hand to mine, palm to palm, our
regular embrace. Sometimes he asked to go for a ride before we
went back to Murdoch. When we got in the car, he arranged the

new CD player so that he could listen to U2's "Bullet the Blue Sky" over and over again. I'd turn north from town and drive up to Oxford and cruise past the big old houses on College Avenue and ask Chase which one he would buy, if he had the money. Sometimes he answered. Usually he did not. Sometimes we just drove east, past old farms and new developments, where tobacco had given way to some kind of real-estate boom signified by the cheap, pale yellow houses that had mushroomed everywhere. After a time, Chase patted my arm and peered at me as I drove and said, "Can we go back now?" Once we stopped for the cheapest gas I'd seen in months and after I ran my credit card through the slot, Chase pumped the gas, leaning lightly against the car as if this was something he'd done all his life.

In the beginning, he kept his eyes trained on the sky, as if things the rest of us could not see might still come in from the horizon. He still talked about bridges falling and terrorist attacks and bombs in the lobby nearly all of the time. He also talked about space travel and time travel, and how World War III came upon us in 1987 and he had to resurrect the dead so there would be a human race to go on living. If I asked him questions about these things, he turned his face away and said, "Never mind." Sometimes he laughed in an incongruous way and shook his head and held one hand up and palm out in my direction and said, "No, man, no, no," as if I were asking him to do something he chose not to do. I wondered if he thought I would return him to the hospital if I knew what was in his head.

But he could answer questions. If I asked him about his lunch, he could tell me if he liked it or not. He pointed to the burger he wanted me to order at the burger place. He answered when I asked him about his job. "It's fine," he'd say. "I'm fine," he'd say. "Things are fine, Mom."

He made slow, steady progress. He grew an inch. He put on ten pounds and then another five. Suddenly he was six feet eight and weighed almost 180; while he was still very thin, his painful look of emaciation was gone. To make sure he didn't lose weight, he was allowed to have unlimited calories each day.

Every three months, the treatment team got together and talked about his meds and we agreed that we would try to cut them back as much as we possibly could. "We'll keep pushing him until he pushes back," Dr. LJ said, and that seemed right to me. Over the course of the first year, we stopped one of the anticonvulsants altogether; by the end of his second year, we had tapered the Clozaril to a dose that was barely in the therapeutic range.

After two years, Chase had a weekend home visit every month; he'd come to Chapel Hill and sleep one night in his room. At first, he wanted to look at all of the things in the boxes in his closet as if to make sure that these things were still there. He sat on the floor and spread his action figures out around him and made one of his Star Wars planes fly through the air, just as he had when he was younger, its wings dipping and tilting and I heard him make a rushing sound under his breath, quietly, like a ten-year-old restored. When he was finished with the plane, he examined the boxes that held his trains and he had me set up his solar system so he could look at the planets that turned around the sun. He opened the box of comics and looked inside. He reached into his dresser drawer and carefully cradled the Eagleman comic book his father had drawn for him, years before, in the Midwest.

But he asked for these things less and less, for time had passed and Chase was no longer a child. He was nineteen and he shaved and the toys he once loved were now souvenirs of a long-ago childhood. Eventually, we found another rhythm: pizza for dinner on the night he came home, a DVD, bed, a day's outing the next day.

Sometimes he rode out to the barn with me and watched Haley ride. Sometimes he just wanted to go to places he used to go: the comic-book store on Franklin Street, Schoolkids Records, the coffee shop where he and Melissa used to get juice. Usually, he just wanted to stay home and listen to music in his room. Sometimes he'd nap on the sofa, as if being at home allowed him a peace he could not find elsewhere. He told me that he liked it at our house because it was so quiet. Still, by four o'clock on the second day, he was anxious to be on his way back to Murdoch and would grow agitated and restless if we were delayed, and pace through the living room and dining room and say, "Is it time to go yet?" In these moments, I knew that while he liked to visit us at home, he still felt safest at BART.

EARLY ONE EVENING, AS we waited for pizza to be delivered, Chase paced up and down in the living room, patting his thigh and patting his thigh. I called to him and asked him if he wanted to watch TV, but he didn't respond. I heard low words under his breath, but I couldn't make sense of them. Whenever Chase spoke in public, people often turned to me for translation, but I had no private Rosetta stone for his language.

Haley came down the stairs, took a plastic cup from the cupboard, filled the bottom with chocolate syrup, poured milk into the cup, and stirred her drink with a table knife. She'd put fresh streaks of turquoise in her hair and wore a T-shirt that read "Strange Is Not a Crime." The phone rang, and she reached up and lifted the receiver. She frowned, and then she said, "This is Haley." The person on the other end said something and she held the receiver out to me.

"It's for you. It's Dad," she said.

I took the phone from her.

"Hi," said Zip.

"Hi," I said. "Hi. Zip."

"It's been a long time," he said.

Nine years, I thought. "Yes, it has," I said.

"I wanted to call," he said. "My apartment burned down two weeks ago. They said it was a fire in the bathroom fan."

"Are you all right?" I said.

"I'm all right," he said. "My stuff. That's another thing."

I heard Haley go into the living room. "Chase," she said. "Chase. Dad's on the phone."

Chase rushed into the kitchen, his dark eyes shiny. "Dad?" he said. "Dad?"

"Chase's right here," I said. "If you want to talk to him."

"Sure I do," Zip said. "Of course I do."

I handed the phone to Chase.

"Dad?" he said. "Dad? I haven't talked to you in a really long time." He waited, eyes alight. "I'm fine," he said. A pause. "Yeah." Another pause, longer this time. "Rage Against the Machine. And Korn." Pause. "Yeah, I go to school. I work at rehab." He paced up and down and smiled and smiled and smiled. "Okay," he said. "Yup. Okay, Dad. Bye, Dad."

He handed the phone back to me.

"How's he doing?" Zip said.

"Better."

"Aw, he's all right," said Zip. "He's fine."

"Well," I said. "No. I wouldn't say fine."

"I know some of what happened," Zip said. "My mother wrote me letters."

I thought of all the times Peggy told me that she wrote to Zip and tried to explain what had happened to Chase. She never heard from him, so she told me she thought he'd never read a word of it.

"He's just visiting this weekend," I said flatly. "He doesn't live here all the time."

"Then I called at a good time," he said.

I heard him light a cigarette, and then I heard the familiar sound of an exhalation of smoke. He told me about the fire. The firefighters woke him and got him out. It turned out to be a four-alarm blaze. The whole apartment building was wrecked. The landlord put him in a new apartment, and the people at work took up a collection for him and bought him new furniture and pots and pans and dishes. He said that in many ways, he was better off than he had been before. People checked in on him and told him they would help him with anything he needed.

"Did everything burn?" I asked.

He exhaled again. "No. I know the landlord put my stuff in another apartment."

I thought of Zip's nine guitars, including a vintage hollow-body Gretsch, and his digital recording equipment, and his big amp. I was sure his landlord had taken care of this stuff, but good, and as it turned out, Zip never saw these things again. But that night, on the phone, when I felt a swift, sharp pain on his behalf, I had to remind myself that this — thinking about this — was not and could not be my job anymore.

"Do you want to talk to Haley?"

"If she wants to talk to me," Zip said.

She had spoken to him once before, when she was twelve. She had come to me very gravely and said that she was ready to talk to her father now, as if she had not been ready before, as if he had not been the one who failed to call her. I called Zip at work and arranged a time for the two of them to speak. They stayed on the phone for twenty-five minutes. Afterward, I asked Haley if she wanted to talk with him again. She shook her head. "No, thank you," she said.

Now she stood with the phone next to her ear and answered his questions. Then she handed the phone back to me. The doorbell rang and the pizza guy delivered the pizza, and Chase and Haley came in and loaded up their plates. I listened to Zip's voice in my ear while I handed out napkins, and for a moment I felt what I thought it would feel like for the four of us to be a family again. The next week I sent him pictures of the kids, and he called again and we talked some more. He told me that he worked most of the time and spent the rest of the time at home, except on Friday evenings, when he went for a beer with a woman he knew from work. It didn't take much for me to picture Zip in a dingy little bar drinking himself blind with a woman who shared his inclinations. He told me that he never expected that we would move away. I wanted to remind him that he'd promised to follow us south, for the kids' sake. I wanted to remind him that he could have called us. But these were things I would have said to a man who had done something intentional and mean. When Zip spoke, I heard nothing but pain and bafflement, as if he truly had no idea what had happened, or what his responsibility in any of it might have been. And when I spoke to him, the thing I felt more than anything else was sorrow.

It turned out that my suspicions were correct: he needed someone to care for him, because he really could not care for himself. I was glad the people around him recognized that and made a point of looking after him. Years before, when the kids were younger, when I was entirely susceptible to self-skewering through guilt, I felt responsible, as if I had abandoned Zip in the rural Midwest. I didn't recognize his illness. I only thought of the man who had descended into near silence and, when he spoke at all, made claims that were unsupported by fact: the water bill unpaid, even though he assured me he had paid it, and the water turned off; the gas bill unpaid, even though he assured me he had paid it, and the gas nearly turned off in the dead of a Midwestern winter. By the time Zip called me to tell me that his apartment had burned, I had long since realized that I was no more the origin of what had happened to Zip than I was the origin of what had happened to Chase. Our brains do as they will, just as our hearts beat or fail.

AT CHRISTMASTIME, I TOOK Chase to see a matinee of *King Kong* at a local mall. When the show let out in the late afternoon, we stepped outside into a square where a tall Christmas tree stood in the blue basin of a dry fountain, its lights twinkling merrily around frosted green and blue and red glass ornaments the size of soccer balls, and loudspeakers shrieked "Deck the Halls" at us. Chase stood next to the tree in the blue light of dusk and looked around and spotted a restaurant across the way, with huge cheesecakes turning on slowly spinning platters in the yellow window.

"Can we go there?" he asked and patted my arm.

Inside, it was crowded so the hostess seated us at the long marble bar. When Chase sat down, all of the people who saw him stared at him. He was extremely tall and very thin, of course, but he wore his hair buzzed short and his coat collar open, so it was easy to see the two huge red scars, a long lateral scar bisected by a shorter horizontal scar, that made a ragged cross to the left of his throat. When he took his coat off, the scar that ran from the base of his skull to the top of his shoulders in a divet as deep as the circumference of a big man's thumb made a purple-red channel. When the people around us saw me looking at them as they stared at Chase, they turned their faces back to their menus but still they spoke to one another and shot glances at him and some looked back at me, belligerent and defiant, as if staring at Chase was an entitlement of some sort.

Chase carefully studied his menu with its long lists of different kinds of cheesecake available by the slice and then turned to me, confused. "What do I get if I just want cheesecake?" he said.

"Just plain cheesecake?"

He nodded.

"It's right here." I pointed to the first entry on the menu. "Do you want me to order for you?"

"I'll do it," he said slowly.

When the cheesecake arrived, Chase ate fast and I had to ask him to slow down. He stopped and put his fork by his plate. "Is this place expensive?" he asked.

"Kind of," I said. "It's not too bad. It costs more than Wendy's."

He didn't say anything but turned back to his cheesecake. I looked past him out the window behind the bar and saw that the sun had gone down fully and families hurried along with their parcels. I knew it must be late and I had to have Chase back at Murdoch by six.

When the check arrived in its black vinyl case tricked out to look like leather, Chase picked it up and said, "I pay."

"What?"

"I pay," said Chase. He showed me the check and he showed me the money in his pocket. "Do I have enough?"

I started to tell him to save his money, that I would take care of this, but then I saw the look on his face.

"Just right," I said. "Thank you, Chase." Chase laid three fives on the counter for a fourteen-dollar check and then added three quarters.

"Good job," I said. We gathered our things and made for the door. Halfway to the car, Chase said, "Why are you crying?"

"I'm not crying," I said stupidly and wiped ferociously at my eyes with the heels of my hands.

"What's that?" said Chase and lifted his index finger to point at the tears on my face.

"Okay," I said. "Okay. I'm crying. Sometimes moms feel so happy that they cry."

He didn't say anything but, when he got in the car, I could see that he kept ducking his head and smiling.

ONE MORNING IN THE late fall, Chase and I drove Haley out to the barn. We walked around the upper ring while she went out to the field to catch Willy, and Chase asked about the horses. I pointed out Kure and Romeo and Bandit and Babette and Caramel and Oliver and Prissy and Red Scooter. I asked him if he wanted to walk through the barns and see the horses stabled in their stalls but he was tapping and patting and staring up into the clouds over the pines, his eyes squinting, as if he was waiting for something to appear, so I took him back to the car.

Haley stood in the upper barn with Willy half tacked up in the cross ties. She had just lifted the bit to his teeth when I came in and she glanced over at me.

"Where's Chase?"

"He's waiting for me in the car. I think we're going to head home after all."

She nodded. "I didn't think he could do this," she said.

"At least not today," I said. "I think we're going to rake leaves when we get home. We'll save some for you."

She made a face.

"Have a good ride," I said. Outside, I could hear her instructor calling for the girls to bring their horses into the ring. Willy shook his head and his tack clinked and jingled and Haley took him by the reins and led him cloppety-clop out into the morning light. I crossed the dirt drive to our car and after I buckled up and made sure Chase was buckled up, I looked back at the ring and watched

Haley laugh as another girl came by and said something to her. I saw her focused anywhere but on us and I breathed and was glad, because this was the way it was meant to be.

When we got home, I gave Chase a pair of canvas work gloves and a rake, and I got my work gloves and the other rake and pulled the plastic tarp from the utility shed.

"If we work together, we can get the leaves here in the backyard out to the curb," I said. "Can you help me?"

He nodded and I helped him pull the work gloves on and showed him that we needed to rake from under the trees out onto the grass, where we would spread our tarp so that we could rake the leaves onto the tarp and then haul the tarp to the street.

At first Chase patted uncertainly at the ground with his rake but when I showed him how to move his rake in a long stroke over the grass, he caught on quickly and set to work raking out the lawn along the fence. Leaves had spun down and carpeted the yard, and covered the daylilies and the hostas, had pressed themselves against the neighbor's fence, and grown listless in the corners of the house. For a time, all I could hear was the susuruss of the rakes moving through the leaves. When Chase had amassed a pile and I had amassed a pile, I showed him how to rake the leaves onto the tarp and then we each took a corner and dragged the tarp up to the street, where we spilled them into the gutter for the town leaf vacuum. It was a cold day and we worked like this for an hour or so, until the sun came out from behind the clouds and I felt sweat trickle down my neck. I looked over at Chase. His upper lip was beaded with moisture.

"Hey Chase," I said. "Chase. Let's stop for a minute."

But he didn't hear me. He just kept raking and raking and raking, and I followed along behind him as he cut his path through the world.

ACKNOWLEDGMENTS

I wish to thank Tobias Wolff, Pam Durban, Michael Fitzgerald, John McGowan, James Leloudis, Lynn York, Anna Gemrich, and Joan Gantz for their unswerving support. I also wish to express deep and abiding thanks to my brilliant editor, Kathy Pories, and to my agent, Julie Barer. Each has been generous, tireless, and insightful. I'm very grateful to the Wildacres Residency Program, which supported the writing of this book through a number of long silent weeks in the North Carolina mountains, and to Rachel Willis, who told me the time had come to get started. My family and friends provided help in the way of encouragement and kindnesses of every description. I thank them all.

Above all, I wish to thank my beloved children. Nothing I write could ever match their courage, strength, and hope.